PENGUIN BOOKS

MORNINGS IN MEXICO
AND
ETRUSCAN PLACES

David Herbert Lawrence was born at Eastwood, Nottingham-shire, in 1885, fourth of the five children of a miner and his middle-class wife. He attended Nottingham High School and Nottingham University College. His first novel, *The White Peacock*, was published in 1911, just a few weeks after the death of his mother to whom he had been abnormally close. At this time he finally ended his relationship with Jessie Chambers (the Miriam of *Sons and Lovers*) and became engaged to Louie Burrows. His career as a schoolteacher was ended in 1911 by the illness which was ultimately diagnosed as tuberculosis.

In 1912 Lawrence eloped to Germany with Frieda Weekley, the German wife of his former modern languages tutor. They were married on their return to England in 1914. Lawrence was now living, precariously, by his writing. His greatest novels, *The Rainbow* and *Women in Love*, were completed in 1915 and 1916. The former was suppressed, and he could not find a publisher for the latter.

After the war Lawrence began his 'savage pilgrimage' in search of a more fulfilling mode of life than industrial Western civilization could offer. This took him to Sicily, Ceylon, Australia and, finally, New Mexico. The Lawrences returned to Europe in 1925. Lawrence's last novel, *Lady Chatterley's Lover*, was banned in 1928, and his paintings confiscated in 1929. He died in Vence in 1930 at the age of 44.

Lawrence spent most of his short life living. Nevertheless he produced an amazing quantity of work – novels, stories, poems, plays, essays, travel books, translations and letters . . . After his death Frieda wrote: 'What he had seen and felt and known he gave in his writing to his fellow men, the splendour of living, the hope of more and more life . . . a heroic and immeasurable gift.'

D. H. LAWRENCE

Mornings in Mexico
AND
Etruscan Places

PENGUIN BOOKS

in association with William Heinemann Ltd

Penguin Books Ltd, Harmondsworth, Middlesex, England
Penguin Books Australia Ltd, Ringwood, Victoria, Australia

—

Mornings in Mexico first published by Martin Secker 1927
Etruscan Places first published by Martin Secker 1932
and published in Penguin Books 1950
Published together in Penguin Books 1960
Reprinted 1967, 1971, 1973, 1974

—

Made and printed in Great Britain
by C. Nicholls & Company Ltd
Set in Monotype Garamond

Contents

List of Plates

MORNINGS IN MEXICO

Corasmin and the Parrots

ONE says Mexico: one means, after all, one little town away South in the Republic: and in this little town, one rather crumbly adobe house built round two sides of a garden *patio*: and of this house, one spot on the deep, shady veranda facing inwards to the trees, where there are an onyx table and three rocking-chairs and one little wooden chair, a pot with carnations, and a person with a pen. We talk so grandly, in capital letters, about Morning in Mexico. All it amounts to is one little individual looking at a bit of sky and trees, then looking down at the page of his exercise book.

It is a pity we don't always remember this. When books come out with grand titles, like *The Future of America*, or *The European Situation*, it's a pity we don't immediately visualize a thin or a fat person, in a chair or in bed, dictating to a bob-haired stenographer or making little marks on paper with a fountain pen.

Still, it is morning, and it is Mexico. The sun shines. But then, during the winter, it always shines. It is pleasant to sit out of doors and write, just fresh enough and just warm enough. But then it is Christmas next week, so it ought to be just right.

There is a little smell of carnations, because they are the nearest thing. And there is a resinous smell of ocote wood, and a smell of coffee, and a faint smell of leaves, and of Morning, and even of Mexico. Because when all is said and done, Mexico has a faint, physical scent of her own, as each human being has. And this is a curious, inexplicable scent, in which there are resin and perspiration and sunburned earth and urine among other things.

And cocks are still crowing. The little mill where the natives have their own corn ground is puffing rather languidly. And because some women are talking in the entrance-way, the two tame parrots in the trees have started to whistle.

The parrots, even when I don't listen to them, have an extraordinary effect on me. They make my diaphragm convulse with little laughs, almost mechanically. They are a quite commonplace pair of green birds, with bits of bluey red, and round, disillusioned eyes, and heavy, overhanging noses. But they listen intently. And they reproduce. The pair whistle now like Rosalino, who is sweeping the *patio* with a twig broom; and yet it is so unlike him, to be whistling full vent, when any of us is around, that one looks at him to see. And the moment one sees him, with his black head bent rather drooping and hidden as he sweeps, one laughs.

The parrots whistle exactly like Rosalino, only a little more so. And this little-more-so is extremely sardonically funny. With their sad old long-jowled faces and their flat disillusioned eyes, they reproduce Rosalino and a little-more-so without moving a muscle. And Rosalino, sweeping the *patio* with his twig broom, scraping and tittering leaves into little heaps, covers himself more and more with the cloud of his own obscurity. He doesn't rebel. He is powerless. Up goes the wild, sliding Indian whistle into the morning, very powerful, with an immense energy seeming to drive behind it. And always, always a little more than life-like.

Then they break off into a cackling chatter, and one knows they are shifting their clumsy legs, perhaps hanging on with their beaks and clutching with their cold, slow claws, to climb to a higher bough, like rather raggedy green buds climbing to the sun. And suddenly the penetrating, demonish mocking voices:

'Perro! Oh, Perro! Perr-rro! Oh, Perr-rro! Perro!'

They are imitating somebody calling the dog. *Perro* means dog. But that any creature should be able to pour such a suave, prussic-acid sarcasm over the voice of a human being calling a dog, is incredible. One's diaphragm chuckles involuntarily.

And one thinks: *Is it possible?* Is it possible that we are so absolutely, so innocently, so *ab ovo* ridiculous?

And not only is it possible, it is patent. We cover our heads in confusion.

Now they are yapping like a dog: exactly like Corasmin. Corasmin is a little fat, curly white dog who was lying in the sun a minute ago, and has now come into the veranda shade, walking with slow resignation, to lie against the wall near-by my chair. 'Yap-yap-yap! Wouf! Wouf! Yapyapyapyap!' go the parrots, exactly like Corasmin when some stranger comes into the *zaguán*, Corasmin and a little-more-so.

With a grin on my face I look down at Corasmin. And with a silent, abashed resignation in his yellow eyes, Corasmin looks up at me, with a touch of reproach. His little white nose is sharp, and under his eyes there are dark marks, as under the eyes of one who has known much trouble. All day he does nothing but walk resignedly out of the sun, when the sun gets too hot, and out of the shade, when the shade gets too cool. And bite ineffectually in the region of his fleas.

Poor old Corasmin: he is only about six, but resigned, unspeakably resigned. Only not humble. He does not kiss the rod. He rises in spirit above it, letting his body lie.

'Perro! Oh, Perr-rro! Perr-rro! Perr-rr-rro!!' shriek the parrots, with that strange penetrating, antediluvian malevolence that seems to make even the trees prick their ears. It is a sound that penetrates one straight at the diaphragm, belonging to the ages before brains were invented. And Corasmin pushes his sharp little nose into his bushy tail, closes his eyes because I am grinning, feigns to sleep and then, in an orgasm of self-consciousness, starts up to bite in the region of his fleas.

'Perr-rro! Perr-rro!' And then a restrained, withheld sort of yapping. The fiendish rolling of the Spanish 'r', malevolence rippling out of all the vanished spiteful aeons. And following it, the small, little-curly-dog sort of yapping. They can make their voices so devilishly small and futile, like a little curly dog. And follow it up with that ringing malevolence that swoops up the ladders of the sunbeams right to the stars, rolling the Spanish 'r'.

Corasmin slowly walks away from the veranda, his head drooped, and flings himself down in the sun. No! He gets up again, in an agony of self-control, and scratches the earth loose a little, to soften his lie. Then flings himself down again.

Invictus! The still-unconquered Corasmin! The sad little white curly pendulum oscillating ever slower between the shadow and the sun.

> In the fell clutch of circumstance
> I have not winced nor cried aloud,
> Under the bludgeonings of chance
> My head is bloody, but unbowed.

But that is human bombast, and a little too ridiculous even for Corasmin. Poor old Corasmin's clear yellow eyes! He is going to be master of his own soul, under all the vitriol those parrots pour over him. But he's not going to throw out his chest in a real lust of self-pity. That belongs to the next cycle of evolution.

I wait for the day when the parrots will start throwing English at us, in the pit of our stomachs. They cock their heads and listen to our gabble. But so far they haven't got it. It puzzles them. Castilian, and Corasmin, and Rosalino come more natural.

Myself, I don't believe in evolution, like a long string hooked on to a First Cause, and being slowly twisted in unbroken continuity through the ages. I prefer to believe in what the Aztecs called Suns: that is, Worlds successively created and destroyed. The sun itself convulses, and the worlds go out like so many candles when somebody coughs in the middle of them. Then subtly, mysteriously, the sun convulses again, and a new set of worlds begins to flicker alight.

This pleases my fancy better than the long and weary twisting of the rope of Time and Evolution, hitched on to the revolving hook of a First Cause. I like to think of the whole show going bust, *bang!* – and nothing but bits of chaos flying about. Then out of the dark, new little twinklings reviving from nowhere, nohow.

I like to think of the world going pop! when the lizards had grown too unwieldy, and it was time they were taken down a peg or two. Then the little humming birds beginning to spark in the darkness, and a whole succession of birds shaking themselves clean of the dark matrix, flamingoes rising upon one leg like dawn commencing, parrots shrieking about at midday, *almost* able to talk, then peacocks unfolding at evening like the night with stars. And apart from these little pure birds, a lot of unwieldy skinny-necked monsters bigger than crocodiles, barging through the mosses; till it was time to put a stop to them. When someone mysteriously touched the button, and the sun went bang, with smithereens of birds bursting in all directions. On a few parrots' eggs and peacocks' eggs and eggs of flamingoes smuggling in some safe nook, to hatch on the next Day, when the animals arose.

Up reared the elephant, and shook the mud off his back. The birds watched him in sheer stupefaction. What? *What in heaven's name is this wingless, beakless old perambulator?*

No good, oh birds! Curly, little white Corasmin ran yapping out of the undergrowth, the new undergrowth, till parrots, going white at the gills, flew off into the ancientest recesses. Then the terrific neighing of the wild horse was heard in the twilight for the first time, and the bellowing of lions through the night.

And the birds were sad. What is this? they said. A whole vast gamut of new noises. A universe of new voices.

Then the birds under the leaves hung their heads and were dumb. No good our making a sound, they said. We are superseded.

The great big, booming, half-naked birds were blown to smithereens. Only the real little feathery individuals hatched out again and remained. This was a consolation. The larks and warblers cheered up, and began to say their little say, out of the old 'Sun', to the new sun. But the peacock, and the turkey, and the raven, and the parrot above all, they could not get over it. Because, in the old days of the Sun of Birds, they had been the big guns. The parrot had been the old boss of the flock. He was so clever.

Now he was, so to speak, up a tree. Nor dare he come down, because of the toddling little curly white Corasmin, and such-like, down below. He felt absolutely bitter. That wingless, beakless, featherless, curly, misshapen bird's nest of a Corasmin had usurped the face of the earth, waddling about, whereas his Grace, the heavy-nosed old Duke of a parrot, was forced to sit out of reach up a tree, dispossessed.

So, like the riff-raff up in the gallery at the theatre, aloft in the Paradiso of the vanished Sun, he began to whistle and jeer. '*Yap-yap!*' said his new little lordship of a Corasmin. 'Ye Gods!' cried the parrot. 'Hear him forsooth! *Yap-yap!* he says! Could anything be more imbecile? Yap-yap! Oh, Sun of the Birds, hark at that! *Yap-yap-yap!* Perro! *Perro! Perr-rro!* Oh, *Perr-rr-rro!*'

The parrot had found his cue. Stiff-nosed, heavy-nosed old duke of the birds, he wasn't going to give in and sing a new song, like those fool brown thrushes and nightingales. Let them twitter and warble. The parrot was a gentleman of the old school. He was going to jeer now! Like an ineffectual old aristocrat.

'*Oh, Perr-rro! Perr-rro-o-o-!*'

The Aztecs say there have been four Suns and ours is the fifth. The first Sun, a tiger, or a jaguar, a night-spotted monster of rage, rose out of nowhere and swallowed it, with all its huge, mercifully forgotten insects along with it. The second Sun blew up in a great wind: that was when the big lizards must have collapsed. The third Sun burst in water, and drowned all the animals that were considered unnecessary, together with the first attempts at animal men.

Out of the floods rose our own Sun, and little naked man. 'Hello!' said the old elephant. 'What's that noise?' And he pricked his ears, listening to a new voice on the face of the earth. The sound of man, and *words* for the first time. Terrible, unheard-of sound. The elephant dropped his tail and ran into the deep jungle, and there stood looking down his nose.

But little white curly Corasmin was fascinated. '*Come on! Perro! Perro!*' called the naked two-legged one. And Corasmin, fascinated, said to himself: 'Can't stand out against that name. Shall have to go!' so off he trotted, at the heels of the naked one. Then came the horse, then the elephant, spell-bound at being given a name. The other animals ran for their lives and stood quaking.

In the dust, however, the snake, the oldest dethroned king of all, bit his tail once more and said to himself: '*Here's another! No end to these new lords of creation! But I'll bruise his heel! Just as I swallow the eggs of the parrot, and lick up the little Corasmin-pups.*'

And in the branches, the parrot said to himself: '*Hello! What's this new sort of half-bird? Why, he's got Corasmin trotting at his heels! Must be a new sort of boss! Let's listen to him, and see if I can't take him off.*'

Perr-rro! Perr-rr-rro-oo! Oh, Perro!

The parrot had hit it.

And the monkey, cleverest of creatures, cried with rage when he heard men speaking. '*Oh, why couldn't I do it!*' he chattered. But no good, he belonged to the old Sun. So he sat and gibbered across the invisible gulf in time, which is the 'other dimension' that clever people gas about: calling it 'fourth dimension', as if you could measure it with a foot-rule, the same as the obedient other three dimensions.

If you come to think of it, when you look at the monkey, you are looking straight into the other dimension. He's got length and breadth and height all right, and he's in the same universe of Space and Time as you are. But there's another dimension. He's different. There's no rope of evolution linking him to you, like a navel string. No! Between you and him there's a cataclysm and another dimension. It's no good. You can't link him up. Never will. It's the other dimension.

He mocks at you and gibes at you and imitates you.

Sometimes he is even more *like* you than you are yourself. It's funny, and you laugh just a bit on the wrong side of your face. It's the other dimension.

He stands in one Sun, you in another. He whisks his tail in one Day, you scratch your head in another. He jeers at you, and is afraid of you. You laugh at him and are frightened of him.

What's the length and the breadth, what's the height and the depths between you and me? says the monkey.

You get out a tape-measure, and he flies into an obscene mockery of you.

It's the other dimension, put the tape-measure away, it won't serve.

'Perro! Oh, Perr-rro!' shrieks the parrot.

Corasmin looks up at me, as much as to say:

'It's the other dimension. There's no help for it. Let us agree about it.'

And I look down into his yellow eyes, and say:

'You're quite right, Corasmin, it's the other dimension. You and I, we admit it. But the parrot won't, and the monkey won't, and the crocodile won't, neither the earwig. They all wind themselves up and wriggle inside the cage of the other dimension, hating it. And those that have voices jeer, and those that have mouths bite, and the insects that haven't even mouths, they turn up their tails and nip with them, or sting. Just behaving according to their own dimension: which, for me, is the other dimension.'

And Corasmin wags his tail mildly, and looks at me with real wisdom in his eyes. He and I, we understand each other in the wisdom of the other dimension.

But the flat, saucer-eyed parrot won't have it. Just won't have it.

'Oh, Perro! Perr-rro! Perr-rro-o-o-o! Yap-yap-yap!'

And Rosalino, the Indian *mozo*, looks up at me with his eyes veiled by their own blackness. We won't have it either: he is hiding and repudiating. Between us also is the gulf of the other dimension, and he wants to bridge it with the foot-rule of the three-dimensional space. He knows it can't be done. So do I. Each of us knows the other knows.

But he can imitate me, even more than life-like. As the parrot can him. And I have to laugh at his *me*, a bit on the wrong side of my face, as he has to grin on the wrong side of his face when I catch his eye as the parrot is whistling *him*. With a grin, with a laugh we pay tribute to the other dimension. But Corasmin is wiser. In his clear, yellow eyes is the self-possession of full admission.

The Aztecs said this world, our Sun, would blow up from inside, in earthquakes. Then what will come, in the other dimension, when we are superseded?

2

Walk to Huayapa

CURIOUS is the psychology of Sunday. Humanity enjoying itself is on the whole a dreary spectacle, and holidays are more disheartening than drudgery. One makes up one's mind: On Sundays and on *fiestas* I will stay at home, in the hermitage of the *patio*, with the parrots and Corasmin and the reddening coffee-berries. I will avoid the sight of people 'enjoying themselves' – or try to, without much success.

Then comes Sunday morning, with the peculiar looseness of its sunshine. And even if *you* keep mum, the better-half says: Let's go somewhere.

But, thank God, in Mexico at least one can't set off in the 'machine'. It is a question of a meagre horse and a wooden saddle; on a donkey; or what we called, as children, 'Shanks' pony' – the shanks referring discourteously to one's own legs.

We will go out of the town. 'Rosalino, we are going for a walk to San Felipe de las Aguas. Do you want to go, and carry the basket?'

'*Come no, Señor?*'

It is Rosalino's inevitable answer, as inevitable as the parrot's 'Perro!' '*Come no, Señor?*' – 'How not, Señor?'

The *Norte*, the north-wind, was blowing last night, rattling the worm-chewed window-frames.

'Rosalino, I am afraid you will be cold in the night.'

'*Come no, Señor?*'

'Would you like a blanket?'

'*Come no, Señor?*'

'With this you will be warm?'

'*Come no, Señor?*'

But the morning is perfect; in a moment we are clear out of the town. Most towns in Mexico, saving the capital, end in themselves, at once. As if they had been lowered from heaven in a napkin, and deposited, rather foreign, upon the wild plain. So we walk round the wall of the church and the huge old monastery enclosure that is now barracks for the scrap-heap soldiery, and at once there are the hills.

'I will lift up my eyes unto the hills, whence cometh my strength.' At least one can always do *that*, in Mexico. In a stride, the town passes away. Before us lies the gleaming, pinkish-ochre of the valley flat, wild and exalted with sunshine. On the left, quite near, bank the stiffly pleated mountains, all the foot-hills, that press savannah-coloured into the savannah of the valley. The mountains are clothed smokily with pine, *ocote*, and, like a woman in a gauze *rebozo*, they rear in a rich blue fume that is almost cornflower-blue in the clefts. It is their characteristic that they are darkest blue at the top. Like some splendid lizard with a wavering, royal-blue crest down the ridge of his back, and pale belly, and soft, pinky-fawn claws, no the plain.

Between the pallor of the claws, a dark spot of trees, and white dots of a church with twin towers. Further away, along the foot-hills, a few scattered trees, white dot and stroke of a *hacienda*, and a green, green square of sugar-cane. Further off still, at the mouth of a cleft of a canyon, a dense little green patch of trees, and two spots of proud church.

'Rosalino, which is San Felipe?'

'*Quien sabe, Señor?*' says Rosalino, looking at the villages beyond the sun of the savannah with black, visionless eyes. In his voice is the inevitable flat resonance of aloofness. touched with resignation, as if to say: It is not becoming to a man to know these things. – Among the Indians it is not becoming to know anything, not even one's own name.

Rosalino is a mountain boy, an Indian from a village two days' walk away. But he has been two years in the little city, and has learnt his modicum of Spanish.

'Have you never been to any of these villages?'

'No, Señor, I never went.'

'Didn't you want to?'

'*Come no, Señor?*'

The Americans would call him a dumb-bell.

We decide for the farthest speck of a village in a dark spot of trees. It lies so magical, alone, tilted in the fawn-pink slope, again as if the dark-green napkin with a few white tiny buildings had been lowered from heaven and left, there at the foot of the mountains, with the deep groove of a canyon slanting in behind. So alone and, as it were, detached from the world in which it lies, a spot.

Nowhere more than in Mexico does human life become isolated, external to its surroundings, and cut off tinily from the environment. Even as you come across the plain to a big city like Guadalajara, and see the twin towers of the cathedral peering around in loneliness like two lost birds side by side on a moor, lifting their white heads to look around in the wilderness, your heart gives a clutch, feeling the pathos, the isolated tininess of human effort. As for building a church with one tower only, it is unthinkable. There must be two towers, to keep each other company in this wilderness world.

The morning is still early, the brilliant sun does not burn too much. Tomorrow is the shortest day. The savannah valley is shadeless, spotted only with the thorny ravel of mesquite bushes. Down the trail that has worn grooves in the turf – the rock is near the surface – occasional donkeys with a blue-hooded woman perched on top come tripping in silence, twinkling, a shadow. Just occasional women taking a few vegetables to market. Practically no men. It is Sunday.

Rosalino, prancing behind with the basket, plucks up his courage to speak to one of the women passing on a donkey. 'Is that San Felipe where we are going?' – 'No, that is not San Felipe.' – 'What, then, is it called?' – 'It is called Huayapa.' – 'Which, then, is San Felipe?' – 'That one' – and she points to her right.

They have spoken to each other in half-audible, crushed tones, as they always do, the woman on the donkey and the woman with her on foot swerving away from the basket-carrying Rosalino. They all swerve away from us, as if we were potential bold brigands. It really gets one's pecker up. The presence of the Señora only half reassures them. For the Señora, in a plain hat of bluey-green woven grass, and a dress of white cotton with black squares on it, is almost a monster of unusualness. *Prophet art thou, bird, or devil?* the women seem to say, as they look at her with keen black eyes. I think they choose to decide she is more of the last.

The women look at the woman, the men look at the man. And always with that same suspicious, inquiring, wondering look, the same with which Edgar Allan Poe must have looked at his momentous raven:

'*Prophet art thou, bird, or devil?*'

Devil, then, to please you! one longs to answer, in a tone of *Nevermore.*

Ten o'clock, and the sun getting hot. Not a spot of shade, apparently, from here to Huayapa. The blue getting thinner on the mountains, and an indiscernible vagueness, of too much light, descending on the plain.

The road suddenly dips into a little crack, where runs a creek. This again is characteristic of these parts of America. Water keeps out of sight. Even the biggest rivers, even the tiny brooks. You look across a plain on which the light sinks down, and you think: Dry! Dry! Absolutely dry! You travel along, and suddenly come to a crack in the earth, and a little stream is running in a little walled-in valley bed, where is a half-yard of green turf, and bushes, the *palo-blanco* with leaves, and with big white flowers like pure white, crumpled cambric. Or you may come to a river a thousand feet below, sheer below you. But not in this valley. Only the stream.

'Shade!' says the Señora, subsiding under a steep bank.

'*Mucho calor!*' says Rosalino, taking off his extra-jaunty straw hat, and subsiding with the basket.

Down the slope are coming two women on donkeys. Seeing the terrible array of three people sitting under a bank, they pull up.

'*Adios!*' I say, with firm resonance.

'*Adios!*' says the Señora, with diffidence.

'*Adios!*' says the reticent Rosalino, his voice the shadow of ours.

'*Adios! Adios! Adios!*' say the women, in suppressed voices, swerving, neutral, past us on their self-contained, sway-eared asses.

When they have passed, Rosalino looks at me to see if I shall laugh. I give a little grin, and he gives me back a great explosive grin, throwing back his head in silence, opening his wide mouth and showing his soft pink tongue, looking along his cheeks with his saurian black eyes, in an access of *farouche* derision.

A great hawk, like an eagle, with white bars at the end of its wings, sweeps low over us, looking for snakes. One can hear the hiss of its pinions.

'*Gabilán,*' says Rosalino.

'What is it called in the *idioma*?'

'*Psia!*' – He makes the consonants explode and hiss.

'Ah!' says the Señora. 'One hears it in the wings. *Psia!*'

'Yes,' says Rosalino, with black eyes of incomprehension.

Down the creek, two native boys, little herdsmen, are bathing, stooping with knees together and throwing water over themselves, rising, gleaming dark coffee-red in the sun, wetly. They are very dark, and their wet heads are so black, they seem to give off a bluish light, like dark electricity.

The great cattle they are tending slowly plunge through the

bushes, coming up-stream. At the place where the path fords—
the stream, a great ox stoops to drink. Comes a cow after him,
and a calf, and a young bull. They all drink a little at the
stream, their noses delicately touching the water. And then
the young bull, horns abranch, stares fixedly, with some of the
same Indian wonder-and-suspicion stare, at us sitting under
the bank.

Up jumps the Señora, proceeds uphill, trying to save her
dignity. The bull, slowly leaning into motion, moves across-
stream like a ship unmoored. The bathing lad on the bank is
hastily fastening his calico pantaloons round his ruddy-dark
waist. The Indians have a certain rich physique, even this lad.
He comes running short-step down the bank, uttering a bird-
like whoop, his dark hair gleaming bluish. Stooping for a
moment to select a stone, he runs athwart the bull, and aims
the stone sideways at him. There is a thud, the ponderous,
adventurous young animal swerves docilely round towards the
stream. '*Becerro!*' cries the boy, in his bird-like, piping tone,
selecting a stone to throw at the calf.

We proceed in the blazing sun up the slope. There is a white
line at the foot of the trees. It looks like water running white
over a weir. The supply of the town water comes this way.
Perhaps this is a reservoir. A sheet of water! How lovely it
would be, in this country, if there was a sheet of water with a
stream running out of it! And those dense trees of Huayapa
behind.

'What is that white, Rosalino? Is it water?'

'*El blanco? Sí, agua, Señora,*' says that dumb-bell.

Probably, if the Señora had said: Is it milk? he would have
replied in exactly the same way: *Sí es leche, Señora!* – Yes, it's
milk.

Hot, silent, walking only amidst a weight of light, out of
which one hardly sees, we climb the spurs towards the dark
trees. And as we draw nearer, the white slowly resolves into a
broken, whitewashed wall.

'Oh!' exclaims the Señora, in real disappointment. 'It isn't
water! It's a wall!'

'*Sí, Señora. Es panteón.*' (They call a cemetery a *panteón*, down here.)

'It is a cemetery,' announces Rosalino, with a certain ponderous, pleased assurance, and without afterthought. But when I suddenly laugh at the absurdity, he also gives a sudden broken yelp of laughter. – They laugh as if it were against their will, as if it hurt them, giving themselves away.

It was nearing midday. At last we got into a shady lane, in which were puddles of escaped irrigation-water. The ragged semi-squalor of a half-tropical lane, with naked trees sprouting into spiky scarlet flowers, and bushes with biggish yellow flowers, sitting rather wearily on their stems, led to the village.

We were entering Huayapa. *Iª Calle de las Minas*, said an old notice. *Iª Calle de las Minas*, said a new, brand-new notice, as if in confirmation. *First Street of the Mines*. And every street had the same old and brand-new notice: 1st Street of the Magnolia: 4th Street of Enriquez Gonzalez: very fine!

But the First Street of the Mines was just a track between the stiff living fence of organ cactus, with poinsettia trees holding up scarlet mops of flowers, and mango trees, tall and black, stonily drooping the strings of unripe fruit. The Street of the Magnolia was a rocky stream-gutter, disappearing to nowhere from nowhere, between cactus and bushes. The Street of the Vasquez was a stony stream-bed, emerging out of tall, wildly tall reeds.

Not a soul anywhere. Through the fences, half deserted gardens of trees and banana plants, each enclosure with a half-hidden hut of black adobe bricks crowned with a few old tiles for a roof, and perhaps a new wing made of twigs. Everything hidden, secret, silent. A sense of darkness among the silent mango trees, a sense of lurking, of unwillingness. Then actually some half-bold curs barking at us across the stile of one garden, a forked bough over which one must step to enter the chicken-bitten enclosure. And actually a man crossing the proudly labelled: Fifth Street of the Independence.

If there were no churches to mark a point in these villages, there would be nowhere at all to make for. The sense of nowhere is intense, between the dumb and repellent living fence of cactus. But the Spaniards, in the midst of these black, mud-brick huts, have inevitably reared the white twin-towered magnificence of a big and lonely, hopeless church; and where there is a church there will be a *plaza*. And a *plaza* is a *zócalo*, a hub. Even though the wheel does not go round, a hub is still a hub. Like the old Forum.

So we stray diffidently on, in the maze of streets which are only straight tracks between cactuses, till we see *Reforma*, and at the end of *Reforma*, the great church.

In front of the church is a rocky *plaza* leaking with grass, with water rushing into two big, oblong stone basins. The great church stands rather ragged, in a dense forlornness, for all the world like some big white human being, in rags, held captive in a world of ants.

On the uphill side of the *plaza*, a long low white building with a shed in front, and under the shed crowding, all the short-statured men of the *pueblo*, in their white cotton clothes and big hats. They are listening to something: but the silence is heavy, furtive, secretive. They stir like white-clad insects.

Rosalino looks sideways at them, and sheers away. Even we lower our voices to ask what is going on. Rosalino replies, *sotto voce*, that they are making *asuntos*. But what business? we insist. The dark faces of the little men under the big hats look round at us suspiciously, like dark gaps in the atmosphere. Our alien presence in this vacuous village, is like the sound of a drum in a churchyard. Rosalino mumbles unintelligibly. We stray across the forlorn yard into the church.

Thursday was the day of the Virgin of the Soledad, so the church is littered with flowers, sprays of wild yellow flowers trailing on the floor. There is a great Gulliver's Travels fresco picture of an angel having a joy-ride on the back of a Goliath. On the left, near the altar steps, is seated a life-size Christ – undersized; seated upon a little table, wearing a pair of woman's frilled knickers, a little mantle of purple silk dangling from His back, and His face bent forward gazing fatuously at

24

His naked knee, which emerges from the needlework frill of the drawers. Across from Him a living woman is half-hidden behind a buttress, mending something, sewing.

We sit silent, motionless, in the whitewashed church ornamented with royal blue and bits of gilt. A barefoot Indian with a high-domed head comes in and kneels with his legs close together, his back stiff, at once very humble and resistant. His cotton jacket and trousers are long-unwashed rag, the colour of dry earth, and torn, so that one sees smooth pieces of brown thigh, and brown back. He kneels in a sort of intense fervour for a minute, then gets up and childishly, almost idiotically, begins to take the pieces of candle from the candlesticks. He is the Verger.

Outside, the gang of men is still pressing under the shed. We insist on knowing what is going on. Rosalino, looking sideways at them, plucks up courage to say plainly that the two men at the table are canvassing for votes: for the Government, for the State, for a new governor, whatever it may be. Votes! Votes! Votes! The farce of it! Already on the wall of the low building, on which one sees, in blue letters, the word *Justizia*, there are pasted the late political posters, with the loud announcement: Vote For This Mark ⊕. Or another: Vote For This Mark ⊖.

My dear fellow, this is when democracy becomes real fun. You vote for one red ring inside another red ring and you get a Julio Echegaray. You vote for a blue dot inside a blue ring, and you get a Socrate Ezequiel Tos. Heaven knows what you get for the two little red circles on top of one another ⊙. Suppose we vote, and try. There's all sorts in the lucky bag. There might come a name like Peregrino Zenon Cocotilla.

Independence! Government by the People, of the People, for the People! We all live in the Calle de la Reforma, in Mexico.

On the bottom of the *plaza* is a shop. We want some fruit. '*Hay frutas?* Oranges or bananas?' – '*No, Señor.*' – 'No fruits?' – '*No hay!*' – 'Can I buy a cup?' – '*No hay.*' – 'Can

25

I buy a *jícara*, a gourd-shell that we might drink from?' '*No hay.*'

No hay means *there isn't any*, and it's the most regular sound made by the dumb-bells of the land.

'What is there, then?' A sickly grin. There are, as a matter of fact, candles, soap, dead and withered chiles, a few dried grasshoppers, dust, and stark, bare wooden pigeon-holes. Nothing, nothing, nothing. Next-door is another little hole of a shop. *Hay frutas? – No hay. – Qué hay? – Hay tepache!*

'*Para borracharse,*' says Rosalino, with a great grin.

Tepache is a fermented drink of pineapple rinds and brown sugar: to get drunk on, as Rosalino says. But mildly drunk. There is probably *mescal* too, to get brutally drunk on.

The village is exhausted in resource. But we insist on fruit. Where, *where* can I buy oranges and bananas? I see oranges on the trees, I see banana plants.

'Up there!' The woman waves with her hand as if she were cutting the air upwards.

'That way?'

'Yes.'

We go up the Street of Independence. They have got rid of us from the *plaza*.

Another black hut with a yard, and orange-trees beyond.

'*Hay frutas?*'

'*No hay.*'

'Not an orange, nor a banana?'

'*No hay.*'

We go on. *She* has got rid of us. We descend the black rocky steps to the stream, and up the other side, past the high reeds. There is a yard with heaps of maize in a shed, and tethered bullocks: and a bare-bosom, black-browed girl.

'*Hay frutas?*'

'*No hay.*'

'But yes! There are oranges – there!'

She turns and looks at the oranges on the trees at the back, and imbecilely answers:

'*No hay.*'

It is a choice between killing her and hurrying away.

We hear a drum and a whistle. It is down a rocky black track that calls itself The Street of Benito Juarez: the same old gent who stands for all this obvious Reform, and Vote for ⊙.

A yard with shade round. Women kneading the maize dough, *masa*, for *tortillas*. A man lounging. And a little boy beating a kettledrum sideways, and a big man playing a little reedy wooden whistle, rapidly, endlessly, disguising the tune of *La Cucuracha*. They won't play a tune unless they can render it almost unrecognizable.

'*Hay frutas?*'

'*No hay.*'

'Then what is happening here?'

A sheepish look, and no answer.

'Why are you playing music?'

'It is a *fiesta*.'

My God, a feast! That weary *masa*, a millstone in the belly. And for the rest, the blank, heavy, dark-grey barrenness, like an adobe brick. The drum-boy rolls his big Indian eyes at us, and beats on, though filled with consternation. The flute man glances, is half appalled and half resentful, so he blows harder. The lounging man comes and mutters to Rosalino, and Rosalino mutters back, four words.

Four words in the *idioma*, the Zapotec language. We retire, pushed silently away.

'What language do they speak here, Rosalino?'

'The *idioma*.'

'You understand them? It is Zapoteca, same as your language?'

'Yes, Señor.'

'Then why do you always speak in Spanish to them?'

'Because they don't speak the *idioma* of my village.'

He means, presumably, that there are dialect differences. Anyhow, he asserts his bit of Spanish, and says *Hay frutas?*

It was like a *posada*. It was like the Holy Virgin on Christmas Eve, wandering from door to door looking for a lodging in which to bear her child: Is there a room here? *No hay!*

The same with us. *Hay frutas? No hay!* We went down every straight ant-run of that blessed village. But at last we pinned a good-natured woman. 'Now tell us, *where* can we buy oranges? We see them on the trees. We want them to eat.'

'Go,' she said, 'to Valentino Ruiz. He has oranges. Yes, he has oranges, and he sells them.' And she cut the air upwards with her hand.

From black hut to black hut went we, till at last we got to the house of Valentino Ruiz. And lo! it was the yard with the *fiesta*. The lounging man was peeping out of the gateless gateway, as we came, at us.

'It is the same place!' cried Rosalino, with a laugh of bashful agony.

But we don't belong to the ruling race for nothing. Into the yard we march.

'Is this the house of Valentino Ruiz? *Hay naranjas?* Are there oranges?'

We had wandered so long, and asked so often, that the *masa* was made into *tortillas*, the *tortillas* were baked, and a group of people were sitting in a ring on the ground, eating them. It was the *fiesta*.

At my question up jumped a youngish man, and a woman as if they had been sitting on a scorpion each.

'Oh, Señor,' said the woman, 'there are few oranges, and they are not ripe, as the Señor would want them. But pass this way.'

We pass up to the garden, past the pink roses, to a little orange-tree, with a few yellowish-green oranges.

'You see, they are not ripe as you will want them,' says the youngish man.

'They will do.' Tropical oranges are always green. These, we found later, were almost insipidly sweet.

Even then, I can only get three of the big, thick-skinned, greenish oranges. But I spy sweet limes, and insist on having five or six of these.

He charges me three cents apiece for the oranges: the

market price is two for five cents: and one cent each for the *limas*.

'In my village,' mutters Rosalino when we get away, 'oranges are five for one cent.'

Never mind! It is one o'clock. Let us get out of the village, where the water will be safe, and eat lunch.

In the *plaza*, the men are just dispersing, one gang coming down the hill. They watch us as if we were a coyote, a *zopilote*, and a white she-bear walking together in the street.

'*Adios!*'

'*Adios!*' comes the low roll of reply, like a roll of cannon shot.

The water rushes downhill in a stone gutter beside the road. We climb up the hill, up the Street of the Camomile, alongside the rushing water. At one point it crosses the road unchannelled, and we wade through it. It is the village drinking supply.

At the juncture of the roads, where the water crosses, another silent white gang of men. Again: *Adios!* and again the low, musical, deep volley of *Adios!*

Up, up wearily. We must get above the village to be able to drink the water without developing typhoid.

At last, the last house, the naked hills. We follow the water across a dry maize-field, then up along a bank. Below is a quite deep gully. Across is an orchard, and some women with baskets of fruit.

'*Hay frutas?*' calls Rosalino, in a half-voice. He is getting bold.

'*Hay,*' says an old woman, in the curious half-voice. 'But not ripe.'

Shall we go down into the gully into the shade? No; someone is bathing among the reeds below, and the aqueduct water rushes along in the gutter here above. On, on, till we spy a wild guava tree over the channel of water. At last we can sit down and eat and drink, on a bank of dry grass, under the wild guava tree.

We put the bottle of lemonade in the aqueduct to cool. I

scoop out a big half-orange, the thick rind of which makes a cup.

'Look, Rosalino! The cup!'

'*La taza!*' he cries, soft-tongued, with a bark of laughter and delight.

And one drinks the soft, rather lifeless, warmish Mexican water. But it is pure.

Over the brink of the water-channel is the gully, and a noise – chock, chock! I go to look. It is a woman, naked to the hips, standing washing her other garments upon a stone. She has a beautiful full back, of a deep orange colour, and her wet hair is divided and piled. In the water a few yards up-stream two men are sitting naked, their brown-orange giving off a glow in the shadow, also washing their clothes. Their wet hair seems to steam blue-blackness. Just above them is a sort of bridge, where the water divides, the channel-water taken from the little river, and led along the top of the bank.

We sit under the wild guava tree in silence, and eat. The old woman of the fruit, with naked breast and coffee-brown naked arms, her under-garment fastened on one shoulder, round her waist an old striped *sarape* for a skirt, and on her head a blue *rebozo* piled against the sun, comes marching down the aqueduct with black bare feet, holding three or four *chirimoyas* to her bosom. *Chirimoyas* are green custard-apples.

She lectures us, in slow, heavy Spanish:

'This water, here, is for drinking. The other, below, is for washing. This, you drink, and you don't wash in it. The other, you wash in, and you don't drink it.' And she looked inquisitively at the bottle of lemonade, cooling.

'Very good. We understand.'

Then she gave us the *chirimoyas*. I asked her to change the *peso*: I had no change.

'No, Señor,' she said. 'No, Señor. You don't pay me. I bring you these, and may you eat well. But the *chirimoyas* are not ripe: in two or three days they will be ripe. Now, they are not. In two or three days they will be. Now, they are not.

You can't eat them yet. But I make a gift of them to you, and may you eat well. Farewell. Remain with God.'

She marched impatiently off along the aqueduct.

Rosalino waited to catch my eye. Then he opened his mouth and showed his pink tongue and swelled out his throat like a cobra, in a silent laugh after the old woman.

'But,' he said in a low tone, 'the *chirimoyas* are not good ones.'

And again he swelled in the silent, delighted, derisive laugh.

He was right. When we came to eat them, three days later, the custard-apples all had worms in them, and hardly any white meat.

'The old woman of Huayapa,' said Rosalino, reminiscent.

However, she had got her bottle. When we had drunk the lemonade, we sent Rosalino to give her the empty wine-bottle, and she made him another sententious little speech. But to her the bottle was a treasure.

And I, going round the little hummock behind the wild guava tree to throw away the papers of the picnic, came upon a golden-brown young man with his shirt just coming down over his head, but over no more of him. Hastily retreating, I thought again what beautiful, suave, rich skins these people have; a sort of richness of the flesh. It goes, perhaps, with the complete absence of what we call 'spirit'.

We lay still for a time, looking at the tiny guavas and the perfect, soft, high blue sky overhead, where the hawks and the ragged-winged *zopilotes* sway and diminish. A long, hot way home. But *mañana es otro dia*. Tomorrow is another day. And even the next five minutes are far enough away, in Mexico, on a Sunday afternoon.

3
The Mozo

ROSALINO really goes with the house, though he has been in service here only two months. When we went to look at the place, we saw him lurking in the *patio*, and glancing furtively under his brows. He is not one of the erect, bantam little Indians that stare with a black, incomprehensible, but somewhat defiant stare. It may be Rosalino has a distant strain of other Indian blood, not Zapotec. Or it may be he is only a bit different. The difference lies in a certain sensitiveness and aloneness, as if he were a mother's boy. The way he drops his head and looks sideways under his black lashes, apprehensive, apprehending, feeling his way, as it were. Not the bold male glare of most of the Indians, who seem as if they had never, never had mothers at all.

The Aztec gods and goddesses are, as far as we have known anything about them, an unlovely and unlovable lot. In their myths there is no grace or charm, no poetry. Only this perpetual grudge, grudge, grudging, one god grudging another, the gods grudging men their existence, and men grudging the animals. The goddess of love is a goddess of dirt and prostitution, a dirt-eater, a horror, without a touch of tenderness. If the god wants to make love to her, she has to sprawl down in front of him, blatant and accessible.

And then, after all, when she conceives and brings forth, what is it she produces? What is the infant-god she tenderly bears? Guess, all ye people, joyful and triumphant!

You never could.

It is a stone knife.

It is a razor-edged knife of blackish-green flint, the knife of all knives, the veritable Paraclete of knives. It is the sacrificial knife with which the priest makes a gash in his victim's breast, before he tears out the heart, to hold it smoking to the sun.

And the Sun, the Sun behind the sun, is supposed to suck the smoking heart greedily with insatiable appetite.

This, then, is a pretty Christmas Eve. Lo, the goddess is gone to bed, to bring forth her child. Lo! ye people, await the birth of the saviour, the wife of a god is about to become a mother.

Tarumm-tarah! Tarumm-tarah! blow the trumpets. The child is born. Unto us a son is given. Bring him forth, lay him on a tender cushion. Show him, then, to all the people. See! See! See him upon the cushion, tenderly new-born and reposing! Ah, *qué bonito!* Oh, what a nice, blackish, smooth, keen stone knife!

And to this day, most of the Mexican Indian women seem to bring forth stone knives. Look at them, these sons of incomprehensible mothers, with their black eyes like flints, and their stiff little bodies as taut and as keen as knives of obsidian. Take care they don't rip you up.

Our Rosalino is an exception. He drops his shoulders just a little. He is a bit bigger, also, than the average Indian down here. He must be about five feet four inches. And he hasn't got the big, obsidian, glaring eyes. His eyes are smaller, blacker, like the quick black eyes of the lizard. They don't look at one with the obsidian stare. They are just a bit aware that there is another being, unknown, at the other end of the glance. Hence he drops his head with a little apprehension, screening himself as if he were vulnerable.

Usually, these people have no correspondence with one at all. To them a white man or white woman is a sort of phenomenon; just as a monkey is a sort of phenomenon; something to watch, and wonder at, and laugh at, but not to be taken on one's own plane.

Now the white man is a sort of extraordinary white monkey that, by cunning, has learnt lots of semi-magical secrets of the universe, and made himself boss of the show. Imagine a race of big white monkeys got up in fantastic clothes, and able to kill a man by hissing at him; able to leap through the air in great hops, covering a mile in each leap; able to transmit his thoughts by a moment's effort of concentration to some great white monkey or monkeyess, a thousand miles away: and you have, from our point of view, something of the picture that the Indian has of us.

The white monkey has curious tricks. He knows, for example, the time. Now to a Mexican, and an Indian, time is a vague, foggy reality. There are only three times: *en la mañana, en la tarde, en la noche*. in the morning, in the afternoon, in the night. There is even no midday, and no evening.

But to the white monkey, horrible to relate, there are exact spots of time, such as five o'clock, half past nine. The day is a horrible puzzle of exact spots of time.

The same with distance: horrible invisible distances called two miles, ten miles. To the Indians, there is near and far, and very near and very far. There is two days or one day. But two miles are as good as twenty to him, for he goes entirely by his feeling. If a certain two miles feels far to him, then it *is* far, it is *muy lejos!* But if a certain twenty miles *feels* near and familiar, then it is not far. Oh, no, it is just a little distance. And he will let you set off in the evening, for night to overtake you in the wilderness, without a qualm. It is not far.

But the white man has a horrible, truly horrible, monkey-like passion for invisible exactitudes. *Mañana,* to the native, may mean tomorrow, three days hence, six months hence, and never. There are no fixed points in life, save birth, and death, and the *fiestas*. The fixed points of birth and death evaporate spontaneously into vagueness. And the priests fix the *fiestas*. From time immemorial priests have fixed the *fiestas*, the festivals of the gods, and men have had no more to do with time. What should men have to do with time?

The same with money. These *centavos* and these *pesos*, what do they mean, after all? Little discs that have no charm. The natives insist on reckoning in invisible coins, coins that don't exist here, like *reales* or *pesetas*. If you buy two eggs for a *real*, you have to pay twelve and a half *centavos*. Since also half a *centavo* doesn't exist, you or the vendor forfeit the non-existent.

The same with honesty, the *meum* and the *tuum*. The white

man has a horrible way of remembering, even to a *centavo*, even to a thimbleful of *mescal*. Horrible! The Indian, it seems to me, is not naturally dishonest. He is not naturally avaricious, has not even any innate cupidity. In this he is unlike the old people of the Mediterranean, to whom possessions have a mystic meaning, and a silver coin a mystic white halo, a *lueur* of magic.

To the real Mexican, no! He doesn't care. He doesn't even *like* keeping money. His deep instinct is to spend it at once, so that he needn't have it. He doesn't really want to keep anything, not even his wife and children. Nothing that he has to be responsible for. Strip, strip, strip away the past and the future, leave the naked moment of the present disentangled. Strip away memory, strip away forethought and care; leave the moment, stark and sharp and without consciousness, like the obsidian knife. The before and the after are the stuff of consciousness. The instant moment is for ever keen with a razor-edge of oblivion, like the knife of sacrifice.

But the great white monkey has got hold of the keys of the world, and the black-eyed Mexican has to serve the great white monkey, in order to live. He has to learn the tricks of the white monkey-show: time of the day, coin of money, machines that start at a second, work that is meaningless and yet is paid for with exactitude, in exact coin. A whole existence of monkey-tricks and monkey-virtues. The strange monkey-virtue of charity, the white monkeys nosing round to *help*, to *save!* Could any trick be more unnatural? Yet it is one of the tricks of the great white monkey.

If an Indian is poor, he says to another: I have no food; give me to eat. Then the other hands the hungry one a couple of *tortillas*. That is natural. But when the white monkey comes round, they peer at the house, at the woman, at the children. They say: Your child is sick. *Sí, Señor*. What have you done for it – *Nothing. What is to be done?* – You must make a poultice. I will show you how.

Well, it was very amusing, this making hot dough to dab on

the baby. Like plastering a house with mud. But why do it twice? Twice is not amusing. The child will die. Well, then, it will be in Paradise. How nice for it! That's just what God wants of it, that it shall be a cheerful little angel among the roses of Paradise. What could be better?

How tedious of the white monkey coming with the trick of salvation, to rub oil on the baby, and put poultices on it, and make you give it medicine in a spoon at morning, noon, and night. Why morning and noon and night? Why not just anytime, anywhen? It will die tomorrow if you don't do these things today! But tomorrow is another day, and it is not dead now, so if it dies at another time, it must be because the other times are out of hand.

Oh, the tedious, exacting white monkeys, with their yesterdays and todays and tomorrows! Tomorrow is always another day, and yesterday is part of the encircling never. Why think outside the moment? And inside the moment one does not think. So why pretend to think? It is one of the white-monkey-tricks. He is a clever monkey. But he is ugly, and he has nasty, white flesh. We are not ugly, with screwed-up faces, and we have good warm-brown flesh. If we have to work for the white monkey, we don't care. His tricks are half-amusing. And one may as well amuse oneself that way as any other. So long as one is amused.

So long as the devil does not rouse in us, seeing the white monkeys for ever mechanically bossing, with their incessant tick-tack of work. Seeing them get the work out of us, the sweat, the money, and then taking the very land from us, the very oil and metal out of our soil.

They do it! They do it all the time. Because they can't help it. Because grasshoppers can but hop, and ants can carry little sticks, and white monkeys can go tick-tack, tick-tack, do this, do that, time to work, time to eat, time to drink, time to sleep, time to walk, time to ride, time to wash, time to look dirty, tick-tack, tick-tack, time, time, time! time! Oh, cut off his nose and make him swallow it.

For the *moment* is as changeless as an obsidian knife, and the heart of the Indian is keen as the moment that divides past from future, and sacrifices them both.

To Rosalino, too, the white monkey-tricks are amusing. He is ready to work for the white monkeys, to learn some of their tricks, their monkey-speech of Spanish, their tick-tack ways. He works for four *pesos* a month, and his food: a few *tortillas*. Four *pesos* are two American dollars: about nine shillings. He owns two cotton shirts, two pairs of calico pantaloons, two blouses, one of pink cotton, one of darkish flannelette, and a pair of sandals. Also, his straw hat that he has curled up to look very jaunty, and a rather old, factory-made, rather cheap shawl, or plaid rug with fringe. *Et praeterea nihil.*

His duty is to rise in the morning and sweep the street in front of the house, and water it. Then he sweeps and waters the broad, brick-tiled verandas, and flicks the chairs with a sort of duster made of fluffy reeds. After which he walks behind the cook – she is very superior, had a Spanish grandfather, and Rosalino must address her as *Señora* – carrying the basket to market. Returned from the market, he sweeps the whole of the *patio*, gathers up the leaves and refuse, fills the pannier-basket, hitches it up on to his shoulders, and holds it by a band across his forehead, and thus, a beast of burden, goes out to deposit the garbage at the side of one of the little roads leading out of the city. Every *little* road leaves the town between heaps of garbage, an avenue of garbage blistering in the sun.

Returning, Rosalino waters the whole of the garden and sprinkles the whole of the *patio*. This takes most of the morning. In the afternoon, he sits without much to do. If the wind has blown or the day is hot, he starts again at about three o'clock, sweeping up leaves, and sprinkling everywhere with an old watering-can.

Then he retreats to the entrance-way, the *zaguán*, which, with its big doors and its cobbled track, is big enough to admit an ox-wagon. The *zaguán* is his home: just the doorway. In one corner is a low wooden bench about four feet long and eighteen inches wide. On this he screws up and sleeps, in his clothes as he is, wrapped in the old *sarape*.

But this is anticipating. In the obscurity of the *zaguán* he sits and pores, pores, pores over a school-book, learning to read and write. He can read a bit, and write a bit. He filled a large sheet of foolscap with writing: quite nice. But I found out that what he had written was a Spanish poem, a love-poem, with *no puedo olvidar* and *voy a cortar* – the rose, of course. He had written the thing straight ahead, without verse-lines or capitals or punctuation at all, just a vast string of words, a whole foolscap sheet full. When I read a few lines aloud, he writhed and laughed in an agony of confused feelings. And of what he had written he understood a small, small amount, parrot-wise, from the top of his head. Actually, it meant just words, sound, noise, to him: noise called *Castellano,* Castilian. Exactly like a parrot.

From seven to eight he goes to the night-school, to cover a bit more of the foolscap. He has been going for two years. If he goes two years more he will perhaps really be able to read and write six intelligible sentences: but only Spanish, which is as foreign to him as Hindustani would be to an English farm-boy. Then if he can speak his quantum of Spanish, and read it and write it to a very uncertain extent, he will return to his village two days' journey on foot into the hills, and then, in time, he may even rise to be an *alcalde,* or headman of the village, responsible to the Government. If he were *alcalde* he would get a little salary. But far more important to him is the glory: being able to boss.

He has a *paisano,* a fellow-countryman, to sleep with him in the *zaguán,* to guard the doors. Whoever gets into the house or *patio* must get through these big doors. There is no other entrance, not even a needle's eye. The windows to the street are heavily barred. Each house is its own small fortress. Ours is a double square, the trees and flowers in the first square, with the two wings of the house. And in the second *patio,* the chickens, pigeons, guinea-pigs, and the big heavy earthenware dish or tub, called an *apaxtle,* in which all the servants can bathe themselves, like chickens in a saucer.

By half past nine at night Rosalino is lying on his little

bench, screwed up, wrapped in his shawl, his sandals, called *huaraches*, on the floor. Usually he takes off his *huaraches* when he goes to bed. That is all his preparation. In another corner, wrapped up, head and all, like a mummy in his thin old blanket, the *paisano*, another lad of about twenty, lies asleep on the cold stones. And at an altitude of five thousand feet, the nights can be cold.

Usually everybody is in by half past nine in our very quiet house. If not, you may thunder at the big doors. It is hard to wake Rosalino. You have to go close to him, and call. That will wake him. But don't touch him. That would startle him terribly. No one is touched unawares, except to be robbed or murdered.

'Rosalino! *están tocando!*' – 'Rosalino! they are knocking!'

At last there starts up a strange, glaring, utterly lost Rosalino. Perhaps he just has enough wit to pull the door-catch. One wonders where he was, and what he was, in his sleep, he starts up so strange and wild and lost.

The first time he had anything to do for me was when the van was come to carry the bit of furniture to the house. There was Aurelio, the dwarf *mozo* of our friends and Rosalino, and the man who drove the wagon. But there *should* have been also a *cargador* – a porter. 'Help them,' said I to Rosalino. 'You give a hand to help.' But he winced away, muttering, '*No quiero!* – I don't want to.'

The fellow, I thought to myself, is a fool. He thinks it's not his job, and perhaps he is afraid of smashing the furniture. Nothing to be done but to leave him alone.

We settled in, and Rosalino seemed to like doing things for us. He liked learning his monkey-tricks from the white monkeys. And since we started feeding him from our own meals, and for the first time in his life he had real soups, meat-stews, or a fried egg, he loved to do things in the kitchen. He would come with sparkling black eyes: '*Hé comido el caldo. Grazias!*' ('I have eaten the soup. Thank you.') – And he would give a strange, excited little yelp of a laugh.

Came the day when we walked to Huayapa, on the Sunday,

and he was very thrilled. But at night, in the evening when we got home, he lay mute on his bench – not that he was really tired. The Indian gloom, which settles on them like a black marsh-fog, had settled on him. He did not bring in the water – let me carry it by myself.

Monday morning, the same black, reptilian gloom, and a sense of hatred. He hated us. This was a bit flabbergasting, because he had been so thrilled and happy the day before. But the revulsion had come. He didn't forgive himself for having felt free and happy with us. He had eaten what we had eaten, hard-boiled eggs and sardine sandwiches and cheese; he had drunk out of the orange-peel *taza*, which delighted him so much. He had had a bottle of *gaseosa*, fizz, with us, on the way home, in San Felipe.

And now, the reaction. The flint knife. He had been happy, *therefore* we were scheming to take another advantage of him. We had some devilish white monkey-trick up our sleeve; we wanted to get at his *soul*, no doubt, and do it the white monkey's damage. We wanted to get at his heart, did we? But his heart was an obsidian knife.

He hated us, and gave off a black steam of hate, that filled the *patio* and made one feel sick. He did not come to the kitchen, he did not carry the water. Leave him alone.

At lunch-time on Monday he said he wanted to leave. Why? He said he wanted to go back to his village.

Very well. He was to wait just a few days, till another *mozo* was found.

At this a glance of pure, reptilian hate from his black eyes.

He sat motionless on his bench all the afternoon, in the Indian stupor of gloom and profound hate. In the evening, he cheered up a little and said he would stay on, at least till Easter.

Tuesday morning. More stupor and gloom and hate. He wanted to go back to his village at once. All right! No one wanted to keep him against his will. Another *mozo* would be found at once.

He went off in the numb stupor of gloom and hate, a very potent hate that could affect one in the pit of one's stomach with nausea.

Tuesday afternoon, and he thought he would stay.

Wednesday morning, and he wanted to go.

Very good. Inquiries made; another *mozo* was coming on Friday morning. It was settled.

Thursday was *fiesta*. Wednesday, therefore, we would go to market, the Niña – that is the mistress – myself, and Rosalino with the basket. He loved to go to market with the *patrones*. We would give him money and send him off to bargain for oranges, *pitahayas*, potatoes, eggs, a chicken, and so forth. This he simply loved to do. It put him into a temper to see us buying without bargaining, and paying ghastly prices.

He bargained away, silent almost, muttering darkly. It took him a long time, but he had far greater success than even Natividad, the cook. And he came back in triumph, with much stuff and little money spent.

So again that afternoon, he was staying on. The spell was wearing off.

The Indians of the hills have a heavy, intense sort of attachment to their villages; Rosalino had not been out of the little city for two years. Suddenly finding himself in Huayapa, a real Indian hill-village, the black Indian gloom of nostalgia must have made a crack in his spirits. But he had been perfectly cheerful – perhaps too cheerful – till we got home.

Again, the Señorita had taken a photograph of him. They are all crazy to have their photographs taken. I had given him an envelope and a stamp, to send a photograph to his mother. Because in his village he had a widow mother, a brother, and a married sister. The family owned a bit of land, with orange-trees. The best oranges come from the hills, where it is cooler. Seeing the photographs, the mother, who had completely forgotten her son, as far as any keen remembering goes, suddenly, like a cracker going off inside her, wanted him: at that very moment. So she sent an urgent message.

But already it was Wednesday afternoon. Arrived a little

fellow in white clothes, smiling hard. It was the brother from the hills. Now, we thought, Rosalino will have someone to walk back with. On Friday, after the *fiesta*, he would go.

Thursday, he escorted us with the basket to the *fiesta*. He bargained for flowers, and for a *sarape* which he didn't get, for a carved *jícara* which he did get, and for a number of toys. He and the Niña and the Señorita ate a great wafer of a pancake with sweet stuff on it. The basket grew heavy. The brother appeared, to carry the hen and the extra things. Bliss.

He was perfectly happy again. He didn't want to go on Friday; he didn't want to go at all. He wanted to stay with us and come with us to England when we went home.

So, another trip to the friend, the Mexican, who had found us the other *mozo*. Now to put off the other boy again: but then, they are like that.

And the Mexican, who had known Rosalino when he first came down from the hills and could speak no Spanish, told us another thing about him.

In the last revolution – a year ago – the revolutionaries of the winning side wanted more soldiers from the hills. The *alcalde* of the hill-village was told to pick out young men and send them down to the barracks in the city. Rosalino was among the chosen.

But Rosalino refused, said again *No quiero!* He is one of those, like myself, who have a horror of serving in a mass of men, or even of being mixed up with a mass of men. He obstinately refused. Whereupon the recruiting soldiers beat him with the butts of their rifles till he lay unconscious, apparently dead.

Then, because they wanted him at once, and he would now be no good for some time, with his injured back, they left him, to get the revolution over without him.

This explains his fear of furniture-carrying, and his fear of being 'caught'.

Yet that little Aurelio, the friend's *mozo*, who is not above four feet six in height, a tiny fellow, fared even worse, He, too, is from the hills. In this village, a cousin of his gave some information to the *losing* side in the revolution. The cousin wisely disappeared.

But in the city, the winning side seized Aurelio, since he was the *cousin* of the delinquent. In spite of the fact that he was the faithful *mozo* of a foreign resident, he was flung into prison. Prisoners in prison are not fed. Either friends or relatives bring them food, or they go very, very thin. Aurelio had a married sister in town, but *she* was afraid to go to the prison lest she and her husband should be seized. The master, then, sent his new *mozo* twice a day to the prison with a basket; the huge, huge prison, for this little town of a few thousands.

Meanwhile the master struggled and struggled with the 'authorities' – friends of the people – for Aurelio's release. Nothing to be done.

One day the new *mozo* arrived at the prison with the basket, to find no Aurelio. A friendly soldier gave the message Aurelio had left. '*Adios a mi patrón. Me llevan.*' Oh, fatal words: '*Me llevan.*' – They are taking me off. The master rushed to the train: it had gone, with the dwarf, plucky little *mozo*, into the void.

Months later, Aurelio reappeared. He was in rags, haggard, and his dark throat was swollen up to the ears. He had been taken off, two hundred miles into Vera Cruz State. He had been hung up by the neck, with a fixed knot, and left hanging for hours. Why? To make the cousin come and save his relative: put his own neck into a running noose. To make the absolutely innocent fellow confess: what? Everybody knew he was innocent. At any rate, to teach everybody better next time. Oh, brotherly teaching!

Aurelio escaped, and took to the mountains. Sturdy little dwarf of a fellow, he made his way back, begging *tortillas* at the villages, and arrived, haggard, with a great swollen neck, to find his master waiting, and another 'party' in power. More friends of the people.

Tomorrow is another day. The master nursed Aurelio well, and Aurelio is a strong, if tiny, fellow, with big, brilliant black eyes that for the moment will trust a foreigner, but none of his own people. A dwarf in stature, but perfectly made, and very strong. And very intelligent, far more quick and intelligent than Rosalino.

Is it any wonder that Aurelio and Rosalino, when they see the soldiers with guns on their shoulders marching towards the prison with some blanched prisoner between them – and one sees it every few days – stand and gaze in a blank kind of horror, and look at the *patrón*, to see if there is any refuge?

Not to be *caught*! Not to be *caught*! It must have been the prevailing motive of Indian-Mexico life since long before Montezuma marched his prisoners to sacrifice.

4

Market Day

THIS is the last Saturday before Christmas. The next year will be momentous, one feels. This year is nearly gone. Dawn was windy, shaking the leaves, and the rising sun shone under a gap of yellow cloud. But at once it touched the yellow flowers that rise above the *patio* wall, and the swaying, glowing magenta of the bougainvillea, and the fierce red outbursts of the poinsettia. The poinsettia is very splendid, the flowers very big, and of a sure stainless red. They call them Noche Buenas, flowers of Christmas Eve. These tufts throw out their scarlet sharply, like red birds ruffling in the wind of dawn as if going to bathe, all their feathers alert. This for Christmas, instead of holly-berries. Christmas seems to need a red herald.

The yucca is tall, higher than the house. It is, too, in flower, hanging an arm's-length of soft creamy bells, like a yard-long grape-cluster of foam. And the waxy bells break on their stems in the wind, fall noiselessly from the long creamy bunch, that hardly sways.

The coffee-berries are turning red. The hibiscus flowers,

rose-coloured, sway at the tips of the thin branches, in rosettes of soft red.

In the second *patio*, there is a tall tree of the flimsy acacia sort. Above itself it puts up whitish fingers of flowers, naked on the blue sky. And in the wind these fingers of flowers in the bare blue sky, sway, sway with the reeling, roundward motion of tree-tips in a wind.

A restless morning, with clouds lower down, moving also with a larger roundward motion. Everything moving. Best to go out in motion too, the slow roundward motion like the hawks.

Everything seems slowly to circle and hover towards a central point, the clouds, the mountains round the valley, the dust that rises, the big, beautiful, white-barred hawks, *gabilanes*, and even the snow-white flakes of flowers upon the dim *palo-blanco* tree. Even the organ cactus, rising in stock-straight clumps, and the candelabrum cactus, seem to be slowly wheeling and pivoting upon a centre, close upon it.

Strange that we should think in straight lines, when there are none, and talk of straight courses, when every course, sooner or later, is seen to be making the sweep round, swooping upon the centre. When space is curved, and the cosmos is sphere within sphere, and the way from any point to any other point is round the bend of the inevitable, that turns as the tips of the broad wings of the hawk turn upwards, leaning upon the air like the invisible half of the ellipse. If I have a way to go, it will be round the swoop of a bend impinging centripetal towards the centre. The straight course is hacked out in wounds, against the will of the world.

Yet the dust advances like a ghost along the road, down the valley plain. The dry turf of the valley-bed gleams like soft skin, sunlit and pinkish ochre, spreading wide between the mountains that seem to emit their own darkness, a dark-blue vapour translucent, sombring them from the humped crests downwards. The many-pleated, noiseless mountains of Mexico.

And away on the footslope lie the white specks of Huayapa,

among its lake of trees. It is Saturday, and the white dots of men are threading down the trail over the bare humps to the plain, following the dark twinkle-movement of asses, the dark nodding of the woman's head as she rides between the baskets. Saturday and market-day, and morning, so the white specks of men, like sea-gulls on plough-land, come ebbing like sparks from the *palo-blanco*, over the fawn undulating of the valley slope.

They are dressed in snow-white cotton, and they lift their knees in the Indian trot, following the ass where the woman sits perched between the huge baskets, her child tight in the *rebozo*, at the brown breast. And girls in long, full, soiled cotton skirts running, trotting, ebbing along after the twinkle-movement of the ass. Down they come in families, in clusters, in solitary ones, threading with ebbing, running, barefoot movement noiseless towards the town, that blows the bubbles of its church-domes above the stagnant green of trees, away under the opposite fawn-skin hills.

But down the valley middle comes the big road, almost straight. You will know it by the tall walking of the dust, that hastens also towards the town, overtaking, overpassing everybody. Overpassing all the dark little figures and the white specks that thread tinily, in a sort of underworld, to the town.

From the valley villages and from the mountains the peasants and the Indians are coming in with supplies, the road is like a pilgrimage, with the dust in greatest haste, dashing for town. Dark-eared asses and running men, running women, running girls, running lads, twinkling donkeys ambling on fine little feet, under twin baskets with tomatoes and gourds, twin great nets of bubble-shaped jars, twin bundles of neat-cut faggots of wood, neat as bunches of cigarettes, and twin net-sacks of charcoal. Donkeys, mules, on they come, great pannier baskets making a rhythm under the perched woman, great bundles bouncing against the sides of the slim-footed animals. A baby donkey trotting naked after its piled-up dam, a white, sandal-footed man following with the silent Indian haste, and a girl running again on light feet.

Onwards, on a strange current of haste. And slowly rowing among the foot-travel, the ox-wagons rolling solid wheels below the high net of the body. Slow oxen, with heads pressed down nosing to the earth, swaying, swaying their great horns as a snake sways itself, the shovel-shaped collar of solid wood pressing down on their necks like a scoop. On, on between the burnt-up turf and the solid, monumental green of the organ cactus. Past the rocks and the floating *palo-blanco* flowers, past the towsled dust of the mesquite bushes. While the dust once more, in a greater haste than anyone, comes tall and rapid down the road, overpowering and obscuring all the little people, as in a cataclysm.

They are mostly small people, of the Zapotec race: small men with lifted chests and quick, lifted knees, advancing with heavy energy in the midst of dust. And quiet, small, round-headed women running barefoot, tightening their blue *rebozos* round their shoulders, so often with a baby in the fold. The white cotton clothes of the men so white that their faces are invisible places of darkness under their big hats. Clothed darkness, faces of night, quickly, silently, with inexhaustible energy advancing to the town.

And many of the *serranos*, the Indians from the hills, wearing their little conical black felt hats, seem capped with night, above the straight white shoulders. Some have come far, walking all yesterday in their little black hats and black-sheathed sandals. Tomorrow they will walk back. And their eyes will be just the same, black and bright and wild, in the dark faces. They have no goal, any more than the hawks in the air, and no course to run, any more than the clouds.

The market is a huge roofed-in place. Most extraordinary is the noise that comes out, as you pass along the adjacent street. It is a huge noise, yet you may never notice it. It sounds as if all the ghosts in the world were talking to one another, in ghost-voices, within the darkness of the market structure. It is a noise something like rain, or banana leaves in a wind. The market, full of Indians, dark-faced, silent-footed, hush-spoken, but pressing in in countless numbers. The queer hissing murmurs of the Zapotec *idioma*, among the sounds of Spanish, the quiet, aside, voices of the Mixtecas.

To buy and to sell, but above all, to commingle. In the old world, men make themselves two great excuses for coming together to a centre, and commingling freely in a mixed, unsuspicious host. Market and religion. These alone bring men, unarmed, together since time began. A little load of firewood, a woven blanket, a few eggs and tomatoes are excuse enough for men, women, and children to cross the foot-weary miles of valley and mountain. To buy, to sell, to barter, to exchange. To exchange, above all things, human contact.

That is why they like you to bargain, even if it's only the difference of a *centavo*. Round the centre of the covered market where there is a basin of water, are the flowers: red, white, pink roses in heaps, many-coloured little carnations, poppies, bits of larkspur, lemon and orange marigolds, buds of madonna lilies, pansies, a few forget-me-nots. They don't bring the tropical flowers. Only the lilies come wild from the hills, and the mauve red orchids.

'How much this bunch of cherry-pie heliotrope?'

'Fifteen *centavos*.'

'Ten.'

'Fifteen.'

You put back the cherry-pie, and depart. But the woman is quite content. The contact, so short even, brisked her up.

'Pinks?'

'The red one, Señorita? Thirty *centavos*.'

'No. I don't want red ones. The mixed.'

'Ah!' The woman seizes a handful of little carnations of all colours, carefully puts them together. 'Look, Señorita! No more?'

'No, no more. How much?'

'The same. Thirty *centavos*.'

'It is much.'

'No, Señorita, it is not much. Look at this little bunch. It is eight centavos.' – Displays a scrappy little bunch. 'Come then, twenty-five.'

'No! Twenty-two.'

'Look!' She gathers up three or four more flowers, and claps them to the bunch. 'Two *reales*, Señorita.'

It is a bargain. Off you go with multicoloured pinks, and the woman has had one more moment of contact, with a stranger, a perfect stranger. An intermingling of voices, a threading together of different wills. It is life. The *centavos* are an excuse.

The stalls go off in straight lines, to the right, brilliant vegetables, to the left, bread and sweet buns. Away at the one end, cheese, butter, eggs, chicken, turkeys, meat. At the other, the native-woven blankets and *rebozos*, skirts, shirts, handkerchiefs. Down the far-side, sandals and leather things.

The *sarape* men spy you, and whistle to you like ferocious birds, and call 'Señor! Señor! Look!' Then with violence one flings open a dazzling blanket, while another whistles more ear-piercingly still, to make you look at *his* blanket. It is the veritable den of lions and tigers, that spot where the *sarape* men have their blankets piled on the ground. You shake your head, and flee.

To find yourself in the leather avenue.

'Señor! Señor! Look! *Huaraches!* Very fine, very finely made! Look, Señor!'

The fat leather man jumps up and holds a pair of sandals at one's breast. They are of narrow woven strips of leather, in the newest Paris style, but a style ancient to these natives. You take them in your hand, and look at them quizzically, while the fat wife of the *huarache* man reiterates, 'Very fine work. Very fine. Much work!'

Leather men usually seem to have their wives with them.

'How much?'

'Twenty *reales*.'

'Twenty!' – in a voice of surprise and pained indignation. 'How much do you give?'

You refuse to answer. Instead you put the *huaraches* to your nose. The *huarache* man looks at his wife, and they laugh aloud.

'They smell,' you say.

'No, Señor, they don't smell!' – and the two go off into fits of laughter.

'Yes, they smell. It is not American leather.'

'Yes, Señor, it is American leather. They don't smell, Señor. No, they don't smell.' He coaxes you till you wouldn't believe your own nose.

'Yes, they smell.'

'How much do you give?'

'Nothing, because they smell.'

And you give another sniff, though it is painfully unnecessary. And in spite of your refusal to bid, the man and wife go into fits of laughter to see you painfully sniffing.

You lay down the sandals and shake your head.

'How much do you offer?' reiterates the man, gaily.

You shake your head mournfully, and move away. The leather man and his wife look at one another and go off into another fit of laughter, because you smelt the *huaraches*, and said they stank.

They did. The natives use human excrement for tanning leather. When Bernal Diaz came with Cortés to the great market-place of Mexico City, in Montezuma's day, he saw the little pots of human excrement in rows for sale, and the leather-makers going round sniffing to see which was the best, before they paid for it. It staggered even a fifteenth-century Spaniard. Yet my leather man and his wife think it screamingly funny that I smell the *huaraches* before buying them. Everything has its own smell, and the natural smell of *huaraches* is what it is. You might as well quarrel with an onion for smelling like an onion.

The great press of the quiet natives, some of them bright and clean, many in old rags, the brown flesh showing through the rents in the dirty cotton. Many wild hillmen, in their little hats of conical black felt, with their wild, staring eyes. And as they cluster round the hat-stall, in a long, long suspense of indecision before they can commit themselves, trying on a new hat, their black hair gleams blue-black, and falls thick and rich over their foreheads, like gleaming bluey-black feathers.

And one is reminded again of the blue-haired Buddha, with the lotus at his navel.

But already the fleas are travelling under one's clothing.

Market lasts all day. The native inns are great dreary yards with little sheds, and little rooms around. Some men and families who have come from far, will sleep in one or other of the little stall-like rooms. Many will sleep on the stones, on the earth, round the market, anywhere. But the asses are there by the hundred, crowded in the inn-yards, drooping their ears with the eternal patience of the beast that knows better than any other beast that every road curves round to the same centre of rest, and hither and thither means nothing.

And towards nightfall the dusty road will be thronged with shadowy people and unladen asses and new-laden mules, urging silently into the country again, their backs to the town, glad to get away from the town, to see the cactus and the pleated hills, and the trees that mean a village. In some village they will lie under a tree, or under a wall, and sleep. Then the next day, home.

It is fulfilled, what they came to market for. They have sold and bought. But more than that, they have had their moment of contact and centripetal flow. They have been part of a great stream of men flowing to a centre, to the vortex of the market-place. And here they have felt life concentrate upon them, they have been jammed between the soft hot bodies of strange men come from afar, they have had the sound of strangers' voices in their ears, they have asked and been answered in unaccustomed ways.

There is no goal, and no abiding-place, and nothing is fixed, not even the cathedral towers. The cathedral towers are slowly leaning, seeking the curve of return. As the natives curved in a strong swirl, towards the vortex of the market. Then on a strong swerve of repulsion, curved out and away again, into space.

Nothing but the touch, the spark of contact. That, no more. That, which is most elusive, still the only treasure. Come, and gone, and yet the clue itself.

True, folded up in the handkerchief inside the shirt, are the copper *centavos*, and maybe a few silver *pesos*. But these too will disappear as the stars disappear at daybreak, as they are meant to disappear. Everything is meant to disappear. Every curve plunges into the vortex and is lost, re-emerges with a certain relief and takes to the open, and there is lost again.

Only that which is utterly intangible, matters. The contact, the spark of exchange. That which can never be fastened upon, for ever gone, for ever coming, never to be detained: the spark of contact.

Like the evening star, when it is neither night nor day. Like the evening star, between the sun and the moon, and swayed by neither of them. The flashing intermediary, the evening star that is seen only at the dividing of the day and night, but then is more wonderful than either.

5

Indians and Entertainment

WE go to the theatre to be entertained. It may be *The Potters*, it may be Max Reinhardt, *King Lear*, or *Electra*. All entertainment.

We want to be taken out of ourselves. Or not entirely that. We want to become spectators at our own show. We lean down from the plush seats like little gods in a democratic heaven, and see ourselves away below there, on the world of the stage, in a brilliant artificial sunlight, behaving comically absurdly, like Pa Potter, yet getting away with it, or behaving tragically absurdly, like King Lear, and not getting away with it: rather proud of not getting away with it.

We see ourselves: we survey ourselves: we laugh at ourselves: we weep over ourselves: we are the gods above of our own destinies. Which is very entertaining.

The secret of it all, is that we detach ourselves from the painful and always sordid trammels of actual existence, and become creatures of memory and of spirit-like consciousness. We are the gods and there's the machine, down below us. Down below, on the stage, our mechanical or earth-bound self stutters or raves, Pa Potter or King Lear. But however Potter-ish or Learian we may be, while we sit aloft in plush seats we are creatures of pure consciousness, pure spirit, surveying those selves of clay who are so absurd or so tragic, below.

Even a little girl trailing a long skirt and playing at being Mrs Paradiso next door, is enjoying the same sensation. From her childish little consciousness she is making Mrs Paradiso, creating her according to her own fancy. It is the little indivi-dual consciousness lording it, for the moment, over the actu-ally tiresome and inflexible world of actuality. Mrs Paradiso in the flesh is a thing to fear. But if I can play at being Mrs Para-diso, why, then I am a little Lord Almighty, and Mrs Paradiso is but a creation from my consciousness.

The audience in the theatre is a little democracy of the ideal consciousness. They all sit there, gods of the ideal mind, and survey with laughter or tears the realm of actuality.

Which is very soothing and satisfying so long as you believe that the ideal mind is the actual arbiter. So long as you in-stinctively feel that there is some supreme, universal Ideal Consciousness swaying all destiny.

When you begin to have misgivings, you sit rather uneasily on your plush seat.

Nobody really believes that destiny is an accident. The very fact that day keeps on following night, and summer winter, establishes the belief in universal law, and from this to a belief in some great hidden mind in the universe is an inevitable step for us.

A few people, the so-called advanced, have grown uneasy in their bones about the Universal Mind. But the mass are abso-lutely convinced. And every member of the mass is absolutely convinced that he is part and parcel of this Universal Mind. Hence his joy at the theatre. His even greater joy at the cinematograph.

In the moving pictures he has detached himself even further

from the solid stuff of earth. There, the people are truly shadows: the shadow-pictures are thinkings of his mind. They live in the rapid and kaleidoscopic realm of the abstract. And the individual watching the shadow-spectacle sits a very god, in an orgy of abstraction, actually dissolved into delighted, watchful spirit. And if his best girl sits beside him, she vibrates in the same ether, and triumphs in the same orgy of abstraction. No wonder this passion of dramatic abstraction becomes a lust.

That is our idea of entertainment.

You come to the Indian and ask him about his. He hasn't got one.

The Indians dance around the drum, singing. They have their great spectacular dances, Eagle dance, Corn dance. They have the dancing, singing procession between the fires at Christmas. They have their sacred races, down the long track.

White people always, or nearly always, write sentimentally about the Indians. Even a man like Adolf Bandelier. He was not a sentimental man. On the contrary. Yet the sentimentality creeps in, when he writes about the thing he knows best, the Indian.

So it is with all of them, anthropologists and myth-transcribers and all. There is that creeping note of sentimentality through it all, which makes one shrug one's shoulders and wish the Indians to hell, along with a lot of other bunk.

You've got to de-bunk the Indians, as you've got to de-bunk the Cowboy. When you've de-bunked the Cowboy, there's not much left. But the Indian bunk is not the Indian's invention. It is ours.

It is almost impossible for the white people to approach the Indian without either sentimentality or dislike. The common healthy vulgar white usually feels a certain native dislike of these drumming aboriginals. The highbrow invariably lapses into sentimentalism like the smell of bad eggs.

Why? – Both the reactions are due to the same feeling in the white man. The Indian is not in line with us. He's not coming our way. His whole being is going a different way from ours. And the minute you set eyes on him you know it.

And then, there's only two things you can do. You can detest the insidious devil for having an utterly different way from our own great way. Or you can perform the mental trick, and fool yourself and others into believing that the befeathered and bedaubed darling is nearer to the true ideal gods than we are.

This last is just bunk, and a lie. But it saves our appearances. The former feeling, of instinctive but tolerant repulsion, the feeling of most ordinary farmers and ranchers and mere individuals in the west, is quite natural, it is only honesty to admit it.

The Indian way of consciousness is different from and fatal to our way of consciousness. Our way of consciousness is different from and fatal to the Indian. The two ways, the two streams are never to be united. They are not even to be reconciled. There is no bridge, no canal of connexion.

The sooner we realize, and accept, this, the better, and leave off trying, with fulsome sentimentalism, to render the Indian in our own terms.

The acceptance of the great paradox of human consciousness is the first step to a new accomplishment.

The consciousness of one branch of humanity is the annihilation of the consciousness of another branch. That is, the life of the Indian, his stream of conscious being, is just death to the white man. And we can understand the consciousness of the Indian only in terms of the death of our consciousness.

And let not this be turned into another sentimentalism. Because the same paradox exists between the consciousness of white men and Hindoos or Polynesians or Bantu. It is the eternal paradox of human consciousness. To pretend that all is one stream is to cause chaos and nullity. To pretend to express one stream in terms of another, so as to identify the two, is false and sentimental. The only thing you can do is to have a little Ghost inside you which sees both ways, or even many ways. But a man cannot *belong* to both ways, or to many ways. One man can belong to one great way of consciousness only. He may even change from one way to another. But he cannot go both ways at once. Can't be done.

So that, to understand the Indian conception of entertainment, we have to destroy our own conception.

Perhaps the commonest entertainment among the Indians is singing round the drum, at evening, when the day is over. European peasants will sit round the fire and sing. But they sing ballads or lyrics, tales about individuals or individual, personal experience. And each individual identifies the emotion of the song with his own emotion.

Or the wild fishermen of the Outer Hebrides will sing in their intense, concentrated way, by the fire. And again, usually, the songs have words. Yet sometimes not. Sometimes the song has merely sounds, and a marvellous melody. It is the seal drifting in to shore on the wave, or the seal-woman, singing low and secret, departing back from the shores of men, through the surf, back to the realm of the outer beasts that rock on the waters and stare through glistening, vivid, mindless eyes.

This is approaching the Indian song. But even this is pictorial, conceptual far beyond the Indian point. The Hebridean still sees himself human, and *outside* the great naturalistic influences, which are the dramatic circumstances of his life.

The Indian, singing, sings without words or vision. Face lifted and sightless, eyes half closed and visionless, mouth open and speechless, the sounds arise in his chest, from the consciousness in the abdomen. He will tell you it is a song of a man coming home from the bear-hunt: or a song to make rain: or a song to make the corn grow: or even, quite modern, the song of the church bell on Sunday morning.

But the man coming home from the bear-hunt is any man, all men, the bear is any bear, every bear, all bear. There is no individual, isolated experience. It is the hunting, tired, triumphant demon of manhood which has won against the squint-eyed demon of all bears. The experience is generic, non-individual. It is an experience of the human bloodstream, not of the mind or spirit. Hence the subtle incessant, insistent rhythm of the drum, which is pulsated like the heart, and soulless, and unescapable. Hence the strange blind unanimity of the Indian men's voices. The experience is one experience, tribal, of the blood-stream. Hence, to our ears, the absence of melody. Melody is individualized emotion, just as orchestral music is the harmonizing again of many separate, individual emotions or experiences. But the real Indian song is non-individual, and without melody. Strange, clapping, crowing, gurgling sounds, in an unseizable subtle rhythm, the rhythm of the heart in her throes: from a parted entranced mouth, from a chest powerful and free, from an abdomen where the great blood-stream surges in the dark, and surges in its own generic experiences.

This may mean nothing to you. To the ordinary white ear, the Indian's singing is a rather disagreeable howling of dogs to a tom-tom. But if it rouses no other sensation, it rouses a touch of fear amid hostility. Whatever the spirit of man may be, the blood is basic.

Or take the song to make the corn grow. The dark faces stoop forward, in a strange race darkness. The eyelashes droop a little in the dark, ageless, vulnerable faces. The drum is a heart beating with insistent thuds. And the spirits of the men go out on the ether, vibrating in waves from the hot, dark, intentional blood, seeking the creative presence that hovers for ever in the ether, seeking the identification, following on down the mysterious rhythms of the creative pulse, on and on into the germinating quick of the maize that lies under the ground, there, with the throbbing, pulsing, clapping rhythm that comes from the dark, creative blood in man, to stimulate the tremulous, pulsating protoplasm in the seed-germ, till it throws forth its rhythms of creative energy into rising blades of leaf and stem.

Or take the round dances, round the drum. These may or may not have a name. The dance, anyhow, is primarily a song. All the men sing in unison, as they move with the soft, yet heavy bird-tread which is the whole of the dance. There is no drama. With bodies bent a little forward, shoulders and breasts loose and heavy, feet powerful but soft, the men tread the rhythm into the centre of the earth. The drums keep up the pulsating heart-beat. The men sing in unison, though some will be silent for moments, or even minutes. And for hours, hours it goes on: the round dance.

It has no name. It has no words. It means nothing at all. There is no spectacle, no spectator.

Yet perhaps it is the most stirring sight in the world, in the dark, near the fire, with the drums going, the pine-trees standing still, the everlasting darkness, and the strange lifting and dropping, surging, crowing, gurgling, aah – h – h – ing! of the male voices.

What are they doing? Who knows? But perhaps they are giving themselves again to the pulsing, incalculable fall of the blood, which for ever seeks to fall to the centre of the earth, while the heart like a planet pulsating in an orbit, keeps up the strange, lonely circulating of the separate human existence.

But what we seek, passively, in sleep, they perhaps seek actively, in the round dance. It is the homeward pulling of the blood, as the feet fall in the soft, heavy rhythm, endlessly. It is the dark blood falling back from the mind, from sight and speech and knowing, back to the great central source where is rest and unspeakable renewal. We whites, creatures of spirit, look upon sleep and see only the dreams that lie as debris of the day, mere bits of wreckage from day-consciousness. We never realize the strange falling back of the dark blood into the downward rhythm, the rhythm of pure forgetting and pure renewal.

Or take the little dances round the fire, the mime dances, when two men put on the eagle feathers and take the shield on their arm, and dance the pantomime of a fight, a spear dance. The rhythm is the same, really, the drums keep up the heart-pulsation, the feet the peculiar bird-tread, the soft, heavy, bird-like step that treads as it were towards the centre of the earth. But there is also the subtle leaping towards each other of the two shield-sheltered naked ones, feathered with the power of an eagle. The leaping together, the coming close, the circling, wary, stealthy avoidance and retreat, always on the same rhythm of drum-beats, the same regular, heavy-soft tread of moccasined feet. It is the dance of the naked blood-being, defending his own isolation in the rhythm of the universe. Not skill nor prowess, not heroism. Not man to man. The creature of the isolated, circulating blood-stream dancing in the peril of his own isolation, in the overweening of his own singleness. The glory in power of the man of single existence. The peril of the man whose heart is suspended, like a single red star, in a great and complex universe, following its own lone course round the invisible sun of our own being, amid the strange wandering array of other hearts.

The other men look on. They may or may not sing. And they see themselves in the power and peril of the lonely heart, the creature of the isolated blood-circuit. They see also, subsidiary, the skill, the agility, the swiftness, the daunting onrush that make the warrior. It is practice as well as mystery.

Or take the big, spectacular dances, like the deer dance, the corn dance. The deer dance in the New Year. The people crowded on the roofs of the pueblo: women, children, old men, watching. The two lines of men, hunters, facing one another. And away at the stream which comes running swiftly from among the cotton-wood trees, the watchers, watching eagerly. At last, over the log bridge, two maidens leading the animals: two maidens in their black shawls and wide white deer-skin top-boots, dancing with a slow, delicate-footed rhythm, facing out, then facing in, and shaking their gourd rattles delicately, marking the rhythm as the drums mark it. Following the maidens, all the animals: men in two columns, and each man an animal, leaning forward each on two slim sticks which are his forelegs, with the deer-skin over him, the antlers branching from his head: or the buffalo hide, from whose shaggy mane his bent head peers out: or a black bear, or a wolf. There they come, the two long lines of wild animals: deer, buffalo, bear, wolf, coyote, and at the back, even tiny boys, as foxes, all stepping on those soft, pointed toes, and moving in slow silence under the winter sun, following the slow, swinging progress of the dancing maidens.

Everything is very soft, subtle, delicate. There is none of the hardness of representation. They are not representing something, not even playing. It is a soft, subtle *being* something.

Yet at the same time it is a game, and a very dramatic naïve spectacle. The old men trot softly alongside, laughing, showing all their wrinkles. But they are experiencing a delicate, wild inward delight, participating in the natural mysteries. They tease the little boys under the fox-skins, and the boys, peeping with their round black eyes, are shy and confused. Yet they keep on in the procession, solemnly, as it moves between the ranks of the wild hunters. And all eyes are round with wonder, and the mystery of participation. Amused, too, on the merely human side of themselves. The gay touch of amusement in buffoonery does not in the least detract from the delicate, pulsing wonder of solemnity, which comes from participating in the ceremony itself.

There you have it all, the pantomime, the buffoonery, the human comicalness. But at the same time, quivering bright and wide-eyed in unchangeable delight of solemnity, you have the participating in a natural wonder. The mystery of the wild creatures led from their fastnesses, their wintry retreats and holes in the ground, docilely fascinated by the delicacy and the commanding wistfulness of the maidens who went out to seek them, to seek food in the winter, and who draw after them, in a following, the wild, the timid, the rapacious animals, following in gentle wonder of bewitchment, right into the haunts of men, right into the camp and up to the hunters. The two long lines of wild animals delicately and slowly stepping behind the slow gyration of the two dark-fringed maidens, who shake their gourd rattles in a delicate, quick, three-pulsed rhythm, and never change their wide dark eyes, under the dark fringe. It is the celebration of another triumph, the triumph of the magical wistfulness of women, the wonderful power of her seeking, her yearning, which can draw forth even the bear from his den.

Drama, we are told, has developed out of these ceremonial dances. Greek drama arose this way.

But from the Indian's ceremonial dance to the Greek's early religious ceremony is still a long step. The Greeks usually had some specified deity, some particular god to whom the ceremony was offered. And this god is the witness, the essential audience of the play. The ceremony is *performed* for the gratification of the god. And here you have the beginning of the theatre, with players and audience.

With the Indians it is different. There is strictly no god. The Indian does not consider himself as created, and therefore external to God, or the creature of God. To the Indian there is no conception of a defined God. Creation is a great flood, for ever flowing, in lovely and terrible waves. In everything, the shimmer of creation, and never the finality of the created. Never the distinction between God and God's creation, or between Spirit and Matter. Everything, everything is the wonderful shimmer of creation, it may be a deadly shimmer like lightning or the anger in the little eyes of the bear, it may be the beautiful shimmer of the moving deer, or the pine-boughs softly swaying under snow. Creation contains the unspeakably terrifying enemy, the unspeakably lovely friend, as the maiden who brings us our food in dead of winter, by her passion of tender wistfulness. Yet even this tender wistfulness is the fearful danger of the wild creatures, deer and bear and buffalo, which find their death in it.

There is, in our sense of the word, no God. But all is godly. There is no Great Mind directing the universe. Yet the mystery of creation, the wonder and fascination of creation shimmers in every leaf and stone, in every thorn and bud, in the fangs of the rattlesnake, and in the soft eyes of a fawn. Things utterly opposite are still pure wonder of creation, the yell of the mountain-lion, and the breeze in the aspen leaves. The Apache warrior in his war-paint, shrieking the war-cry and cutting the throats of old women, still he is part of the mystery of creation. He is godly as the growing corn. And the mystery of creation makes us sharpen the knives and point the arrows in utmost determination against him. It must be so. It is part of the wonder. And to every part of the wonder we must answer in kind.

The Indians accept Jesus on the Cross amid all the rest of the wonders. The presence of Jesus on the Cross, or the pitiful Mary Mother, does not in the least prevent the strange intensity of the war-dance. The brave comes home with a scalp. In the morning he goes to Mass. Two mysteries! The soul of man is the theatre in which every mystery is enacted. Jesus, Mary, the snake-dance, red blood on the knife: it is all the rippling of this untellable flood of creation, which, in a narrow sense, we call Nature.

There is no division between actor and audience. It is all one.

There is no God looking on. The only god there is, is involved all the time in the dramatic wonder and inconsistency of creation. God is immersed, as it were, in creation, not to be separated or distinguished. There can be no Ideal God.

And here finally you see the difference between Indian entertainment and even the earliest form of Greek drama. Right at the beginning of Old World dramatic presentation there was the onlooker, if only in the shape of the God Himself, or the Goddess Herself, to whom the dramatic offering was made. And this God or Goddess resolves, at last, into a Mind occupied by some particular thought or idea. And in the long course of evolution, we ourselves become the gods of our own drama. The spectacle is offered to us. And we sit aloft, enthroned in the Mind, dominated by some one exclusive idea, and we judge the show.

There is absolutely none of this in the Indian dance. There is no God. There is no Onlooker. There is no Mind. There is no dominant idea. And finally, there is no judgement: absolutely no judgement.

The Indian is completely embedded in the wonder of his own drama. It is a drama that has no beginning and no end, it is all-inclusive. It can't be judged, because there is nothing outside it, to judge it.

The mind is there merely as a servant, to keep a man pure and true to the mystery, which is always present. The mind bows down before the creative mystery, even of the atrocious Apache warrior. It judges, not the good and the bad, but the lie and the true. The Apache warrior in all his atrocity, is true to his own creative mystery. And as such, he must be fought. But he cannot be called a *lie* on the face of the earth. Hence he cannot be classed among the abominations, the cowards, and the liars: those who betray the wonder.

The Indian, so long as he is pure, has only two great negative commandments.

Thou shalt not lie.

Thou shalt not be a coward.

Positively, his one commandment is:

Thou shalt acknowledge the wonder.

Evil lies in lying and in cowardice. Wickedness lies in witchcraft; that is, in seeking to prostitute the creative wonder to the individual mind and will, the individual conceit.

And virtue? Virtue lies in the heroic response to the creative wonder, the utmost response. In the man, it is a valiant putting forth of all his strength to meet and to run forward with the wonder. In woman it is the putting forth of all herself in a delicate, marvellous sensitiveness, which draws forth the wonder to herself, and draws the man to the wonder in her, as it drew even the wild animals from the lair of winter.

You see this so plainly in the Indian races. Naked and daubed with clay to hide the nakedness, and to take the anointment of the earth; stuck over with bits of fluff of eagle's down, to be anointed with the power of the air, the youths and men whirl down the racing track, in relays. They are not racing to win a race. They are not racing for a prize. They are not racing to show their prowess.

They are putting forth all their might, all their strength, in a tension that is half anguish, half ecstasy, in the effort to gather into their souls more and more of the creative fire, the creative energy which shall carry their tribe through the year, through the vicissitudes of the months, on, on, in the unending race of humanity along the track of trackless creation. It is the heroic effort, the sacred heroic effort which men *must* make and must keep on making. As if hurled from a catapult the Indian youth throws himself along the course, working his body strangely incomprehensibly. And when his turn comes again, he hurls himself forward with greater intensity, to greater speed, driving himself, as it were, into the heart of the fire. And the old men along the track encourage him, urge him with their green twigs, laughingly, mockingly, teasingly, but at the same time with an exquisite pure anxiety and concern.

And he walks away at last, his chest lifting and falling heavily, a strange look in his eyes, having run with the changeless god who will give us nothing unless we overtake him.

6

Dance of the Sprouting Corn

PALE, dry, baked earth, that blows into dust of fine sand. Low hills of baked pale earth, sinking heavily, and speckled sparsely with dark dots of cedar bushes. A river on the plain of drought, just a cleft of dark, reddish-brown water, almost a flood. And over all, the blue, uneasy, alkaline sky.

A pale, uneven, parched world, where a motor-car rocks and lurches and churns in sand. A world pallid with dryness, inhuman with a faint taste of alkali. Like driving in the bed of a great sea that dried up unthinkable ages ago, and now is drier than any other dryness, yet still reminiscent of the bottom of the sea, sandhills sinking, and straight, cracked mesas, like cracks in the dry-mud bottom of the sea.

So, the mud church standing discreetly outside, just outside the pueblo, not to see too much. And on its façade of mud, under the timbered mud-eaves, two speckled horses rampant, painted by the Indians, a red piebald and a black one.

Swish! Over the logs of the ditch-bridge, where brown water is flowing full. There below is the pueblo, dried mud like mud-pie houses, all squatting in a jumble, prepared to crumble into dust and be invisible, dust to dust returning, earth to earth.

That they don't crumble is the mystery. That these little squarish mud-heaps endure for centuries after centuries, while Greek marble tumbles asunder, and cathedrals totter, is the wonder. But then, the naked human hand with a bit of new soft mud is quicker than time, and defies the centuries.

Roughly the low, square, mud-pie houses make a wide street where all is naked earth save a doorway or a window with a pale-blue sash. At the end of the street, turn again into a parallel wide, dry street. And there, in the dry, oblong aridity, there tosses a small forest that is alive: and thud – thud – thud goes the drum, and the deep sound of men singing is like the deep soughing of the wind, in the depths of a wood.

You realize that you had heard the drum from the distance, also the deep, distant roar and boom of the singing, but that you had not heeded, as you don't heed the wind.

It all tosses like young, agile trees in a wind. This is the dance of the sprouting corn, and everybody holds a little, beating branch of green pine. Thud – thud – thud – thud – thud! goes the drum, heavily the men hop and hop and hop, sway, sway, sway, sway go the little branches of green pine. It tosses like a little forest, and the deep sound of men's singing is like the booming and tearing of a wind deep inside a forest. They are dancing the Spring Corn Dance.

This is the Wednesday after Easter, after Christ Risen and the corn germinated. They dance on Monday and on Tuesday. Wednesday is the third and last dance of this green resurrection.

You realize the long line of dancers, and a solid cluster of men singing near the drum. You realize the intermittent black-and-white fantasy of the hopping Koshare, the jesters, the Delight-Makers. You become aware of the ripple of bells on the knee-garters of the dancers, a continual pulsing ripple of little bells; and of the sudden wild, whooping yells from near the drum. Then you become aware of the seed-like shudder of the gourd-rattles, as the dance changes, and the swaying of the tufts of green pine-twigs stuck behind the arms of all the dancing men, in the broad green arm-bands.

Gradually come through to you the black, stable solidity of the dancing women, who poise like solid shadow, one woman behind each rippling, leaping male. The long, silky black hair of the women streaming down their backs, and the equally long, streaming, gleaming hair of the males, loose over broad, naked, orange-brown shoulders.

Then the faces, the impassive, rather fat, golden-brown faces of the women, with eyes cast down, crowned above with the green *tableta*, like a flat tiara. Something strange and noble about the impassive, barefoot women in the short black cassocks, as they subtly tread the dance, scarcely moving, and yet edging rhythmically along, swaying from each hand the green spray of pine-twig out – out – out, to the thud of the drum, immediately behind the leaping fox-skin of the men dancers. And all the emerald-green, painted *tabletas*, the flat wooden tiaras shaped like a castle gateway, rise steady and noble from the soft, slightly bowed heads of the women, held by a band under the chin. All the *tabletas* down the line, emerald green, almost steady, while the bright black heads of the men leap softly up and down, between.

Bit by bit you take it in. You cannot get a whole impression, save of some sort of wood tossing, a little forest of trees in motion, with gleaming black hair and gold-ruddy breasts that somehow do not destroy the illusion of forest.

When you look at the women, you forget the men. The bare-armed, bare-legged, barefoot women with streaming hair and lofty green tiaras, impassive, downward-looking faces, twigs swaying outwards from subtle, rhythmic wrists; women clad in the black, prehistoric short gown fastened over one shoulder, leaving the other shoulder bare, and showing at the arm-place a bit of pink or white undershirt; belted also round the waist with a woven woollen sash, scarlet and green on the hand-woven black cassock. The noble, slightly submissive bending of the tiara-ed head. The subtle measure of the bare, breathing, bird-like feet, that are flat, and seem to cleave to earth softly, and softly lift away. The continuous outward swaying of the pine-sprays.

But when you look at the men, you forget the women. The men are naked to the waist, and ruddy-golden, and in the rhythmic hopping leap of the dance their breasts shake downwards, as the strong, heavy body comes down, down, down, down, in the downward plunge of the dance. The black hair streams loose and living down their backs, the black brows are level, the black eyes look out unchanging from under the silky lashes. They are handsome, and absorbed with a deep rhythmic absorption, which still leaves them awake and aware. Down, down, down they drop, on the heavy, ceaseless leap of the dance, and the great necklaces of shell-cores spring on the naked breasts, the neck-shell flaps up and down, the short white kilt of woven stuff, with the heavy woollen embroidery, green and red and black, opens and shuts slightly to the strong lifting of the knees: the heavy whitish cords that hang from the kilt-band at the side sway and coil for ever down the side of the right leg, down to the ankle, the bells on the red-woven garters under the knees ripple without end, and the feet, in buckskin boots furred round the ankle with a beautiful band of skunk fur, black with a white tip, come down with a lovely, heavy, soft precision, first one, then the other, dropping always plumb to earth. Slightly bending forward, a black gourd rattle in the right hand, a small green bough in the left, the dancer dances the eternal drooping leap, that brings his life down, down, down, down from the mind, down from the broad, beautiful shaking breast, down to the powerful pivot of the knees, then to the ankles, and plunges deep from the ball of the foot into the earth, towards the earth's red centre, where these men belong, as is signified by the red earth with which they are smeared.

And meanwhile, the shell-cores from the Pacific sway up and down, ceaselessly on their breasts.

Mindless, without effort, under the hot sun, unceasing, yet never perspiring nor even breathing heavily, they dance on and on. Mindless, yet still listening, observing. They hear the deep, surging singing of the bunch of old men, like a great wind soughing. They hear the cries and yells of the man waving his bough by the drum. They catch the word of the song, and at a moment, shudder the black rattles, wheel, and the line breaks, women from men, they thread across to a new formation. And as the men wheel round, their black hair gleams and shakes, and the long fox-skin sways, like a tail. And always, when they form into line again, it is a beautiful long straight line, flexible as life, but straight as rain.

The men round the drum are old, or elderly. They are all in a bunch, and they wear day dress, loose cotton drawers, pink or white cotton shirt, hair tied up behind with the red cords, and banded round the head with a strip of pink rag, or white rag, or blue. There they are, solid like a cluster of bees, their black heads with the pink rag circles all close together, swaying their pine-twigs with rhythmic, wind-swept hands, dancing slightly, mostly on the right foot, ceaselessly, and singing, their black bright eyes absorbed, their dark lips pushed out, while the deep strong sound rushes like wind, and the unknown words form themselves in the dark.

Suddenly the solitary man pounding the drum swings his drum round, and begins to pound on the other end, on a higher note, pang – pang – pang! instead of the previous brumm! brumm! brumm! of the bass note. The watchful man next the drummer yells and waves lightly, dancing on bird-feet. The Koshare make strange, eloquent gestures to the sky.

And again the gleaming bronze-and-dark men dancing in the rows shudder their rattles, break the rhythm, change into a queer, beautiful two-step, the long lines suddenly curl into rings, four rings of dancers, the leaping, gleaming-seeming men between the solid, subtle, submissive blackness of the women who are crowned with emerald-green tiaras, all going subtly round in rings. Then slowly they change again, and form a star. Then again, unmingling, they come back into rows.

And all the while, all the while the naked Koshare are threading about. Of bronze-and-dark men-dancers there are some forty-two, each with a dark, crowned woman attending him like a shadow. The old men, the bunch of singers in shirts and tied-up black hair, are about sixty in number, or sixty-four. The Koshare are about twenty-four.

They are slim and naked, daubed with black and white earth, their hair daubed white and gathered upwards to a great knot on top of the head, whence springs a tuft of corn-husks, dry corn-leaves. Though they wear nothing but a little black square cloth, front and back, at their middle, they do not seem naked, for some are white with black spots, like a leopard, and some have broad black lines or zigzags on their smeared bodies, and all their faces are blackened with triangle or lines till they look like weird masks. Meanwhile their hair, gathered straight up and daubed white and sticking up from the top of the head with corn-husks, completes the fantasy. They are anything but natural. Like blackened ghosts of a dead corn-cob, tufted at the top.

And all the time, running like queer spotted dogs, they weave nakedly, through the unheeding dance, comical, weird, dancing the dance-step naked and fine, prancing through the lines, up and down the lines, and making fine gestures with their flexible hands, calling something down from the sky, calling something up from the earth, and dancing forward all the time. Suddenly as they catch a word from the singers, name of a star, of a wind, a name for the sun, for a cloud, their hands soar up and gather in the air, soar down with a slow motion. And again, as they catch a word that means earth, earth deeps, water within the earth, or red-earth-quickening, the hands flutter softly down, and draw up the water, draw up the earth-quickening, earth to sky, sky to earth, influences above to influences below, to meet in the germ-quick of corn, where life is.

And as they dance, the Koshare watch the dancing men.

And if a fox-skin is coming loose at the belt, they fasten it as the man dances, or they stoop and tie another man's shoe. For the dancer must not hesitate to the end.

And then, after some forty minutes, the drum stops. Slowly the dancers file into one line, woman behind man, and move away, threading towards their kiva, with no sound but the tinkle of knee-bells in the silence.

But at the same moment the thud of an unseen drum, from beyond, the soughing of deep song approaching from the unseen. It is the other half, the other half of the tribe coming to continue the dance. They appear round the kiva – one Koshare and one dancer leading the rows, the old men all abreast, singing already in a great strong burst.

So, from ten o'clock in the morning till about four in the afternoon, first one-half then the other. Till at last, as the day wanes, the two halves meet, and the two singings like two great winds surge one past the other, and the thicket of the dance becomes a real forest. It is the close of the third day.

Afterwards, the men and women crowd on the roofs of the two low round towers, the kivas, while the Koshare run round jesting and miming, and taking big offerings from the women, loaves of bread and cakes of blue-maize meal. Women come carrying big baskets of bread and guayava, on two hands, an offering.

And the mystery of germination, not procreation, but *putting forth*, resurrection, life springing within the seed, is accomplished. The sky has its fire, its waters, its stars, its wandering electricity, its winds, its fingers of cold. The earth has its reddened body, its invisible hot heart, its inner waters and many juices and unaccountable stuffs. Between them all, the little seed: and also man, like a seed that is busy and aware. And from the heights and from the depths man, the caller, calls: man, the knower, brings down the influences and brings up the influences, with his knowledge: man, so vulnerable, so subject, and yet even in his vulnerability and subjection, a master, commands the invisible influences and is obeyed. Commands in that song, in that rhythmic energy of dance, in that still-submissive mockery of the Koshare. And he accomplishes his end, as master. He partakes in the springing of the corn, in the rising and budding and earing of the corn. And when he eats his bread at last, he recovers all he once sent forth, and partakes again of the energies he called to the corn, from out of the wide universe.

7

The Hopi Snake Dance

THE Hopi country is in Arizona, next the Navajo country, and some seventy miles north of the Santa Fé railroad. The Hopis are Pueblo Indians, village Indians, so their reservation is not large. It consists of a square track of greyish, unappetizing desert, out of which rise three tall arid mesas, broken off in ragged pallid rock. On the top of the mesas perch the ragged, broken, greyish pueblos, identical with the mesas on which they stand.

The nearest village, Walpi, stands in half-ruin high, high on a narrow rock-top where no leaf of life ever was tender. It is all grey, utterly grey, utterly pallid stone and dust, and very narrow. Below it all the stark light of the dry Arizona sun.

Walpi is called the 'first mesa'. And it is at the far edge of Walpi you see the withered beaks and claws and bones of sacrificed eagles, in a rock-cleft under the sky. They sacrifice an eagle each year, on the brink, by rolling him out and crushing him so as to shed no blood. Then they drop his remains down the dry cleft in the promontory's farthest grey tip.

The trail winds on, utterly bumpy and horrible, for thirty miles, past the second mesa, where Chimopova is, on to the third mesa. And on the Sunday afternoon of 17th August black automobile after automobile lurched and crawled across the grey desert, where low, grey, sage-scrub was coming to pallid yellow. Black hood followed crawling after black hood, like a funeral cortège. The motor-cars, with all the tourists wending their way to the third and farthest mesa, thirty miles across this dismal desert where an odd water-windmill spun, and odd patches of corn blew in the strong desert wind, like dark-green women with fringed shawls blowing and fluttering, not far from the foot of the great, grey, up-piled mesa.

The snake dance (I am told) is held once a year, on each of the three mesas in succession. This year of grace 1924 it was to be held in Hotevilla, the last village on the farthest western tip of the third mesa.

On and on bumped the cars. The lonely second mesa lay in the distance. On and on, to the ragged ghost of the third mesa.

The third mesa has two main villages, Oraibi, which is on the near edge, and Hotevilla, on the far. Up scrambles the car, on all its four legs, like a black-beetle straddling past the school-house and store down below, up the bare rock and over the changeless boulders, with a surge and a sickening lurch to the sky-brim, where stands the rather foolish church. Just beyond, dry, grey, ruined, and apparently abandoned, Oraibi, its few ragged stone huts. All these cars come all this way, and apparently nobody at home.

You climb still, up the shoulder of rock, a few more miles, across the lofty, wind-swept mesa, and so you come to Hotevilla, where the dance is, and where already hundreds of motor-cars are herded in an official camping-ground, among the piñon bushes.

Hotevilla is a tiny little village of grey little houses, raggedly built with undressed stone and mud around a little oblong *plaza*, and partly in ruins. One of the chief two-storey houses on the small square is a ruin, with big square window-holes.

It is a parched, grey country of snakes and eagles, pitched up against the sky. And a few dark-faced, short, thickly built Indians have their few peach trees among the sand, their beans and squashes on the naked sand under the sky, their springs of brackish water.

Three thousand people came to see the little snake dance this year, over miles of desert and bumps. Three thousand, of all sorts, cultured people from New York, Californians, onward-pressing tourists, cowboys, Navajo Indians, even Negroes; fathers, mothers, children, of all ages, colours, sizes of stoutness, dimensions of curiosity.

What had they come for? Mostly to see men hold *live rattlesnakes* in their mouths. '*I never did see a rattlesnake and I'm crazy to see one!*' cried a girl with bobbed hair.

There you have it. People trail hundreds of miles, avidly, to see this circus-performance of men handling live rattlesnakes that may bite them any minute – even do bite them. Some show, that!

There is the other aspect, of the ritual dance. One may look on from the angle of culture, as one looks on while Anna Pavlova dances with the Russian Ballet.

Or there is still another point of view, the religious. Before the snake dance begins, on the Monday, and the spectators are packed thick on the ground round the square, and in the window-holes, and on all the roofs, all sorts of people greedy with curiosity, a little speech is made to them all, asking the audience to be silent and respectful, as this is a sacred religious ceremonial of the Hopi Indians, and not a public entertainment. Therefore, please, no clapping or cheering or applause, but remember you are, as it were, in a church.

The audience accepts the implied rebuke in good faith, and looks round with a grin at the 'church'. But it is a good-humoured, very decent crowd, ready to respect any sort of feelings. And the Indian with his 'religion' is a sort of public pet.

From the cultured point of view, the Hopi snake dance is almost nothing, not much more than a circus turn, or the games that children play in the street. It has none of the impressive beauty of the Corn Dance at Santo Domingo, for example. The big pueblos of Zuni, Santo Domingo, Taos have a cultured instinct which is not revealed in the Hopi snake dance. This last is uncouth rather than beautiful, and rather uncouth in its touch of horror. Hence the thrill, and the crowd.

As a cultured spectacle, it is a circus turn: men actually

dancing round with snakes, poisonous snakes, dangling from their mouths.

And as a religious ceremonial: well, you can either be politely tolerant like the crowd to the Hopis; or you must have some spark of understanding of the sort of religion implied.

'Oh, the Indians,' I heard a woman say, 'they believe we are all brothers, the snakes are the Indians' brothers, and the Indians are the snakes' brothers. The Indians would never hurt the snakes, they won't hurt any animal. So the snakes won't bite the Indians. They are all brothers, and none of them hurt anybody.'

This sounds very nice, only more Hindoo than Hopi. The dance itself does not convey much sense of fraternal communion. It is not in the least like St Francis preaching to the birds.

The animistic religion, as we call it, is not the religion of the Spirit. A religion of spirits, yes. But not of Spirit. There is no One Spirit. There is no One God. There is no Creator. There is strictly no God at all: because all is alive. In our conception of religion there exists God and His Creation: two things. We are creatures of God, therefore we pray to God as the Father, the Saviour, the Maker.

But strictly, in the religion of aboriginal America, there is no Father, and no Maker. There is the great living source of life: say the Sun of existence: to which you can no more pray than you can pray to Electricity. And emerging from this Sun are the great potencies, the invincible influences which make shine and warmth and rain. From these great interrelated potencies of rain and heat and thunder emerge the seeds of life itself, corn, and creatures like snakes. And beyond these, men, persons. But all emerge separately. There is no oneness, no sympathetic identifying oneself with the rest. The law of isolation is heavy on every creature.

Now the Sun, the rain, the shine, the thunder, they are alive. But they are not persons or people. They are alive. They are manifestations of living activity. But they are not personal Gods.

Everything lives. Thunder lives, and rain lives, and sunshine lives. But not in the personal sense.

How is man to get himself into relation with the vast living convulsions of rain and thunder and sun, which are conscious and alive and potent, but like vastest of beasts, inscrutable and incomprehensible. How is man to get himself into relation with these, the vastest of cosmic beasts?

It is the problem of the ages of man. Our religion says the cosmos is Matter, to be conquered by the Spirit of Man. The yogi, the fakir, the saint try conquest by abnegation and by psychic powers. The real conquest of the cosmos is made by science.

The American-Indian sees no division into Spirit and Matter, God and not-God. Everything is alive, though not personally so. Thunder is neither Thor nor Zeus. Thunder is the vast living thunder asserting itself like some incomprehensible monster, or some huge reptile-bird of the pristine cosmos.

How to conquer the dragon-mouthed thunder! How to capture the feathered rain!

We make reservoirs, and irrigation ditches and artesian wells. We make lightning conductors, and build vast electric plants. We say it is a matter of science, energy, force.

But the Indian says No! It all lives. We must approach it fairly, with profound respect, but also with desperate courage. Because man must conquer the cosmic monsters of living thunder and live rain. The rain that slides down from its source, and ebbs back subtly, with a strange energy generated between its coming and going, an energy which, even to our science, is of life: this, man has to conquer. The serpent-striped, feathery Rain.

We made the conquest by dams and reservoirs and windmills. The Indian, like the old Egyptian, seeks to make the conquest from the mystic will within him, pitted against the Cosmic Dragon.

We must remember, to the animistic vision there is no perfect God behind us, who created us from his knowledge, and foreordained all things. No such God. Behind lies only the terrific, terrible, crude Source, the mystic Sun, the well-head of all things. From this mystic Sun emanate the Dragons, Rain, Wind, Thunder Shine, Light. The Potencies of Powers. These bring forth Earth, then reptiles, birds, and fishes.

The Potencies are not Gods. They are Dragons. The Sun of Creation itself is a dragon most terrible, vast, and most powerful, yet even so, less in being than we. The only gods on earth are men. For gods, like man, do not exist beforehand. They are created and evolved gradually, with aeons of effort, out of the fire and smelting of life. They are the highest thing created, smelted between the furnace of the Life-Sun, and beaten on the anvil of the rain, with hammers or thunder and bellows of rushing wind. The cosmos is a great furnace, a dragon's den, where the heroes and demi-gods, men, forge themselves into being. It is a vast and violent matrix, where souls form like diamonds in earth, under extreme pressure.

So that gods are the outcome, not the origin. And the best gods that have resulted, so far, are men. But gods frail as flowers; which have also the godliness of things that have won perfection out of the terrific dragon-clutch of the cosmos. Men are frail as flowers. Man is as a flower, rain can kill him or succour him, heat can flick him with a bright tail, and destroy him: or, on the other hand, it can softly call him into existence, out of the egg of chaos. Man is delicate as a flower, godly beyond flowers, and his lordship is a ticklish business.

He has to conquer, and hold his own, and again conquer all the time. Conquer the powers of the cosmos. To us, science is our religion of conquest. Hence through science, we are the conquerors and resultant gods of our earth. But to the Indian, the so-called mechanical processes do not exist. All lives. And the conquest is made by the means of the living will.

This is the religion of all aboriginal America. Peruvian, Aztec, Athabascan: perhaps the aboriginal religion of all the word. In Mexico, men fell into horror of the crude, pristine gods, the dragons. But to the pueblo Indian, the most terrible dragon is still somewhat gentle-hearted.

This brings us back to the Hopi. He has the hardest task, the stubbornest destiny. Some inward fate drove him to the top of these parched mesas, all rocks and eagles, sand and snakes, and wind and sun and alkali. These he had to conquer. Not merely, as we should put it, the natural conditions of the place. But the mysterious life-spirit that reigned there. The eagle and the snake.

It is a destiny as well as another. The destiny of the animistic soul of man, instead of our destiny of Mind and Spirit. We have undertaken the scientific conquest of forces, of natural conditions. It has been comparatively easy, and we are victors. Look at our black motor-cars like beetles working up the rock-face at Oraibi. Look at our three thousand tourists gathered to gaze at the twenty lonely men who dance in the tribe's snake dance!

The Hopi sought the conquest by means of the mystic, living will that is in man, pitted against the living will of the dragon-cosmos. The Egyptians long ago made a partial conquest by the same means. We have made a partial conquest by other means. Our corn doesn't fail us: we have no seven years' famine, and apparently need never have. But the other thing fails us, the strange inward sun of life; the pellucid monster of the rain never shows us his stripes. To us, heaven switches on daylight, or turns on the shower-bath. We little gods are gods of the machine only. It is our highest. Our cosmos is a great engine. And we die of *ennui*. A subtle dragon stings us in the midst of plenty. *Quos vult perdere Deus, dementat prius.*

On the Sunday evening is a first little dance in the plaza at Hotevilla, called the Antelope dance. There is the hot, sandy, oblong little place, with a tuft of green cotton-wood boughs stuck like a plume at the south end, and on the floor at the foot of the green, a little lid of a trap-door. They say the snakes are under there.

They say that the twelve officiating men of the snake clan of the tribe have for nine days been hunting snakes in the rocks. They have been performing the mysteries for nine days, in the kiva, and for two days they have fasted completely. All these days they have tended the snakes, washed them with repeated lustrations, soothed them, and exchanged spirits with them. The spirit of man soothing and seeking and making interchange with the spirits of the snakes. For the snakes are more rudimentary, nearer to the great convulsive powers. Nearer to the nameless Sun, more knowing in the slanting tracks of the rain, the pattering of the invisible feet of the rain-monster from the sky. The snakes are man's next emissaries to the rain-gods. The snakes lie nearer to the source of potency, the dark, lurking, intense sun at the centre of the earth. For to the cultured animist, and the pueblo Indian is such, the earth's dark centre holds its dark sun, our source of isolated being, round which our world coils its folds like a great snake. The snake is nearer the dark sun, and cunning of it.

They say – people say – that rattlesnakes are not travellers. They haunt the same spots on earth, and die there. It is said also that the snake priest (so-called) of the Hopi probably capture the same snakes year after year.

Be that as it may. At sundown before the real dance, there is the little dance called the Antelope Dance. We stand and wait on a house-roof. Behind us is tethered an eagle; rather dishevelled he sits on the coping, and looks at us in unutterable resentment. See him, and see how much 'brotherhood' the Indian feels with animals – at best the silent tolerance that acknowledges dangerous difference. We wait without event. There are no drums, no announcements. Suddenly into the *plaza*, with rude, intense movements, hurried a little file of men. They are smeared all with grey and black, and are naked save for little kilts embroidered like the sacred dance-kilts in other pueblos, red and green and black on a white fibre-cloth. The fox-skins hangs behind. The feet of the dancers are pure ash-grey. Their hair is long.

The first is a heavy old man with heavy, long, wild grey hair and heavy fringe. He plods intensely forward in the silence, followed in a sort of circle by the other grey-smeared, long-haired, naked, concentrated men. The oldest men are first: the last is a short-haired boy of fourteen or fifteen. There are only eight men – the so-called antelope priests. They pace round in a circle, rudely, absorbedly, till the first heavy, intense old man with his massive grey hair flowing, comes to the lid on the ground, near the tuft of kiva-boughs. He rapidly shakes from the hollow of his right hand a little white meal on the lid, stamps heavily, with naked right foot, on the meal, so the wood resounds, and paces heavily forward. Each man, to the boy, shakes meal, stamps, paces absorbedly on in the circle, comes to the lid again, shakes meal, stamps, paces absorbedly on, comes a third time to the lid, or trap-door, and this time spits on the lid, stamps, and goes on. And this time the eight men file away behind the lid, between it and the tuft of green boughs. And there they stand in a line, their backs to the kiva-tuft of green; silent, absorbed, bowing a little to the ground.

Suddenly paces with rude haste another file of men. They are naked, and smeared with red 'medicine', with big black lozenges of smeared paint on their backs. Their wild heavy hair hangs loose, the old, heavy, grey-haired men go first, then the middle-aged, then the young men, then last, two short-haired, slim boys, schoolboys. The hair of the young men, growing after school, is bobbed round.

The grown men are all heavily built, rather short, with heavy but shapely flesh, and rather straight sides. They have not the archaic slim waists of the Taos Indians. They have archaic squareness, and a sensuous heaviness. Their very hair is black, massive, heavy. These are the so-called snake-priests, men of the snake clan. And tonight they are eleven in number.

They pace rapidly round, with that heavy wild silence of concentration characteristic of them, and cast meal and stamp upon the lid, cast meal and stamp in the second round, come round and spit and stamp in the third. For to the savage, the animist, to spit may be a kind of blessing, a communion, a sort of embrace.

The eleven snake-priests form silently in a row, facing the eight grey smeared antelope-priests across the little lid, and bowing forward a little, to earth. Then the antelope-priests, bending forward, begin a low, sombre chant, or call, that sounds wordless, only a deep, low-toned, secret Ay-a! Ay-a! Ay-a! And they bend from right to left, giving two shakes to the little, flat, white rattle in their left hand, at each shake, and stamping the right foot in heavy rhythm. In their right hand, that held the meal, is grasped a little skin bag, perhaps also containing meal.

They lean from right to left, two seed-like shakes of the rattle each time and the heavy rhythmic stamp of the foot, and the low, sombre, secretive chant-call each time. It is a strange low sound, such as we never hear, and it reveals how deep, how deep the men are in the mystery they are practising, how sunk deep below our world, to the world of snakes, and dark ways in the earth, where the roots of corn, and where the little rivers of unchannelled, uncreated life-passion run like dark, trickling lightning, to the roots of the corn and to the feet and loins of men, from the earth's innermost dark sun. They are calling in the deep, almost silent snake-language, to the snakes and the rays of dark emission from the earth's inward 'Sun'.

At this moment, a silence falls on the whole crowd of listeners. It is that famous darkness and silence of Egypt, the touch of the other mystery. The deep concentration of the 'priests' conquers for a few seconds our white-faced flippancy, and we hear only the deep Hah-há! Hah-ha! speaking to snakes and the earth's inner core.

This lasts a minute or two. Then the antelope-priests stand bowed and still, and the snake-priests take up the swaying and the deep chant, that sometimes is so low, it is like a mutter underground, inaudible. The rhythm is crude, the swaying unison is all uneven. Culturally, there is nothing. If it were not for that mystic, dark-sacred concentration.

Several times in turn, the two rows of daubed, long-haired, insunk men facing one another take up the swaying and the chant. Then that too is finished. There is a break in the formation. A young snake-priest takes up something that may be a corn-cob – perhaps an antelope-priest hands it to him – and comes forward, with an old, heavy, but still shapely snake-priest behind him dusting his shoulders with the feathers, eagle-feathers presumably, which are the Indians' hollow prayer-sticks. With the heavy, stamping hop they move round in the previous circle, the young priest holding the cob curiously, and the old priest prancing strangely at the young priest's back, in a sort of incantation, and brushing the heavy young shoulders delicately with the prayer-feathers. It is the God-vibration that enters us from behind, and is transmitted to the hands, from the hands to the corn-cob. Several young priests emerge, with the bowed heads and the cob in their hands and the heavy older priests hanging over them behind. They tread round the rough curve and come back to the kiva, take perhaps another cob, and tread round again.

That is all. In ten or fifteen minutes it is over. The two files file rapidly and silently away. A brief, primitive performance.

The crowd disperses. They were not many people. There were no venomous snakes on exhibition, so the mass had nothing to come for. And therefore the curious immersed intensity of the priests was able to conquer the white crowd.

By afternoon of the next day the three thousand people had massed in the little *plaza*, secured themselves places on the roof and in the window-spaces, everywhere, till the small pueblo seemed built of people instead of stones. All sorts of people, hundreds and hundreds of white women, all in breeches like half-men, hundreds and hundreds of men who had been driving motor-cars, then many Navajos, the women in their full, long skirts and tight velvet bodices, the men rather lanky, long-waisted, real nomads. In the hot sun and the wind which blows the sand every day, every day in volumes round the corners, the three thousand tourists sat for hours, waiting for the show. The Indian policeman cleared the central oblong, in front of the kiva. The front rows of onlookers sat thick on the ground. And at last, rather early, because of the masses awaiting them, suddenly, silently, in the same rude haste, the antelope-priests filed absorbedly in, and made the rounds over the lid, as before. Today, the eight antelope-priests were very grey. Their feet ashed pure grey, like suède soft boots: and their lower jaw was pure suède grey, while the rest of their face was blackish. With that pale-grey jaw, they looked like corpse-faces with swathing-bands. And all their bodies ash-grey smeared, with smears of black, and a black cloth today at the loins.

They made their rounds, and took their silent position behind the lid, with backs to the green tuft: an unearthly grey row of men with little skin bags in their hands. They were the lords of shadow, the intermediate twilight, the place of after-life and before-life, where house the winds of change. Lords of the mysterious, fleeting power of change.

Suddenly, with abrupt silence, in paced the snake-priests, headed by the same heavy man with solid grey hair like iron. Today they were twelve men, from the old one, down to the slight, short-haired, erect boy of fourteen. Twelve men, two for each of the six worlds, or quarters: east, north, south, west, above, and below. And today they were in a queer ecstasy. Their faces were black, showing the whites of the eyes. And they wore small black loin-aprons. They were the hot living men of the darkness, lords of the earth's inner rays, the black sun of the earth's vital core, from which dart the speckled snakes, like beams.

Round they went, in rapid, uneven, silent absorption, the three rounds. Then in a row they faced the eight ash-grey men, across the lid. All kept their heads bowed towards earth, except the young boys.

Then, in the intense, secret, muttering chant the grey men began their leaning from right to left, shaking the hand, one-two, one-two, and bowing the body each time from right to left, left to right, above the lid in the ground, under which were the snakes. And their low, deep, mysterious voices spoke to the spirits under the earth, not to men above the earth.

But the crowd was on tenterhooks for the snakes, and could hardly wait for the mummery to cease. There was an atmosphere of inattention and impatience. But the chant and the swaying passed from the grey men to the black-faced men, and back again, several times.

This was finished. The formation of the lines broke up.

There was a slight crowding to the centre, round the lid. The old antelope-priest (so called) was stooping. And before the crowd could realize anything else a young priest emerged, bowing reverently, with the neck of a pale, delicate rattlesnake held between his teeth, the little, naïve, bird-like head of the rattlesnake quite still, near the black cheek, and the long, pale, yellowish, spangled body of the snake dangling like some thick, beautiful cord. On passed the black-faced young priest, with the wondering snake dangling from his mouth, pacing in the original circle, while behind him, leaping almost on his shoulders, was the oldest heavy priest, dusting the young man's shoulders with the feather-prayer-sticks, in an intense, earnest anxiety of concentration such as I have only seen in the old Indian men during a religious dance.

Came another young black-faced man out of the confusion, with another snake dangling and writhing a little from his mouth, and an elder priest dusting him from behind with the feathers: and then another, and another: till it was all confusion, probably, of six, and then four young priests with snakes dangling from their mouths, going round, apparently, three times in the circle. At the end of the third round the young priest stooped and delicately laid his snake on the earth, waving him away, away, as it were, into the world. He must not wriggle back to the kiva bush.

And after wondering a moment, the pale, delicate snake steered away with a rattlesnake's beautiful movement, rippling and looping, with the small, sensitive head lifted like antennae, across the sand to the massed audience squatting solid on the ground around. Like soft, watery lightning went the wondering snake at the crowd. As he came nearer, the people began to shrink aside, half-mesmerized. But they betrayed no exaggerated fear. And as the little snake drew very near, up rushed one of the two black-faced young priests who held the snake-stick, poised a moment over the snake, in the prayer-concentration of reverence which is at the same time conquest, and snatched the pale, long creature delicately from the ground, waving him in a swoop over the heads of the seated crowd, then delicately smoothing down the length of the snake with his left hand, stroking and smoothing and soothing the long, pale, bird-like thing; and returning with it to the kiva, handed it to one of the grey-jawed antelope-priests.

Meanwhile, all the time, the other young priests were emerging with a snake dangling from their mouths. The boy had finished his rounds. He launched his rattlesnake on the ground, like a ship, and like a ship away it steered. In a moment, after it went one of those two black-faced priests who carried snake-sticks and were the snake-catchers. As it neared the crowd, very close, he caught it up and waved it dramatically, his eyes glaring strangely out of his black face. And in the interim that youngest boy had been given a long, handsome bull-snake, by the priest at the hole under the kiva boughs. The bull-snake is not poisonous. It is a constrictor. This one was six feet long, with a sumptuous pattern. It waved its pale belly, and pulled its neck out of the boy's mouth. With two hands he put it back. It pulled itself once more free. Again he got it back, and managed to hold it. And then as he went round in his looping circle, it coiled its handsome folds twice round his knee. He stooped, quietly, and as quietly as if he were untying his garter, he unloosed the folds. And all the time, an old priest was intently brushing the boy's thin straight shoulders with the feathers. And all the time, the snakes seemed strangely gentle, naïve, wondering and almost willing, almost in harmony with the man. Which of course was the sacred aim. While the boy's expression remained quite still and simple, as it were candid, in a candour where he and the snake should be in unison. The only dancers who showed signs of being wrought-up were the two young snake-catchers, and one of these, particularly, seemed in a state of actor-like uplift, rather ostentatious. But the old priests had that immersed, religious intentness which is like a spell, something from another world.

The young boy launched his bull-snake. It wanted to go back to the kiva. The snake-catcher drove it gently forward. Away it went, towards the crowd, and at the last minute was caught up into the air. Then this snake was handed to an old man sitting on the ground in the audience, in the front row. He was an old Hopi of the Snake clan.

Snake after snake had been carried round in the circles, dangling by the neck from the mouths of one young priest or another, and writhing and swaying slowly, with the small, delicate snake-head held as if wondering and listening. There had been some very large rattlesnakes, unusually large, two or three handsome bull-snakes, and some racers, whipsnakes. All had been launched, after their circuits in the mouth, all had been caught up by the young priests with the snake-sticks, one or two had been handed to old-snake clan men in the audience, who sat holding them in their arms as men hold a kitten. The most of the snakes, however, had been handed to the grey antelope-men who stood in the row with their backs to the kiva bush. Till some of these ash-smeared men held armfuls of snakes, hanging over their arms like wet washing. Some of the snakes twisted and knotted round one another, showing pale bellies.

Yet most of them hung very still and docile. Docile, almost sympathetic, so that one was struck only by their clean, slim length of snake nudity, their beauty, like soft, quiescent lightning. They were so clean, because they had been washed and anointed and lustrated by the priests, in the days they had been in the kiva.

At last all the snakes had been mouth-carried in the circuits, and had made their little outrunning excursion to the crowd, and had been handed back to the priests in the rear. And now the Indian policemen, Hopi and Navajo, began to clear away the crowd that sat on the ground, five or six rows deep, around the small *plaza*. The snakes were all going to be set free on the ground. We must clear away.

We recoiled to the farther end of the *plaza*. There, two Hopi women were scattering white corn-meal on the sandy ground. And thither came the two snake-catchers, almost at once, with their arms full of snakes. And before we who stood had realized it, the snakes were all writhing and squirming on the ground, in the white dust of meal, a couple of yards from our feet. Then immediately, before they could writhe clear of each other and steer away, they were gently, swiftly snatched up again, and with their arms full of snakes, the two young priests went running out of the *plaza*.

We followed slowly, wondering, towards the western, or north-western edge of the mesa. There the mesa dropped steeply, and a broad trail wound down to the vast hollow of desert brimmed up with strong evening light, up out of which jutted a perspective of sharp rock and further mesas and distant sharp mountains: the great, hollow, rock-wilderness space of that part of Arizona, submerged in light.

Away down the trail, small, dark, naked, rapid figures with arms held close, went the two young men, running swiftly down to the hollow level, and diminishing, running across the hollow towards more stark rocks of the other side. Two small, rapid, intent, dwindling little human figures. The tiny, dark sparks of men. Such specks of gods.

They disappeared, no bigger than stones, behind rocks in shadow. They had gone, it was said, to lay down the snakes before a rock called the snake-shrine, and let them all go free. Free to carry the message and thanks to the dragon-gods who can give and withhold. To carry the human spirit, the human breath, the human prayer, the human gratitude, the human command which had been breathed upon them in the mouths of the priests, transferred into them from those feather-prayer-sticks which the old wise men swept upon the shoulders of the young, snake-bearing men, to carry this back, into the vaster, dimmer, inchoate regions where the monsters of rain and wind alternated in beneficence and wrath. Carry the human prayer and will-power into the holes of the winds, down into the octopus heart of the rain-source. Carry the corn-meal which the women had scattered, back to that terrific, dread, and causeful dark sun which is at the earth's core, that which sends us corn out of the earth's nearness, sends us food or death, according to our strength of vital purpose, our power of sensitive will, our courage.

It is a battle, a wrestling all the time. The Sun, the nameless

Sun, source of all things, which we call sun because the other name is too fearful, this, this vast dark protoplasmic sun from which issues all that feeds our life, this original One is all the time willing and unwilling. Systole, diastole, it pulses its willingness and its unwillingness that we should live and move on, from being to being, manhood to further manhood. Man, small, vulnerable man, the farthest adventurer from the dark heart of the first of suns, into the cosmos of creation. Man, the last god won into existence. And all the time, he is sustained and threated, menaced and sustained from the Source, the innermost sun-dragon. And all the time, he must submit and he must conquer. Submit to the strange beneficence from the Source, whose ways are past finding out. And conquer the strange malevolence of the Source, which is past comprehension also.

For the great dragons from which we draw our vitality are all the time willing and unwilling that we should have being. Hence only the heroes snatch manhood, little by little, from the strange den of the Cosmos.

Man, little man, with his consciousness and his will, must both submit to the great origin-powers of his life, and conquer them. Conquered by man who has overcome his fears, the snakes must go back into the earth with his messages of tenderness, of request, and of power. They go back as rays of love to the dark heart of the first of suns. But they go back also as arrows shot clean by man's sapience and courage, into the resistant, malevolent heart of the earth's oldest, stubborn core. In the core of the first of suns, whence man draws his vitality, lies poison as bitter as the rattlesnake's. This poison man must overcome, he must be master of its issue. Because from the first of suns come travelling the rays that make men strong and glad and gods who can range between the known and the unknown. Rays that quiver out of the earth as serpents do, naked with vitality. But each ray charged with poison for the unwary, the irreverent, and the cowardly. Awareness, wariness, is the first virtue in primitive man's morality. And his awareness must travel back and forth, back and forth, from the darkest origins out to the brightest edifices of creation.

And amid all its crudity, and the sensationalism which comes chiefly out of the crowd's desire for thrills, one cannot help pausing in reverence before the delicate, anointed bravery of the snake-priests (so called), with the snakes.

They say the Hopis have a marvellous secret cure for snake-bites. They say the bitten are given an emetic drink, after the dance, by the old women, and that they must lie on the edge of the cliff and vomit, vomit, vomit. I saw none of this. The two snake-men who ran down into the shadow came soon running up again, running all the while, and steering off at a tangent, ran up the mesa once more, but beyond a deep, impassable cleft. And there, when they had come up to our level, we saw them across the cleft distance washing, brown and naked, in a pool; washing off the paint, the medicine, the ecstasy, to come back into daily life and eat food. Because for two days they had eaten nothing, it was said. And for nine days they had been immersed in the mystery of snakes, and fasting in some measure.

Men who have lived many years among the Indians say they do not believe the Hopi have any secret cure. Sometimes priests do die of bites, it is said. But a rattlesnake secretes his poison slowly. Each time he strikes he loses his venom, until if he strikes several times, he has very little wherewithal to poison a man. Not enough, not half enough to kill. His glands must be very full charged with poison, as they are when he merges from winter-sleep, before he can kill a man outright. And even then, he must strike near some artery.

Therefore, during the nine days of the kiva, when the snakes are bathed and lustrated, perhaps they strike their poison away into some inanimate object. And surely they are soothed and calmed with such things as the priests, after centuries of experience, know how to administer to them.

We dam the Nile and take the railway across America. The Hopi smooths the rattlesnake and carries him in his mouth, to send him back into the dark places of the earth, an emissary to the inner powers.

To each sort of man his own achievement, his own victory, his own conquest. To the Hopi, the origins are dark and dual, cruelty is coiled in the very beginnings of all things, and circle after circle creation emerges towards a flickering, revealed Godhead. With Man as the godhead so far achieved, waveringly and for ever incomplete, in this world.

To us and to the Orientals, the Godhead was perfect to start with, and man makes but a mechanical excursion into a created and ordained universe, an excursion of mechanical achievement, and of yearning for the return to the perfect Godhead of the beginning.

To us, God was in the beginning, Paradise and the Golden Age have been long lost, and all we can do is to win back.

To the Hopi, God is not yet, and the Golden Age lies far ahead. Out of the dragon's den of the cosmos, we have wrested only the beginnings of our being, the rudiments of our Godhead.

Between the two visions lies the gulf of mutual negations. But ours was the quickest way, so we are conquerors for the moment.

The American aborigines are radically, innately religious. The fabric of their life is religion. But their religion is animistic, their sources are dark and impersonal, their conflict with their 'gods' is slow, and unceasing.

This is true of the settled pueblo Indian and the wandering Navajo, the ancient Maya, and the surviving Aztec. They are all involved at every moment, in their old, struggling religion.

Until they break in a kind of hopelessness under our cheerful, triumphant success. Which is what is rapidly happening. The young Indians who have been to school for many years are losing their religion, becoming discontented, bored, and rootless. An Indian with his own religion inside him *cannot* be bored. The flow of the mystery is too intense all the time, too intense, even, for him to adjust himself to circumstances which really are mechanical. Hence his failure. So he, in his great religious struggle for the Godhead of man, falls back beaten. The Personal God who ordained a mechanical cosmos gave the victory to his sons, a mechanical triumph.

Soon after the dance is over, the Navajo begin to ride down the Western trail, into the light. Their women, with velvet bodices and full, full skirts, silver and turquoise tinkling thick on their breasts, sit back on their horses and ride down the steep slope, looking wonderingly around from their pleasant, broad, nomadic, Mongolian faces. And the men, long, loose, thin, long-waisted, with tall hats on their brows and low-sunk silver belts on their hips, come down to water their horses at the spring. We say they look wild. But they have the remoteness of their religion, their animistic vision, in their eyes, they can't see as we see. And they cannot accept us. They stare at us as the coyotes stare at us: the gulf of mutual negation between us.

So in groups, in pairs, singly, they ride silently down into the lower strata of light, the aboriginal Americans riding into their shut-in reservations. While the white Americans hurry back to their motor-cars, and soon the air buzzes with starting engines, like the biggest of rattlesnakes buzzing.

8

A Little Moonshine with Lemon

'Ye Gods, he doth bestride the narrow world
Like a Colossus . . . !'

THERE is a bright moon, so that even the vines make a shadow, and the Mediterranean has a broad white shimmer between its dimness. By the shore, the lights of the old houses twinkle quietly, and out of the wall of the headland advances the glare of a locomotive's lamps. It is a feast day, St Catherine's Day, and the men are all sitting round the little tables, down below, drinking wine or vermouth.

And what about the ranch, the little ranch in New Mexico? The time is different there: but I too have drunk my glass to St Catherine, so I can't be bothered to reckon. I consider that there, too, the moon is in the south-east, standing, as it were, over Santa Fé, beyond the bend of those mountains of Picoris.

Sono io! say the Italians. I am I! Which sounds simpler than it is.

Because which I am I, after all, now that I have drunk a glass also to St Catherine, and the moon shines over the sea, and my thoughts, just because they are fleetingly occupied by the moon on the Mediterranean, and ringing with the last farewell: *Dunque, Signore! di nuovo!* – must needs follow the moontrack south-west, to the great South-west, where the ranch is.

They say: *in vino veritas.* Bah! They say so much! But in the wine of St Catherine, my little ranch, and the three horses down among the timber. Or if it has snowed, the horses are gone away, and it is snow, and the moon shines on the alfalfa slope, between the pines, and the cabins are blind. There is nobody there. Everything shut up. Only the big pine tree in front of the house, standing still and unconcerned, alive.

Perhaps when I have a *Weh* at all, my *Heimweh* is for the tree in front of the house, the overshadowing tree whose green top one never looks at. But on the trunk one hangs the various odds and ends of iron things. It is so near. One goes out of the door, and the tree-trunk is there, like a guardian angel.

The tree-trunk, and the long work table, and the fence! Then beyond, since it is night, and the moon shines, for me at least, away beyond is a light, at Taos, or at Ranchos de Taos. Here, the castle of Noli is on the western skyline. But there, no doubt it has snowed, since even here the wind is cold. There it has snowed, and the nearly full moon blazes wolf-like, as here it never blazes; risen like a were-wolf over the mountains. So there is a faint hoar shagginess of pine trees, away at the foot of the alfalfa field, and a grey gleam of snow in the night, on the level desert, and a ruddy point of human light, in Ranchos de Taos.

And beyond, you see them even if you don't see them, the circling mountains, since there is a moon.

So, one hurries indoors, and throws more logs on the fire.

One doesn't either. One hears Giovanni calling from below, to say good-night! He is going down to the village for a spell. *Vado giù Signor Lorenzo! Buona notte!*

And the Mediterranean whispers in the distance, a sound like in a shell. And save that somebody is whistling, the night is very bright and still. The Mediterranean, so eternally young, the very symbol of youth! And Italy, so reputedly old, yet for ever so child-like and naïve! Never, never for a moment able to comprehend the wonderful, hoary age of America, the continent of the afterwards.

I wonder if I am here, or if I am just going to bed at the ranch. Perhaps looking in Montgomery Ward's catalogue for something for Christmas, and drinking moonshine and hot water, since it is cold. Go out and look if the chickens are shut up warm: if the horses are in sight: if Susan, the black cow, has gone to her nest among the trees, for the night. Cows don't eat much at night. But Susan will wander in the moon. The moon makes her uneasy. And the horses stamp around the cabins.

In a cold like this, the stars snap like distant coyotes, beyond the moon. And you'll see the shadow of actual coyotes, going across the alfalfa field. And the pine trees make little noises, sudden and stealthy, as if they were walking about. And the place heaves with ghosts. That place, the ranch, heaves with ghosts. But when one has got used to one's own home-ghosts, be they never so many, and so potent, they are like one's own family, but nearer than the blood. It is the ghosts one misses most, the ghosts there, of the Rocky Mountains, that never go beyond the timber and that linger, like the animals, round the water-spring. I know them, they know me: we go well together. But they reproach me for going away. They are resentful too.

Perhaps the snow is in tufts on the greasewood bushes. Perhaps the blue jay falls in a blue metallic cloud out of the pine trees in front of the house, at dawn, in the terrific cold, when the dangerous light comes watchful over the mountains, and touches the desert far-off, far-off, beyond the Rio Grande.

And I, I give it up. There is a choice of vermouth, Marsala, red wine or white. At the ranch, tonight, because it is cold, I should have moonshine, not very good moonshine, but still warming: with hot water and lemon, and sugar, and a bit of cinnamon from one of those little red Schilling's tins. And I should light my little stove in the bedroom, and let it roar a bit, sucking the wind. Then dark to bed, with all the ghosts of the ranch cosily round me, and sleep till the very coldness of my emerged nose wakes me. Waking, I shall look at once through the glass panels of the bedroom door, and see the trunk of the great pine tree, like a person on guard, and a low star just coming over the mountain, very brilliant, like someone swinging an electric lantern.

Si vedrà la primavera.

Fiorann' i mandorlini –

Ah, well, let it be vermouth, since there's no moonshine with lemon and cinnamon. Supposing I called Giovanni, and told him I wanted:

'*Un poco di chiar' di luna, con canella e limone …*'

ETRUSCAN PLACES

Cerveteri

THE Etruscans, as everyone knows, were the people who occupied the middle of Italy in early Roman days and whom the
Romans, in their usual neighbourly fashion, wiped out entirely
in order to make room for Rome with a very big R. They
couldn't have wiped them all out, there were too many of
them. But they did wipe out the Etruscan existence as a nation
and a people. However, this seems to be the inevitable result
of expansion with a big E, which is the sole *raison d'être* of
people like the Romans.

Now, we know nothing about the Etruscans except what
we find in their tombs. There are references to them in Latin
writers. But of first-hand knowledge we have nothing except
what the tombs offer.

So to the tombs we must go: or to the museums containing
the things that have been rifled from the tombs.

Myself, the first time I consciously saw Etruscan things, in
the museum at Perugia, I was instinctively attracted to them.
And it seems to be that way. Either there is instant sympathy,
or instant contempt and indifference. Most people despise
everything B.C. that isn't Greek, for the good reason that it
ought to be Greek if it isn't. So Etruscan things are put down
as a feeble Greco-Roman imitation. And a great scientific
historian like Mommsen hardly allows that the Etruscans
existed at all. Their existence was antipathetic to him. The
Prussian in him was enthralled by the Prussian in the all-
conquering Romans. So being a great scientific historian, he
almost denies the very existence of the Etruscan people. He
didn't like the idea of them. That was enough for a great
scientific historian.

Besides, the Etruscans were vicious. We know it, because their enemies and exterminators said so. Just as we knew the unspeakable depths of *our* enemies in the late war. Who isn't vicious to his enemy? To my detractors I am a very effigy of vice. *À la bonne heure!*

However, those pure, clean-living, sweet-souled Romans, who smashed nation after nation and crushed the free soul in people after people, and were ruled by Messalina and Heliogabalus and such-like snowdrops, they said the Etruscans were vicious. So *basta! Quand le maître parle, tout le monde se tait.* The Etruscans were vicious! The only vicious people on the face of the earth presumably. You and I, dear reader, we are two unsullied snowflakes, aren't we? We have every right to judge.

Myself, however, if the Etruscans were vicious, I'm glad they were. To the Puritan all things are impure, as somebody says. And those naughty neighbours of the Romans at least escaped being Puritans.

But to the tombs, to the tombs! On a sunny April morning we set out for the tombs. From Rome, the eternal city, now in a black bonnet. It was not far to go – about twenty miles over the Campagna towards the sea, on the line to Pisa.

The Campagna, with its great green spread of growing wheat, is almost human again. But still there are damp empty tracts, where now the little narcissus stands in clumps, or covers whole fields. And there are places green and foam-white, all with camomile, on a sunny morning in early April.

We are going to Cerveteri, which was the ancient Caere, or Cere, and which had a Greek name too, Agylla. It was a gay and gaudy Etruscan city when Rome put up her first few hovels: probably. Anyhow, there are tombs there now.

The inestimable big Italian railway-guide says the station is Palo, and Cerveteri is eight and a half kilometres away: about five miles. But there is a post-omnibus.

We arrive at Palo, a station in nowhere, and ask if there is a bus to Cerveteri. No! An ancient sort of wagon with an ancient white horse stands outside. Where does that go? To Ladispoli. We know we don't want to go to Ladispoli, so we stare at the landscape. Could we get a carriage of any sort? It would be difficult. That is what they always say: difficult! Meaning impossible. At least they won't lift a finger to help. Is there an hotel at Cerveteri? They don't know. They have none of them ever been, though it is only five miles away, and there are tombs. Well, we will leave our two bags at the station. But they cannot accept them. Because they are not locked. But when did a hold-all ever lock? Difficult! Well then, let us leave them, and steal if you want to. Impossible! Such a moral responsibility! Impossible to leave an unlocked small hold-all at the station. So much for the officials!

However, we try the man at the small buffet. He is very laconic, but seems all right. We abandon our things in a corner of the dark little eating-place, and set off on foot. Luckily it is only something after ten in the morning.

A flat, white road with a rather noble avenue of umbrella-pines for the first few hundred yards. A road not far from the sea, a bare, flattish, hot white road with nothing but a tilted oxen-wagon in the distance like a huge snail with four horns. Beside the road the tall asphodel is letting off its spasmodic pink sparks, rather at random, and smelling of cats. Away to the left is the sea, beyond the flat green wheat, the Mediterranean glistening flat and deadish, as it does on the low shores. Ahead are hills, and a ragged bit of a grey village with an ugly big grey building: that is Cerveteri. We trudge on along the dull road. After all, it is only five miles and a bit.

We creep nearer, and climb the ascent. Caere, like most Etruscan cities, lay on the crown of a hill with cliff-like escarpments. Not that this Cerveteri is an Etruscan city. Caere, the Etruscan city, was swallowed by the Romans, and after the fall of the Roman Empire it fell out of existence altogether. But it feebly revived, and today we come to an old Italian village, walled in with grey walls, and having a few new, pink, box-shaped houses and villas outside the walls.

We pass through the gateway, where men are lounging talking and mules are tied up, and in the bits of crooked grey streets look for a place where we can eat. We see the notice,

Vini e Cucina, Wines and Kitchen; but it is only a deep cavern where mule-drivers are drinking blackish wine.

However, we ask the man who is cleaning the post-omnibus in the street if there is any other place. He says no, so in we go, into the cavern, down a few steps.

Everybody is perfectly friendly. But the food is as usual, meat broth, very weak, with thin macaroni in it: the boiled meat that made the broth: and tripe: also spinach. The broth tastes of nothing, the meat tastes almost of less, the spinach, alas! has been cooked over in the fat skimmed from the boiled beef. It is a meal – with a piece of so-called sheep's cheese, that is pure salt and rancidity, and probably comes from Sardinia; and wine that tastes like, and probably is, the black wine of Calabria wetted with a good proportion of water. But it is a meal. We will go to the tombs.

Into the cavern swaggers a spurred shepherd wearing goat-skin trousers with the long, rusty brown goat's hair hanging shaggy from his legs. He grins and drinks wine, and immediately one sees again the shaggy-legged faun. His face is a faun-face, not deadened by morals. He grins quietly, and talks very subduedly, shyly, to the fellow who draws the wine from the barrels. It is obvious fauns are shy, very shy, especially of moderns like ourselves. He glances at us from a corner of his eye, ducks, wipes his mouth on the back of his hand, and is gone, clambering with his hairy legs on to his lean pony, swirling, and rattling away with a neat little clatter of hoofs, under the ramparts and away to the open. He is the faun escaping again out of the city precincts, far more shy and evanescent than any Christian virgin. You cannot hard-boil him.

It occurs to me how rarely one sees the faun-face now, in Italy, that one used to see so often before the war: the brown, rather still, straight-nosed face with a little black moustache and often a little tuft of black beard; yellow eyes, rather shy under long lashes, but able to glare with a queer glare, on occasion; and mobile lips that had a queer way of showing the teeth when talking, bright white teeth. It was an old, old type, and rather common in the South. But now you will hardly see one of these men left, with the unconscious, ungrimacing faun-face. They were all, apparently, killed in the war: they would be sure not to survive such a war. Anyway the last one I know, a handsome fellow of my own age – forty and a bit – is going queer and morose, crushed between war memories, that have revived, and remorseless go-ahead women-folk. Probably when I go South again he will have disappeared. They can't survive, the faun-faced men, with their pure outlines and their strange non-moral calm. Only the deflowered faces survive.

So much for a Maremma shepherd! We went out into the sunny April street of this Cerveteri, Cerevetus, the old Caere. It is a worn-out little knot of streets shut in inside a wall. Rising on the left is the citadel, the acropolis, the high place, that which is the arx in Etruscan cities. But now the high place is forlorn, with a big, weary building like a governor's palace, or a bishop's palace, spreading on the crest behind the castle gate, and a desolate sort of yard tilting below it, surrounded by ragged, ruinous enclosure. It is forlorn beyond words, dead, and still too big for the grey knot of inhabited streets below.

The girl of the cavern, a nice girl but a bad cook, has found us a guide, obviously her brother, to take us to the necropolis. He is a lad of about fourteen, and like everybody in this abandoned place shy and suspicious, holding off. He bids us wait while he runs away somewhere. So we drink coffee in the tiny café outside which the motor-omnibus reposes all day long, till the return of our guide and another little boy, who will come with him and see him through. The two boys cotton together, make a little world secure from us, and move on ahead of us, ignoring us as far as possible. The stranger is always a menace. B. and I are two very quiet-mannered harmless men. But that first boy could not have borne to go alone with us. Not alone! He would have been afraid, as if he were in the dark.

They led us out of the only gate of the old town. Mules and ponies were tied up in the sloping, forlorn place outside, and pack-mules arrived, as in Mexico. We turned away to the left, under the rock cliff from whose summit the so-called palace goes up flush, the windows looking out on to the world. It seems as if the Etruscans may once have cut this low rock-face, and as if the whole crown on which the wall-girt village of Cerveteri now stands may once have been the arx, the ark, the inner citadel and holy place of the city of Caere, or Agylla, the splendid Etruscan city, with its Greek quarters. There was a whole suburb of Greek colonists, from Ionia, or perhaps from Athens, in busy Caere when Rome was still a rather crude place. About the year 390 B.C. the Gauls came swooping down on Rome. Then the Romans hurried the Vestal Virgins and other women and children away to Caere, and the Etruscans took care of them, in their rich city. Perhaps the refugee Vestals were housed on this rock. And perhaps not. The site of Caere may not have been exactly here. Certainly it stretched away on this same hilltop, east and south, occupying the whole of the small plateau, some four or five miles round, and spreading a great city thirty times as big as the present Cerveteri. But the Etruscans built everything of wood – houses, temples – all save walls for fortification, great gates, bridges, and drainage works. So that the Etruscan cities vanished as completely as flowers. Only the tombs, the bulbs, were underground. But the Etruscans built their cities, whenever possible, on a long narrow plateau or headland above the surrounding country, and they liked to have a rocky cliff for their base, as in Cerveteri. Round the summit of this cliff, this headland, went the enclosure wall, sometimes miles of the great cincture. And within the walls they liked to have one inner high place, the arx, the citadel. Then outside they liked to have a sharp dip or ravine, with a parallel hill opposite. And on the parallel hill opposite they liked to have their city of the dead, the necropolis. So they could stand on their ramparts and look over the hollow where the stream flowed among its bushes, across from the city of life, gay with its painted houses and temples, to the near-at-hand city of their dear dead, pleasant with its smooth walks and stone symbols, and painted fronts.

So it is at Cerveteri. From the sea-plain – and the sea was

probably a mile or two miles nearer in, in Etruscan days – the land leaves the coast in an easy slope to the low-crowned cliffs of the city. But behind, turning out of the gate away from the sea, you pass under the low but sheer cliff of the town, down the stony road to the little ravine, full of bushes.

Down here in the gully, the town – village, rather – has built its wash-house, and the women are quietly washing the linen. They are good-looking women, of the old world, with that very attractive look of noiselessness and inwardness, which women must have had in the past. As if, within the woman, there were again something to seek, that the eye can never search out. Something that can be lost, but can never be found out.

Up the other side of the ravine is a steep, rocky little climb along a sharp path, the two lads scrambling sub-duedly ahead. We pass a door cut in the rock-face. I peep in to the damp, dark cell of what was apparently once a tomb. But this must have been for unimportant people, a little room in a cliff-face, now all deserted. The great tombs in the Banditaccia are covered with mounds, tumuli. No one looks at these damp little rooms in the low cliff-face, among the bushes. So I scramble on hastily, after the others.

To emerge on to the open, rough, uncultivated plain. It was like Mexico, on a small scale: the open, abandoned plain; in the distance little, pyramid-shaped mountains set down straight upon the level, in the not-far distance; and between, a mounted shepherd galloping round a flock of mixed sheep and goats, looking very small. It was just like Mexico, only much smaller and more human.

The boys went ahead across the fallow land, where there were many flowers, tiny purple verbena, tiny forget-me-nots, and much wild mignonette, that had a sweet little scent. I asked the boys what they called it. They gave the usual dumb-bell answer: 'It is a flower!' On the heaping banks towards the edge of the ravine the asphodel grew wild and thick, with tall flowers up to my shoulder, pink and rather spasmodic. These asphodels are very noticeable, a great feature in all this coast landscape. I thought the boys surely would have a name for it. But no! Sheepishly they make the same answer: '*È un fiore! Puzza!*' – It is a flower. It stinks! – Both facts being self-evident, there was no contradicting it. Though the smell of the asphodel is not objectionable, to me: and I find the flower, now I know it well, very beautiful, with its way of opening some pale, big, starry pink flowers, and leaving many of its buds shut, with their dark, reddish stripes.

Many people, however, are very disappointed with the Greeks, for having made so much of this flower. It is true, the word 'asphodel' makes one expect some tall and mysterious lily, not this sparky, assertive flower with just a touch of the onion about it. But for me, I don't care for mysterious lilies, not even for that weird shyness the mariposa lily has. And having stood on the rocks in Sicily, with the pink asphodel proudly sticking up like clouds at sea, taller than myself, letting off pink different flowerets with such sharp and vivid *éclat*, and saving up such a store of buds in ear, stripey, I confess I admire the flower. It has a certain reckless glory, such as the Greeks loved.

One man said he thought we were mistaken in calling this the Greek asphodel, as somewhere in Greek the asphodel is called yellow. Therefore, said this scholastic Englishman, the asphodel of the Greeks was probably the single daffodil.

But not it! There is a very nice and silky yellow asphodel on Etna, pure gold. And heaven knows how common the wild daffodil is in Greece. It does not seem a very Mediterranean flower. The narcissus, the polyanthus narcissus, is pure Mediterranean, and Greek. But the daffodil, the Lent lily!

However, trust an Englishman and a modern for wanting to turn the tall, proud, sparky, dare-devil asphodel into the modest daffodil! I believe we don't like the asphodel because we don't like anything proud and sparky. The myrtle opens her blossoms in just the same way as the asphodel, explosively, throwing out the sparks of her stamens. And I believe it was just this that the Greeks *saw*. They were that way themselves.

However, this is all on the way to the tombs: which lie ahead, mushroom-shaped mounds of grass, great mushroom-shaped mounds, along the edge of the ravine. When I say ravine, don't expect a sort of Grand Canyon. Just a modest, Italian sort of ravine-gully, that you could almost jump down.

When we come near we see the mounds have bases of stone masonry, great girdles of carved and bevelled stone, running round touching the earth in flexible, uneven lines, like the girdles on big, uneasy buoys half sunk in the sea. And they are sunk a bit in the ground. And there is an avenue of mounds, with a sunken path between, parallel to the ravine. This was evidently the grand avenue of the necropolis, like the million-dollar cemetery in New Orleans. *Absit omen!*

Between us and the mounds is a barbed-wire fence. There is a wire gate on which it says you mustn't pick the flowers, whatever that may mean, for there are no flowers. And another notice says, you mustn't tip the guide, as he is gratuitous.

The boys run to the new little concrete house just by, and bring the guide: a youth with red eyes and a bandaged hand. He lost a finger on the railway a month ago. He is shy, and muttering, and neither prepossessing nor cheerful, but he turns out quite decent. He brings keys and an acetylene lamp, and we go through the wire gate into the place of tombs.

There is a queer stillness and a curious peaceful repose about the Etruscan places I have been to, quite different from the weirdness of Celtic places, the slightly repellent feeling of Rome and the old Campagna, and the rather horrible feeling of the great pyramid places in Mexico, Teotihuacan and Cholula, and Mitla in the south; or the amiably idolatrous Buddha places in Ceylon. There is a stillness and a softness in these great grassy mounds with their ancient stone girdles, and down the central walk there lingers still a kind of home-liness and happiness. True, it was a still and sunny afternoon in April, and larks rose from the soft grass of the tombs. But there was a stillness and a soothingness in all the air, in that sunken place, and a feeling that it was good for one's soul to be there.

The same when we went down the few steps, and into the chambers of rock, within the tumulus. There is nothing left. It is like a house that has been swept bare: the inmates have left: now it waits for the next comer. But whoever it is that has departed, they have left a pleasant feeling behind them, warm to the heart, and kindly to the bowels.

They are surprisingly big and handsome, these homes of the dead. Cut out of the living rock, they are just like houses. The roof has a beam cut to imitate the roof-beam of the house. It is a house, a home.

As you enter, there are two small chambers, one to the right, one to the left, antechambers. They say that here the ashes of the slaves were deposited, in urns, upon the great benches of rock. For the slaves were always burned, presumably. Whereas at Cerveteri the masters were laid full-length, sometimes in the great stone sarcophagi, sometimes in big coffins of terra-cotta, in all their regalia. But most often they were just laid there on the broad rock-bed that goes round the tomb, and is empty now, laid there calmly upon an open bier, not shut in sarcophagi, but sleeping as if in life.

The central chamber is large; perhaps there is a great square column of rock left in the centre, apparently supporting the solid roof as a roof-tree supports the roof of a house. And all round the chamber goes the broad bed of rock, sometimes a double tier, on which the dead were laid, in their coffins, or lying open upon carved litters of stone or wood, a man glittering in golden armour, or a woman in white and crimson robes, with great necklaces round their necks, and rings on their fingers. Here lay the family, the great chiefs and their wives, the Lucumones, and their sons and daughters, many in one tomb.

Beyond again is a rock doorway, rather narrow, and narrowing upwards, like Egypt. The whole thing suggests Egypt: but on the whole, here all is plain, simple, usually with no decoration, and with those easy natural proportions whose beauty one hardly notices, they come so naturally, physically. It is the natural beauty of proportion of the phallic consciousness, contrasted with the more studied or ecstatic proportion of the mental and spiritual Consciousness we are accustomed to.

Through the inner doorway is the last chamber, small and dark and culminative. Facing the door goes the stone bed on which was laid, presumably, the Lucumo and the sacred treasures of the dead, the little bronze ship of death that should bear him over to the other world, the vases of jewels for his arraying, the vases of small dishes, the little bronze statuettes and tools, the weapons, the armour: all the amazing impedimenta of the important dead. Or sometimes in this inner room lay the woman, the great lady, in all her robes, with the mirror in her hand, and her treasures, her jewels and combs and silver boxes of cosmetics, in urns or vases ranged alongside. Splendid was the array they went with, into death.

One of the most important tombs is the tomb of the Tarquins, the family that gave Etruscan kings to early Rome. You go down a flight of steps, and into the underworld home of the Tarchne, as the Etruscans wrote it. In the middle of the great chamber there are two pillars, left from the rock. The walls of the big living-room of the dead Tarquins, if one may put it so, are stuccoed, but there are no paintings. Only there are the writings on the wall, and in the burial niches in the wall above the long double-tier stone bed; little sentences freely written in red paint or black, or scratched in the stucco with the finger, slanting with the real Etruscan carelessness and fullness of life, often running downwards, written from right to left. We can read these debonair inscriptions, that look as if someone had just chalked them up yesterday without a thought, in the archaic Etruscan letters, quite easily. But when we have read them we don't know what they mean. *Avle – Tarchnas – Larthal – Clan.* That is plain enough. But what does it mean? Nobody knows precisely. Names, family names, family connexions, titles of the dead – we may assume so much. 'Aule, son of Larte Tarchna,' say the scientists, having got so far. But we cannot read one single sentence. The Etruscan language is a mystery. Yet in Caesar's day it was the everyday language of the bulk of the people in central Italy – at least, east-central. And many Romans spoke Etruscan as we speak French. Yet now the language is entirely lost. Destiny is a queer thing.

The tomb called the Grotta Bella is interesting because of the low-relief carvings and stucco reliefs on the pillars and the walls round the burial niches and above the stone death-bed that goes round the tomb. The things represented are mostly warriors' arms and insignia: shields, helmets, corselets, greaves for the legs, swords, spears, shoes, belts, the necklace of the noble: and then the sacred drinking bowl, the sceptre, the dog who is man's guardian even on the death journey, the two lions that stand by the gateway of life or death, the triton, or merman, and the goose, the bird that swims on the waters and thrusts its head deep into the flood of the Beginning and the End. All these are represented on the walls. And all these, no doubt, were laid, the actual objects, or figures to represent them, in this tomb. But now nothing is left. But when we remember the great store of treasure that every notable tomb must have contained: and that every large tumulus covered several tombs: and that in the necropolis of Cerveteri we can still discover hundreds of tombs: and that other tombs exist in great numbers on the other side of the old city, towards the sea; we can have an idea of the vast mass of wealth this city could afford to bury with its dead, in days when Rome had very little gold, and even bronze was precious.

The tombs seem so easy and friendly, cut out of rock underground. One does not feel oppressed, descending into them. It must be partly owing to the peculiar charm of natural proportion which is in all Etruscan things of the unspoilt, unromanized centuries. There is a simplicity, combined with a most peculiar, free-breasted naturalness and spontaneity, in the shapes and movements of the underworld walls and spaces, that at once reassures the spirit. The Greeks sought to make an impression, and Gothic still more seeks to impress the mind. The Etruscans, no. The things they did, in their easy centuries, are as natural and as easy as breathing. They leave the breast breathing freely and pleasantly, with a certain fullness of life. Even the tombs. And that is the true Etruscan quality: ease, naturalness, and an abundance of life, no need to force the mind or the soul in any direction.

And death, to the Etruscan, was a pleasant continuance of life, with jewels and wine and flutes playing for the dance. It was neither an ecstasy of bliss, a heaven, nor a purgatory of torment. It was just a natural continuance of the fullness of life. Everything was in terms of life, of living.

Yet everything Etruscan, save the tombs, has been wiped out. It seems strange. One goes out again into the April sunshine, into the sunken road between the soft, grassy-mounded tombs, and as one passes one glances down the steps at the doorless doorways of tombs. It is so still and pleasant and cheerful. The place is so soothing.

B., who has just come back from India, is so surprised to see the phallic stones by the doors of many tombs. Why, it's like the Shiva lingam at Benares! It's exactly like the lingam stones in the Shiva caves and the Shiva temples!

And that is another curious thing. One can live one's life, and read all the books about India or Etruria, and never read a single word about the thing that impresses one in the very first five minutes, in Benares or in an Etruscan necropolis: that is, the phallic symbol. Here it is, in stone, unmistakable, and everywhere, around these tombs. Here it is, big and little, standing by the doors, or inserted, quite small, into the rock: the phallic stone! Perhaps some tumuli had a great phallic column on the summit: some perhaps by the door. There are still small phallic stones, only seven or eight inches long, inserted in the rock outside the doors: they always seem to have been outside. And these small lingams look as if they were part of the rock. But no, B. lifts one out. It is cut, and is fitted into a socket, previously cemented in. B puts the phallic stone back into its socket, where it was placed, probably, five or six hundred years before Christ was born.

The big phallic stones that, it is said, probably stood on top of the tumuli, are sometimes carved very beautifully, sometimes with inscriptions. The scientists call them *cippus*, *cippi*. But surely the cippus is a truncated column used usually as a gravestone: a column quite squat, often square, having been cut across, truncated, to represent maybe a life cut short. Some of the little phallic stones are like this – truncated. But others are tall, huge and decorated, and with the double cone that is surely phallic. And little inserted phallic stones are not cut short.

By the doorway of some tombs there is a carved stone house, or a stone imitation chest with sloping lids like the two sides of the roof of an oblong house. The guide-boy, who works on the railway and is no profound scholar, mutters that every woman's tomb had one of these stone houses or chests over it – over the doorway, he says – and every man's tomb had one of the phallic stones, or lingams. But since the great tombs were family tombs, perhaps they had both.

The stone house, as the boy calls it, suggests the Noah's Ark without the boat part: the Noah's Ark box we had as children, full of animals. And that is what it is, the Ark, the *arx*, the womb. The womb of all the world, that brought forth all the creatures. The womb, the *arx*, where life retreats in the last refuge. The womb, the ark of the covenant, in which lies the mystery of eternal life, the manna and the mysteries. There it is, standing displaced outside the doorway of Etruscan tombs at Cerveteri.

And perhaps in the insistence on these two symbols, in the Etruscan world, we can see the reason for the utter destruction and annihilation of the Etruscan consciousness. The new world wanted to rid itself of these fatal, dominant symbols of the old world, the old physical world. The Etruscan consciousness was rooted quite blithely in these symbols, the phallus and the arx. So the whole consciousness, the whole Etruscan pulse and rhythm, must be wiped out.

Now we see again, under the blue heavens where the larks are singing in the hot April sky, why the Romans called the Etruscans vicious. Even in their palmy days the Romans were not exactly saints. But they thought they ought to be. They hated the phallus and the ark, because they wanted empire and dominion and, above all, riches: social gain. You cannot dance gaily to the double flute and at the same time conquer nations or rake in large sums of money. *Delenda est Cartago*. To the greedy man, everybody that is in the way of his greed is vice incarnate.

There are many tombs, though not many of the great mounds are left. Most have been levelled. There are many tombs: some were standing half full of water; some were in process of being excavated, in a kind of quarry-place, though the work for the time was silent and abandoned. Many tombs, many, many, and you must descend to them all, for they are all cut out below the surface of the earth: and where there was a tumulus it was piled above them afterwards, loose earth, within the girdle of stone. Some tumuli have been levelled, yet the whole landscape is lumpy with them. But the tombs remain, here all more or less alike, though some are big and some are small, and some are noble and some are rather mean. But most of them seem to have several chambers, beyond the antechambers. And all these tombs along the dead highway would seem to have been topped, once, by the beautiful roundness of tumuli, the great mounds of fruition, for the dead, with the tall phallic cone rising from the summit.

The necropolis, as far as we are concerned, ends on a waste place of deserted excavations and flood-water. We turn back, to leave the home of dead Etruscans. All the tombs are empty. All have been rifled. The Romans may have respected the dead, for a certain time, while their religion was sufficiently Etruscan to exert a power over them. But later, when the Romans started collecting Etruscan antiques – as we collect antiques today – there must have been a great sacking of the tombs. Even when all the gold and silver and jewels had been pilfered from the urns – which no doubt happened very soon after the Roman dominion – still the vases and the bronze must have remained in their places. Then the rich Romans began to collect vases, 'Greek' vases with the painted scenes. So these were stolen from the tombs. Then the little bronze figures, statuettes, animals, bronze ships, of which the Etruscans put thousands in the tombs, became the rage with the Roman collectors. Some smart Roman gentry would have a thousand or two choice little Etruscan bronzes to boast of. Then Rome fell, and the barbarians pillaged whatever was left. So it went on.

And still some tombs remained virgin, for the earth had washed in and filled the entrance way, covered the stone bases of the mounds; trees, bushes grew over the graves; you had only hilly, humpy, bushy waste country.

Under this the tombs lay silent, either ravaged, or, in a few wonderful cases, still virgin. And still absolutely virgin lay one of the tombs of Cerveteri, alone and apart from the necropolis, buried on the other side of the town, until 1836, when it was discovered: and, of course, denuded. General Galassi and the arch-priest Regolini unearthed it: so it is called the Regolini-Galassi tomb.

It is still interesting: a primitive narrow tomb like a passage, with a partition half-way, and covered with an arched roof, what they call the false arch, which is made by letting the flat horizontal stones of the roof jut out step by step, as they pile upwards, till they almost meet. Then big flat stones are laid as cover, and make the flat top of the almost Gothic arch: an arch built, probably, in the eighth century before Christ.

In the first chamber lay the remains of a warrior, with his bronze armour, beautiful and sensitive as if it had grown in life for the living body, sunk on his dust. In the inner chamber beautiful, frail, pale-gold jewellery lay on the stone bed, earrings where the ears were dust, bracelets in the dust that once was arms, surely of a noble lady, nearly three thousand years ago.

Plate 1. Cerveteri. Entrance to the Chamber Tombs.

Plate 2. Cerveteri. Tomb of the Sarcophagi.

Plate 3. Cerveteri. Tomb of the Stuccos, or the Grotta Bella.

Plate 4. Cerveteri. Terra-cotta Heads on Sarcophagus now in the Villa Giulia Museum, Rome.

Plate 5. Cerveteri. The Regolini-Galassi Tomb.

Plate 6. Tarquinia. Greek Vases with Eye-Pattern and Head of Bacchus.

Plate 7. Tarquinia. Tomb of Hunting and Fishing.

Plate 8. Tarquinia. Tomb of the Leopards.

Plate 9. Tarquinia. Tomb of the Leopards.

Plate 10. Tarquinia. Tomb of the Feast.

Plate 11. Tarquinia. Tomb of the Lionesses.

Plate 12. Tarquinia. Tomb of the Bulls.

Plate 13. Tarquinia. Tomb of the Baron.

Plate 14. Volterra. Porta dell'Arco.

Plate 15. Volterra. Ash-chest showing the Boar-hunt.

Plate 16. Volterra. Ash-chest showing Acteon and the Dogs.

They took away everything. The treasure, so delicate and sensitive and wistful, is mostly in the Gregorian Museum in the Vatican. On two of the little silver vases from the Regolini-Galassi tomb is the scratched inscription – *Mi Larthia*. Almost the first written Etruscan words we know. And what do they mean, anyhow? 'This is Larthia' – Larthia being a lady?

Caere, even seven hundred years before Christ, must have been rich and full of luxury, fond of soft gold and of banquets, dancing, and great Greek vases. But you will find none of it now. The tombs are bare: what treasure they yielded up, and even to us Cerveteri has yielded a great deal, is in the museums. If you go you will see, as I saw, a grey, forlorn little township in tight walls – perhaps having a thousand inhabitants – and some empty burying places.

But when you sit in the post-automobile, to be rattled down to the station, about four o'clock in the sunny afternoon, you will probably see the bus surrounded by a dozen buxom, handsome women, saying good-bye to one of their citizenesses. And in the full, dark, handsome, jovial faces surely you see the lustre still of the life-loving Etruscans! There are some level Greek eyebrows. But surely there are other vivid, warm faces still jovial with Etruscan vitality, beautiful with the mystery of the unrifled ark, ripe with the phallic knowledge and the Etruscan carelessness!

2

Tarquinia

In Cerveteri there is nowhere to sleep, so the only thing to do is to go back to Rome, or forwards to Città Vecchia. The bus landed us at the station of Palo at about five o'clock: in the midst of nowhere: to meet the Rome train. But we were going on to Tarquinia, not back to Rome, so we must wait two hours, till seven.

In the distance we could see the concrete villas and new houses of what was evidently Ladispoli, a seaside place, some two miles away. So we set off to walk to Ladispoli, on the flat sea-road. On the left, in the wood that forms part of the great park, the nightingales had already begun to whistle, and looking over the wall one could see many little rose-coloured cyclamens glowing on the earth in the evening light.

We walked on, and the Rome train came surging round the bend. It misses Ladispoli, whose two miles of branch line runs only in the hot bathing months. As we neared the first ugly villas on the road the ancient wagonette drawn by the ancient white horse, both looking sun-bitten almost to ghostliness, clattered past. It just beat us.

Ladispoli is one of those ugly little places on the Roman coast, consisting of new concrete villas, new concrete hotels, kiosks and bathing establishments; bareness and non-existence for ten months in the year, seething solid with fleshy bathers in July and August. Now it was deserted, quite deserted, save for two or three officials and four wild children.

B. and I lay on the grey-black lava sand, by the flat, low sea, over which the sky, grey and shapeless, emitted a flat, wan evening light. Little waves curled green out of the sea's dark greyness, from the curious low flatness of the water. It is a peculiarly forlorn coast, the sea peculiarly flat and sunken, lifeless-looking, the land as if it had given its last gasp, and was now for ever inert.

Yet this is the Tyrrhenian sea of the Etruscans, where their shipping spread sharp sails, and beat the sea with slave-oars, roving in from Greece and Sicily, Sicily of the Greek tyrants; from Cumae, the city of the old Greek colony of Campania, where the province of Naples now is; and from Elba, where the Etruscans mined their iron ore. The Etruscans sailed the seas. They are even said to have come by sea, from Lydia in Asia Minor, at some date far back in the dim mists before the eighth century B.C. But that a whole people, even a whole host, sailed in the tiny ships of those days, all at once, to people a sparsely peopled central Italy, seems hard to imagine. Probably ships did come – even before Ulysses. Probably men landed on the strange flat coast, and made camps, and then treated with the natives. Whether the newcomers were Lydians or Hittites with hair curled in a roll behind, or men from Mycenae or Crete, who knows. Perhaps men of all these sorts came, in batches. For in Homeric days a restlessness seems to have possessed the Mediterranean basin, and ancient races began shaking ships like seeds over the sea. More people than Greeks, or Hellenes, or Indo-Germanic groups, were on the move.

But whatever little ships were run ashore on the soft, deep, grey-black volcanic sand of this coast, three thousand years ago, and earlier, their mariners certainly did not find those hills inland empty of people. If the Lydians or Hittites pulled up their long little two-eyed ships on to the beach, and made a camp behind a bank, in shelter from the wet strong wind, what natives came down curiously to look at them? For natives there were, of that we may be certain. Even before the fall of Troy, before even Athens was dreamed of, there were natives here. And they had huts on the hills, thatched huts in clumsy groups most probably; with patches of grain, and flocks of goats and probably cattle. Probably it was like coming on an old Irish village, or a village in the Scottish Hebrides in Prince Charlie's day, to come upon a village of these Italian aborigines, by the Tyrrhenian sea, three thousand years ago. But by the time Etruscan history starts in Caere, some eight centuries B.C., there was certainly more than a village on the hill. There was a native city, of that we may be sure; and a busy spinning of linen and beating of gold, long before the Regolini-Galassi tomb was built.

However that may be, somebody came, and somebody was already here: of that we may be certain: and, in the first place, none of them were Greeks or Hellenes. It was the days before Rome rose up: probably when the first comers arrived it was the days even before Homer. The newcomers, whether they were few or many, seem to have come from the east, Asia Minor or Crete or Cyprus. They were, we must feel, of an old, primitive Mediterranean and Asiatic or Aegean stock. The twilight of the beginning of our history was the nightfall of some previous history, which will never be written. Pelasgian is but a shadow-word. But Hittite and Minoan, Lydian, Carian, Etruscan, these words emerge from shadow, and perhaps from one and the same great shadow come the peoples to whom the names belong.

The Etruscan civilization seems a shoot, perhaps the last, from the prehistoric Mediterranean world, and the Etruscans, newcomers and aborigines alike, probably belonged to that ancient world, though they were of different nations and levels of culture. Later, of course, the Greeks exerted a great influence. But that is another matter.

Whatever happened, the newcomers in ancient central Italy found many natives flourishing in possession of the land. These aboriginals, now ridiculously called Villanovans, were neither wiped out nor suppressed. Probably they welcomed the strangers, whose pulse was not hostile to their own. Probably the more highly developed religion of the newcomers was not hostile to the primitive religion of the aborigines: no doubt the two religions had the same root. Probably the aborigines formed willingly a sort of religious aristocracy from the newcomers: the Italians might almost do the same today. And so the Etruscan world arose. But it took centuries to arise. Etruria was not a colony, it was a slowly developed country.

There was never an Etruscan nation: only, in historical times, a great league of tribes or nations using the Etruscan language and the Etruscan script – at least officially – and uniting in their religious feeling and observances. The Etruscan alphabet seems to have been borrowed from the old Greeks, apparently from the Chalcidians of Cumae – the Greek colony just north of where Naples now is. But the Etruscan language is not akin to any of the Greek dialects, nor, apparently, to the Italic. But we don't know. It is probably to a great extent the language of the old aboriginals of southern Etruria, just as the religion is in all probability basically aboriginal, belonging to some vast old religion of the prehistoric world. From the shadow of the prehistoric world emerge dying religions that have not yet invented gods or goddesses, but live by the mystery of the elemental powers in the Universe, the complex vitalities of what we feebly call Nature. And the Etruscan religion was certainly one of these. The gods and goddesses don't seem to have emerged in any sharp definiteness.

But it is not for me to make assertions. Only, that which half emerges from the dim background of time is strangely stirring; and after having read all the learned suggestions, most of them contradicting one another; and then having looked sensitively at the tombs and the Etruscan things that are left, one must accept one's own resultant feeling.

Ships came along this low, inconspicuous sea, coming up from the Near East, we should imagine, even in the days of Solomon – even, maybe, in the days of Abraham. And they kept on coming. As the light of history dawns and brightens, we see them winging along with their white or scarlet sails. Then, as the Greeks came crowding into colonies in Italy, and the Phoenicians began to exploit the western Mediterranean, we begin to hear of the silent Etruscans, and to see them.

Just north of here Caere founded a port called Pyrgi, and we know that the Greek vessels flocked in, with vases and stuffs and colonists coming from Hellas or from Magna Graecia, and that Phoenician ships came rowing sharply, over from Sardinia, up from Carthage, round from Tyre and Sidon; while the Etruscans had their own fleets, built of timber from the mountains, caulked with pitch from northern Volterra, fitted with sails from Tarquinia, filled with wheat from the bountiful plains, or with the famous Etruscan articles of bronze and iron, which they carried away to Corinth or to Athens or to the ports of Asia Minor. We know of the great and finally disastrous sea-battles with the Phoenicians and the tyrant of Syracuse. And we know that the Etruscans, all except those of Caere, became ruthless pirates,

–almost like the Moors and the Barbary corsairs later on. This was part of their viciousness, a great annoyance to their loving and harmless neighbours, the law-abiding Romans – who believed in the supreme law of conquest.

However, all this is long ago. The very coast has changed since then. The smitten sea has sunk and fallen back, the weary land has emerged when, apparently, it didn't want to, and the flowers of the coast-line are miserable bathing-places such as Ladispoli and seaside Ostia, desecration put upon desolation, to the triumphant trump of the mosquito.

The wind blew flat and almost chill from the darkening sea, the dead waves lifted small bits of pure green out of the leaden greyness, under the leaden sky. We got up from the dark grey but soft sand, and went back along the road to the station, peered at by the few people and officials who were holding the place together till the next bathers came.

At the station there was general desertedness. But our things still lay untouched in a dark corner of the buffet, and the man gave us a decent little meal of cold meats and wine and oranges. It was already night. The train came rushing in, punctually.

It is an hour or more to Cività Vecchia, which is a port of not much importance, except that from here the regular steamer sails to Sardinia. We gave our things to a friendly old porter, and told him to take us to the nearest hotel. It was night, very dark as we emerged from the station.

And a fellow came furtively shouldering up to me.

'You are foreigners, aren't you?'

'Yes.'

'What nationality?'

'English.'

'You have your permission to reside in Italy – or your passport?'

'My passport I have – what do you want?'

'I want to look at your passport.'

'It's in the valise! And why? Why is this?'

'This is a port, and we must examine the papers of foreigners.'

'And why? Genoa is a port, and no one dreams of asking for papers.'

I was furious. He made no answer. I told the porter to go on to the hotel, and the fellow furtively followed at our side, half-a-pace to the rear, in the mongrel way these spy-louts have.

In the hotel I asked for a room and registered, and then the fellow asked again for my passport. I wanted to know why he demanded it, what he meant by accosting me outside the station as if I was a criminal, what he meant by insulting us with his requests, when in any other town in Italy one went unquestioned – and so forth, in considerable rage.

He did not reply, but obstinately looked as though he would be venomous if he could. He peered at the passport – though I doubt if he could make head or tail of it – asked where we were going, peered at B.'s passport, half excused himself in a whining, disgusting sort of fashion, and disappeared into the night. A real lout.

I was furious. Supposing I had not been carrying my passport – and usually I don't dream of carrying it – what amount of trouble would that lout have made me! Probably I should have spent the night in prison, and been bullied by half a dozen low bullies.

Those poor rats at Ladispoli had seen me and B. go to the sea and sit on the sand for half-an-hour, then go back to the train. And this was enough to rouse their suspicions, I imagine, so they telegraphed to Città Vecchia. Why are officials always fools? Even when there is no war on? What could they imagine we were doing?

The hotel manager, propitious, said there was a very interesting museum in Città Vecchia, and wouldn't we stay the next day and see it. 'Ah!' I replied. 'But all it contains is Roman stuff, and we don't want to look at that.' It was malice on my part, because the present regime considers itself purely ancient Roman. The man looked at me scared, and I grinned at him. 'But what do they mean,' I said, 'behaving like this to a simple traveller, in a country where foreigners are invited to travel!' 'Ah!' said the porter softly and soothingly. 'It is the Roman province. You will have no more of it when you leave the Provincia di Roma.' And when the Italians give the soft answer to turn away wrath, the wrath somehow turns away.

We walked for an hour in the dull street of Cività Vecchia. There seemed so much suspicion, one would have thought there were several wars on. The hotel manager asked if we were staying. We said we were leaving by the eight-o'clock train in the morning, for Tarquinia.

And, sure enough, we left by the eight-o'clock train. Tarquinia is only one station from Cività Vecchia – about twenty minutes over the flat Maremma country, with the sea on the left, and the green wheat growing luxuriantly, the asphodel sticking up its spikes.

We soon saw Tarquinia, its towers pricking up like antennae on the side of a low bluff of a hill, some few miles inland from the sea. And this was once the metropolis of Etruria, chief city of the great Etruscan League. But it died like all the other Etruscan cities, and had a more or less medieval rebirth, with a new name. Dante knew it, as it was known for centuries, as Corneto – Corgnetum or Cornetium – and forgotten was its Etruscan past. Then there was a feeble sort of wakening to remembrance a hundred years ago, and the town got Tarquinia tacked on to its Corneto: Corneto-Tarquinia. The Fascist regime, however, glorying in the Italian origins of Italy, has now struck out the Corneto, so the town is once more, simply, Tarquinia. As you come up in the motor-bus from the station you see the great black letters, on a white ground, painted on the wall by the city gateway: *Tarquinia*. So the wheel of revolution turns. There stands the Etruscan word – Latinized Etruscan – beside the medieval gate, put up by the Fascist power to name and unname.

But the Fascists, who consider themselves in all things

Roman, Roman of the Caesars, heirs of Empire and world power, are beside the mark restoring the rags of dignity to Etruscan places. For of all the Italian people that ever lived, the Etruscans were surely the least Roman. Just as, of all the people that ever rose up in Italy, the Romans of ancient Rome were surely the most un-Italian, judging from the natives of today.

Tarquinia is only about three miles from the sea. The omnibus soon runs one up, charges through the widened gateway, swirls round in the empty space inside the gateway, and is finished. We descend in the bare place, which seems to expect nothing. On the left is a beautiful stone palazzo – on the right is a café, upon the low ramparts above the gate. The man of the *Dazio*, the town customs, looks to see if anybody has brought food-stuffs into the town – but it is a mere glance. I ask him for the hotel. He says: 'Do you mean to sleep?' I say I do. Then he tells a small boy to carry my bag and takes us to Gentile's.

Nowhere is far off, in these small wall-girdled cities. In the warm April morning the stony little town seems half asleep. As a matter of fact, most of the inhabitants are out in the fields, and won't come in through the gates again till evening. The slight sense of desertedness is everywhere – even in the inn, when we have climbed up the stairs to it, for the ground floor does not belong. A little lad in long trousers, who would seem to be only twelve years old but who has the air of a mature man, confronts us with his chest out. We ask for rooms. He eyes us, darts away for the key, and leads us off upstairs another flight, shouting to a young girl, who acts as chambermaid, to follow on. He shows us two small rooms, opening off a big, desert sort of general assembly room common in this kind of inn. 'And you won't be lonely,' he said briskly, 'because you can talk to one another through the wall. *Toh! Lina!*' He lifts his finger and listens. '*Eh!*' comes through the wall, like an echo, with startling nearness and clearness. '*Fai presto!*' says Albertino. '*È pronto!*' comes the voice of Lina. '*Ecco!*' says Albertino to us.

'You hear!' We certainly did. The partition wall must have been butter-muslin. And Albertino was delighted, having reassured us we should not feel lonely nor frightened in the night.

He was, in fact, the most manly and fatherly little hotel manager I have ever known, and he ran the whole place. He was in reality fourteen years old, but stunted. From five in the morning till ten at night he was on the go, never ceasing, and with a queer, abrupt, sideways-darting alacrity that must have wasted a great deal of energy. The father and mother were in the background – quite young and pleasant. But they didn't seem to exert themselves. Albertino did it all. How Dickens would have loved him! But Dickens would not have seen the queer wistfulness, and trustfulness, and courage in the boy. He was absolutely unsuspicious of us strangers. People must be rather human and decent in Tarquinia, even the commercial travellers: who, presumably, are chiefly buyers of agricultural produce, and sellers of agricultural implements and so forth.

We sallied out, back to the space by the gate, and drank coffee at one of the tin tables outside. Beyond the wall there were a few new villas – the land dropped green and quick, to the strip of coast plain and the indistinct, faintly gleaming sea, which seemed somehow not like a sea at all.

I was thinking, if this were still an Etruscan city, there would still be this cleared space just inside the gate. But instead of a rather forlorn vacant lot it would be a sacred clearing, with a little temple to keep it alert.

Myself, I like to think of the little wooden temples of the early Greeks and of the Etruscans: small, dainty, fragile, and evanescent as flowers. We have reached the stage when we are weary of huge stone erections, and we begin to realize that it is better to keep life fluid and changing than to try to hold it fast down in heavy monuments. Burdens on the face of the earth are man's ponderous erections.

The Etruscans made small temples, like little houses with pointed roofs, entirely of wood. But then, outside, they had friezes and cornices and crests of terra-cotta, so that the upper part of the temple would seem almost made of earthenware, terra-cotta plaques fitted neatly, and alive with freely modelled painted figures in relief, gay dancing creatures, rows of ducks, round faces like the sun, and faces grinning and putting out a big tongue, all vivid and fresh and unimposing. The whole thing small and dainty in proportion, and fresh, somehow charming instead of impressive. There seems to have been in the Etruscan instinct a real desire to preserve the natural humour of life. And that is a task surely more worthy, and even much more difficult in the long run, than conquering the world or sacrificing the self or saving the immortal soul.

Why has mankind had such a craving to be imposed upon? Why this lust after imposing creeds, imposing deeds, imposing buildings, imposing language, imposing works of art? The thing becomes an imposition and a weariness at last. Give us things that are alive and flexible, which won't last too long and become an obstruction and a weariness. Even Michelangelo becomes at last a lump and a burden and a bore. It is so hard to see past him.

Across the space from the café is the Palazzo Vitelleschi, a charming building, now a national museum – so the marble slab says. But the heavy doors are shut. The place opens at ten, a man says. It is nine-thirty. We wander up the steep but not very long street, to the top.

And the top is a fragment of public garden, and a look-out. Two old men are sitting in the sun, under a tree. We walk to the parapet, and suddenly are looking into one of the most delightful landscapes I have ever seen: as it were, into the very virginity of hilly green country. It is all wheat – green and soft and swooping, swooping down and up, and glowing with green newness, and no houses. Down goes the declivity below us, then swerving the curve and up again, to the neighbouring hill that faces in all its greenness and long-running immaculateness. Beyond, the hills ripple away to the mountains, and far in the distance stands a round peak, that seems to have an enchanted city on its summit.

Such a pure, uprising, unsullied country, in the greenness of wheat on an April morning! – and the queer complication of hills! There seems nothing of the modern world here – no houses, no contrivances, only a sort of fair wonder and stillness, an openness which has not been violated.

The hill opposite is like a distinct companion. The near end is quite steep and wild, with evergreen oaks and scrub, and specks of black-and-white cattle on the slopes of common. But the long crest is green again with wheat, running and drooping to the south. And immediately one feels: that hill has a soul, it has a meaning.

Lying thus opposite to Tarquinia's long hill, a companion across a suave little swing of valley, one feels at once that, if this is the hill where the living Tarquinians had their gay wooden houses, then that is the hill where the dead lie buried and quick, as seeds, in their painted houses underground. The two hills are as inseparable as life and death, even now, on the sunny, green-filled April morning with the breeze blowing in from the sea. And the land beyond seems as mysterious and fresh as if it were still the morning of Time.

But B. wants to go back to the Palazzo Vitelleschi: it will be open now. Down the street we go, and sure enough the big doors are open, several officials are in the shadowy courtyard entrance. They salute us in the Fascist manner; *alla romana!* Why don't they discover the Etruscan salute, and salute us *all'etrusca!* But they are perfectly courteous and friendly. We go into the courtyard of the palace.

The museum is exceedingly interesting and delightful, to anyone who is even a bit aware of the Etruscans. It contains a great number of things found at Tarquinia, and important things.

If only we would realize it, and not tear things from their settings. Museums anyhow are wrong. But if one must have museums, let them be small, and above all, let them be local. Splendid as the Etruscan museum is in Florence, how much happier one is in the museum at Tarquinia, where all the

things are Tarquinian, and at least have some association
with one another, and form some sort of *organic* whole.

In an entrance room from the cortile lie a few of the long
sarcophagi in which the nobles were buried. It seems as if
the primitive inhabitants of this part of Italy always burned
their dead, and then put the ashes in a jar, sometimes covering
the jar with the dead man's helmet, sometimes with a shallow
dish for a lid, and then laid the urn with its ashes in a little
round grave like a little well. This is called the Villanovan
way of burial, in the well-tomb.

The newcomers to the country, however, apparently
buried their dead whole. Here, at Tarquinia, you may still
see the hills where the well-tombs of the aboriginal inhabitants
are discovered, with the urns containing the ashes inside.
Then come the graves where the dead were buried unburned,
graves very much like those of today. But tombs of the
same period with cinerary urns are found near to, or in
connexion. So that the new people and the old apparently
lived side by side in harmony, from very early days, and the
two modes of burial continued side by side, for centuries,
long before the painted tombs were made.

At Tarquinia, however, the main practice seems to have
been, at least from the seventh century on, that the nobles
were buried in the great sarcophagi, or laid out on biers,
and placed in chamber-tombs, while the slaves apparently
were cremated, their ashes laid in urns, and the urns often
placed in the family tomb, where the stone coffins of the
masters rested. The common people, on the other hand,
were apparently sometimes cremated, sometimes buried in
graves very much like our graves of today, though the sides
were lined with stone. The mass of the common people was
mixed in race, and the bulk of them were probably serf-
peasants, with many half-free artisans. These must have
followed their own desire in the matter of burial: some
had graves, many must have been cremated, their ashes
saved in an urn or jar which takes up little room in a poor
man's burial-place. Probably even the less important members

of the noble families were cremated, and their remains placed in the vases, which became more beautiful as the connexion with Greece grew more extensive.

It is a relief to think that even the slaves – and the luxurious Etruscans had many, in historical times – had their remains decently stored in jars and laid in a sacred place. Apparently the 'vicious Etruscans' had nothing comparable to the vast dead-pits which lay outside Rome, beside the great highway, in which the bodies of slaves were promiscuously flung.

It is all a question of sensitiveness. Brute force and over-bearing may make a terrific effect. But in the end, that which lives lives by delicate sensitiveness. If it were a question of brute force, not a single human baby would survive for a fortnight. It is the grass of the field, most frail of all things, that supports all life all the time. But for the green grass, no empire would rise, no man would eat bread: for grain is grass; and Hercules or Napoleon or Henry Ford would alike be denied existence.

Brute force crushes many plants. Yet the plants rise again. The Pyramids will not last a moment compared with the daisy. And before Buddha or Jesus spoke the nightingale sang, and long after the words of Jesus and Buddha are gone into oblivion the nightingale still will sing. Because it is neither preaching nor teaching nor commanding nor urging. It is just singing. And in the beginning was not a Word, but a chirrup.

Because a fool kills a nightingale with a stone, is he therefore greater than the nightingale? Because the Roman took the life out of the Etruscan, was he therefore greater than the Etruscan? Not he! Rome fell, and the Roman phenomenon with it. Italy today is far more Etruscan in its pulse than Roman; and will always be so. The Etruscan element is like the grass of the field and the sprouting of corn, in Italy: it will always be so. Why try to revert to the Latin-Roman mechanism and suppression?

In the open room upon the courtyard of the Palazzo Vitelleschi lie a few sarcophagi of stone, with the effigies carved on top, something as the dead crusaders in English churches. And here, in Tarquinia, the effigies are more like crusaders than usual, for some lie flat on their backs, and have a dog at their feet; whereas usually the carved figure of the dead rears up as if alive, from the lid of the tomb, resting upon one elbow, and gazing out proudly, sternly. If it is a man, his body is exposed to just below the navel, and he holds in his hand the sacred *patera*, or *mundum*, the round saucer with the raised knob in the centre, which represents the round germ of heaven and earth. It stands for the plasm, also, of the living cell, with its nucleus, which is the indivisible God of the beginning, and which remains alive and unbroken to the end, the eternal quick of all things, which yet divides and sub-divides, so that it becomes the sun of the firmament and the lotus of the waters under the earth, and the rose of all existence upon the earth: and the sun maintains its own quick, unbroken for ever; and there is a living quick of the sea, and of all the waters; and every living created thing has its own unfailing quick. So within each man is the quick of him, when he is a baby, and when he is old, the same quick; some spark, some unborn and undying vivid life-electron. And this is what is symbolized in the *patera*, which may be made to flower like a rose or like the sun, but which remains the same, the germ central within the living plasm.

And this *patera*, this symbol, is almost invariably found in the hand of a dead man. But if the dead is a woman her dress falls in soft gathers from her throat, she wears splendid jewellery, and she holds in her hand not the *mundum*, but the mirror, the box of essence, the pomegranate, some symbols of her reflected nature, or of her woman's quality. But she, too, is given a proud, haughty look, as is the man: for she belongs to the sacred families that rule and that read the signs.

These sarcophagi and effigies here all belong to the centuries of the Etruscan decline, after there had been long intercourse with the Greeks, and perhaps most of them were made after the conquest of Etruria by the Romans. So that we do not look for fresh, spontaneous works of art, any more than we do in modern memorial stones. The funerary arts are always more or less commercial. The rich man orders his sarcophagus while he is still alive, and the monument-carver makes the work more or less elaborate, according to the price. The figure is supposed to be a portrait of the man who orders it, so we see well enough what the later Etruscans look like. In the third and second centuries B.C., at the fag end of their existence as a people, they look very like the Romans of the same day, whose busts we know so well. And often they are given the tiresomely haughty air of people who are no longer rulers indeed, only by virtue of wealth.

Yet, even when the Etruscan art is Romanized and spoilt; there still flickers in it a certain naturalness and feeling. The Etruscan *Lucumones*, or prince-magistrates, were in the first place religious seers, governors in religion, then magistrates, then princes. They were not aristocrats in the Germanic sense, not even patricians in the Roman. They were first and foremost leaders in the sacred mysteries, then magistrates, then men of family and wealth. So there is always a touch of vital life, of life-significance. And you may look through modern funerary sculpture in vain for anything so good even as the Sarcophagus of the Magistrate, with his written scroll spread before him, his strong, alert old face gazing sternly out, the necklace of office round his neck, the ring of rank on his finger. So he lies, in the museum at Tarquinia. His robe leaves him naked to the hip, and his body lies soft and slack, with the soft effect of relaxed flesh the Etruscan artists render so well, and which is so difficult. On the sculptured side of the sarcophagus the two death-dealers wield the hammer of death, the winged figures wait for the soul, and will not be persuaded away. Beautiful it is, with the easy simplicity of life. But it is late in date. Probably this old Etruscan magistrate is already an official under Roman authority: for he does not hold the sacred *mundum*, the dish, he has only the written scroll, probably of laws. As if he were no longer the religious lord or Lucumo. Though possibly, in this case, the dead man was not one of the Lucumones anyhow.

Upstairs in the museum are many vases, from the ancient crude pottery of the Villanovans to the early black ware decorated in scratches, or undecorated, called *bucchero*, and on to the painted bowls and dishes and amphoras which came from Corinth or Athens, or to those painted pots made by the Etruscans themselves more or less after the Greek patterns. These may or may not be interesting: the Etruscans are not at their best, painting dishes. Yet they must have loved them. In the early days these great jars and bowls, and smaller mixing bowls, and drinking cups and pitchers, and flat winecups formed a valuable part of the household treasure. In very early times the Etruscans must have sailed their ships to Corinth and to Athens, taking perhaps wheat and honey, wax and bronze-ware, iron and gold, and coming back with these precious jars, and stuffs, essences, perfumes, and spice. And jars brought from overseas for the sake of their painted beauty must have been household treasures.

But then the Etruscans made pottery of their own, and by the thousand they imitated the Greek vases. So that there must have been millions of beautiful jars in Etruria. Already in the first century B.C. there was a passion among the Romans for collecting Greek and Etruscan painted jars from the Etruscans, particularly from the Etruscan tombs: jars and the little bronze votive figures and statuettes, the *sigilla Tyrrhena* of the Roman luxury. And when the tombs were first robbed, for gold and silver treasure, hundreds of fine jars must have been thrown over and smashed. Because even now, when a part-rifled tomb is discovered and opened, the fragments of smashed vases lie around.

As it is, however, the museums are full of vases. If one looks for the Greek form of elegance and convention, those elegant 'still-unravished brides of quietness', one is disappointed. But get over the strange desire we have for elegant convention, and the vases and dishes of the Etruscans, especially many of the black bucchero ware, begin to open out like strange flowers, black flowers with all the softness and the rebellion of life against convention, or red-and-black flowers painted with amusing free, bold designs. It is there nearly always in Etruscan things, the naturalness verging on the commonplace, but usually missing it, and often achieving an originality so free and bold, and so fresh, that we, who love convention and things 'reduced to a norm', call it a bastard art, and commonplace.

It is useless to look in Etruscan things for 'uplift'. If you want uplift, go to the Greek and the Gothic. If you want mass, go to the Roman. But if you love the odd spontaneous forms that are never to be standardized, go to the Etruscans. In the fascinating little Palazzo Vitelleschi one could spend many an hour, but for the fact that the very fullness of museums makes one rush through them.

3

The Painted Tombs of Tarquinia

I

WE arranged for the guide to take us to the painted tombs, which are the real fame of Tarquinia. After lunch we set out, climbing to the top of the town, and passing through the south-west gate, on the level hillcrest. Looking back, the wall of the town, medieval, with a bit of more ancient black wall lower down, stands blank. Just outside the gate are one or two forlorn new houses, then ahead, the long, running table-land of the hill, with the white highway dipping and going on to Viterbo, inland.

'All this hill in front,' said the guide, 'is tombs! All tombs! The city of the dead.'

So! Then this hill is the necropolis hill! The Etruscans never buried their dead within the city walls. And the modern cemetery and the first Etruscan tombs lie almost close up to the present city gate. Therefore, if the ancient city of Tarquinia lay on this hill, it can have occupied no more space, hardly, than the present little town of a few thousand people.

Which seems impossible. Far more probably, the city itself lay on that opposite hill there, which lies splendid and unsullied, running parallel to us.

We walk across the wild bit of hilltop, where the stones crop out, and the first rock-rose flutters, and the asphodels stick up. This is the necropolis. Once it had many a tumulus, and streets of tombs. Now there is no sign of any tombs: no tumulus, nothing but the rough bare hill-crest, with stones and short grass and flowers, the sea gleaming away to the right, under the sun, and the soft land inland glowing very green and pure.

But we see a little bit of wall, built perhaps to cover a water-trough. Our guide goes straight towards it. He is a fat, good-natured young man, who doesn't look as if he would be interested in tombs. We are mistaken, however. He knows a good deal, and has a quick, sensitive interest, absolutely unobtrusive, and turns out to be as pleasant a companion for such a visit as one could wish to have.

The bit of wall we see is a little hood of masonry with an iron gate, covering a little flight of steps leading down into the ground. One comes upon it all at once, in the rough nothingness of the hillside. The guide kneels down to light his acetylene lamp, and his old terrier lies down resignedly in the sun, in the breeze which rushes persistently from the southwest, over these long, exposed hilltops.

The lamp begins to shine and smell, then to shine without smelling: the guide opens the iron gate, and we descend the steep steps down into the tomb. It seems a dark little hole underground: a dark little hole, after the sun of the upper world! But the guide's lamp begins to flare up, and we find ourselves in a little chamber in the rock, just a small, bare little cell of a room that some anchorite might have lived in. It is so small and bare and familiar, quite unlike the rather splendid spacious tombs at Cerveteri.

But the lamp flares bright, we get used to the change of light, and see the paintings on the little walls. It is the Tomb of Hunting and Fishing, so called from the pictures on the walls, and it is supposed to date from the sixth century B.C. It is very badly damaged, pieces of the wall have fallen away, damp has eaten into the colours, nothing seems to be left. Yet in the dimness we perceive flights of birds flying through the haze, with the draught of life still in their wings. And as we take heart and look closer we see the little room is frescoed all round with hazy sky and sea, with birds flying and fishes leaping, and little men hunting, fishing, rowing in boats. The lower part of the wall is all a blue-green of sea with a silhouette surface that ripples all round the room. From the sea rises a tall rock, off which a naked man, shadowy but still distinct, is beautifully and cleanly diving into the sea, while a companion climbs up the rock after him, and on the water a boat waits with rested oars in it, three men watching the diver, the middle man standing up naked, holding out his arms. Meanwhile a great dolphin leaps behind the boat, a flight of birds soars upwards to pass the rock, in the clear air. Above all, from the bands of colour that border the wall at the top hang the regular loops of garlands, garlands of flowers and leaves and buds and berries, garlands which belong to maidens and to women, and which represent the flowery circle of the female life and sex. The top border of the wall is formed of horizontal stripes or ribands of colour that go all round the room, red and black and dull gold and blue and primrose, and these are the colours that occur invariably. Men are nearly always painted a darkish red, which is the colour of many Italians when they go naked in the sun, as the Etruscans went. Women are coloured paler, because women did not go naked in the sun.

At the end of the room, where there is a recess in the wall, is painted another rock rising from the sea, and on it a man with a sling is taking aim at the birds which rise scattering this way and that. A boat with a big paddle oar is holding off from the rock, a naked man amidships is giving a queer salute to the slinger, a man kneels over the bows with his back to the others, and is letting down a net. The prow of the boat has a beautifully painted eye, so the vessel shall see where it is going. In Syracuse you will see many a two-eyed boat today come swimming in to quay. One dolphin is diving down into the sea, one is leaping out. The birds fly, and the garlands hang from the border.

It is all small and gay and quick with life, spontaneous as only young life can be. If only it were not so much damaged, one would be happy, because here is the real Etruscan liveliness and naturalness. It is not impressive or grand. But if you are content with just a sense of the quick ripple of life, then here it is.

The little tomb is empty, save for its shadowy paintings. It had no bed of rock around it: only a deep niche for holding vases, perhaps vases of precious things. The sarcophagus on the floor, perhaps under the slinger on the end wall. And it stood alone, for this is an individual tomb, for one person only, as is usual in the older tombs of this necropolis.

In the gable triangle of the end wall, above the slinger and the boat, the space is filled in with one of the frequent Etruscan banqueting scenes of the dead. The dead man, sadly obliterated, reclines upon his banqueting couch with his flat wine-dish in his hand, resting on his elbow, and beside him, also half risen, reclines a handsome and jewelled lady in fine robes, apparently resting her left hand upon the naked breast of the man, and in her right holding up to him the garland – the garland of the female festive offering. Behind the man stands a naked slave-boy, perhaps with music, while another naked slave is just filling a wine-jug from a handsome amphora or wine-jar at the side. On the woman's side stands a maiden, apparently playing the flute: for a woman was supposed to play the flute at classic funerals; and beyond sit two maidens with garlands, one turning round to watch the banqueting pair, the other with her back to it all. Beyond the maidens in the corner are more garlands, and two birds, perhaps doves. On the wall behind the head of the banqueting lady is a problematic object, perhaps a bird-cage.

The scene is natural as life, and yet it has a heavy archaic fullness of meaning. It is the death-banquet; and at the same time it is the dead man banqueting in the underworld; for the underworld of the Etruscans was a gay place. While the living feasted out of doors, at the tomb of the dead, the dead himself feasted in like manner, with a lady to offer him garlands and slaves to bring him wine, away in the underworld. For the life on earth was so good, the life below could but be a continuance of it.

This profound belief in life, acceptance of life, seems characteristic of the Etruscans. It is still vivid in the painted tombs. There is a certain dance and glamour in all the movements, even in those of the naked slave men. They are by no means downtrodden menials, let later Romans say what they will. The slaves in the tombs are surging with full life.

We come up the steps into the upper world, the sea-breeze and the sun. The old dog shambles to his feet, the guide blows out his lamp and locks the gate, we set off again, the dog trundling apathetic at his master's heels, the master speaking to him with that soft Italian familiarity which seems so very different from the spirit of Rome, the strong-willed Latin.

The guide steers across the hilltop, in the clear afternoon sun, towards another little hood of masonry. And one notices there is quite a number of these little gateways, built by the Government to cover the steps that lead down to the separate small tombs. It is utterly unlike Cerveteri, though the two places are not forty miles apart. Here there is no stately tumulus city, with its highroad between the tombs, and inside, rather noble, many-roomed houses of the dead. Here the little one-room tombs seem scattered at random on the hilltop, here and there: though probably, if excavations were fully carried out, here also we should find a regular city of the dead, with its streets and crossways. And probably each tomb had its little tumulus of piled earth, so that even above-ground there were streets of mounds with tomb entraces. But even so, it would be different from Cerveteri, from Caere; the mounds would be so small, the streets surely irregular. Anyhow, today there are scattered little one-room tombs, and we dive down into them just like rabbits popping down a hole. The place is a warren.

It is interesting to find it so different from Cerveteri. The Etruscans carried out perfectly what seems to be the Italian instinct: to have single, independent cities, with a certain surrounding territory, each district speaking its own dialect and feeling at home in its own little capital, yet the whole confederacy of city-states loosely linked together by a common religion and a more-or-less common interest. Even today Lucca is very different from Ferrara, and the language is hardly the same. In ancient Etruria this isolation of cities developing according to their own idiosyncrasy, within the loose union of a so-called nation, must have been complete. The contact between the plebs, the mass of the people, of Caere and Tarquinii must have been almost null. They were, no doubt, foreigners to one another. Only the Lucumones, the ruling sacred magistrates of noble family, the priests and the other nobles, and the merchants, must have kept up an intercommunion, speaking 'correct' Etruscan, while the people, no doubt, spoke dialects varying so widely as to be different languages. To get any idea of the pre-Roman past we must break up the conception of oneness and uniformity, and see an endless confusion of differences.

We are diving down into another tomb, called, says the guide, the Tomb of the Leopards. Every tomb has been given a name, to distinguish it from its neighbours. The Tomb of the Leopards has two spotted leopards in the triangle of the end wall, between the roof-slopes. Hence its name.

The Tomb of the Leopards is a charming, cosy little room, and the paintings on the walls have not been so very much damaged. All the tombs are ruined to some degree by weather and vulgar vandalism, having been left and neglected like common holes, when they had been broken open again and rifled to the last gasp.

But still the paintings are fresh and alive: the ochre-reds and blacks and blues and blue-greens are curiously alive and harmonious on the creamy yellow walls. Most of the tomb walls have had a thin coat of stucco, but it is of the same paste as the living rock, which is fine and yellow, and weathers to a lovely creamy gold, a beautiful colour for a background.

The walls of this little tomb are a dance of real delight. The room seems inhabited still by Etruscans of the sixth century before Christ, a vivid, life-accepting people, who must have lived with real fullness. On come the dancers and the music-players, moving in a broad frieze towards the front wall of the tomb, the wall facing us as we enter from the dark stairs, and where the banquet is going on in all its glory. Above the banquet, in the gable angle, are the two spotted leopards, heraldically facing each other across a little tree. And the ceiling of rock has chequered slopes of red and black and yellow and blue squares, with a roof-beam painted with coloured circles, dark red and blue and yellow. So that all is colour, and we do not seem to be underground at all, but in some gay chamber of the past.

The dancers on the right wall move with a strange, powerful alertness onwards. The men are dressed only in a loose coloured scarf, or in the gay handsome chlamys draped as a mantle. The *subulo* plays the double flute the Etruscans loved so much, touching the stops with big, exaggerated hands, the man behind him touches the seven-stringed lyre, the man in front turns round and signals with his left hand, holding a big wine-bowl in his right. And so they move on, on their long, sandalled feet, past the little berried olive-trees, swiftly going with their limbs full of life, full of life to the tips.

This sense of vigorous, strong-bodied liveliness is characteristic of the Etruscans, and is somehow beyond art. You cannot think of art, but only of life itself, as if this were the very life of the Etruscans, dancing in their coloured wraps with massive yet exuberant naked limbs, ruddy from the air and the sea-light, dancing and fluting along through the little olive-trees, out in the fresh day.

The end wall has a splendid banqueting scene. The feasters recline upon a checked or tartan couch-cover, on the banqueting couch, and in the open air, for they have little trees behind them. The six feasters are bold and full of life like the dancers, but they are strong, they keep their life so beautifully and richly inside themselves, they are not loose, they don't lose themselves even in their wild moments. They lie in pairs, man and woman, reclining equally on the couch, curiously friendly. The two end women are called *hetaerae*, courtesans; chiefly because they have yellow hair, which seems to have been a favourite feature in a woman of pleasure. The men are dark and ruddy, and naked to the waist. The women, sketched in on the creamy rock, are fair, and wear thin gowns, with rich mantles round their hips. They have a certain free bold look, and perhaps really are courtesans.

The man at the end is holding up, between thumb and forefinger, an egg, showing it to the yellow-haired woman who reclines next to him, she who is putting out her left hand as if to touch his breast. He, in his right hand, holds a large wine-dish, for the revel.

The next couple, man and fair-haired woman, are looking round and making the salute with the right hand curved over, in the usual Etruscan gesture. It seems as if they too are saluting the mysterious egg held up by the man at the end; who is, no doubt, the man who has died, and whose feast is being celebrated. But in front of the second couple a naked slave with a chaplet on his head is brandishing an empty wine-jug, as if to say he is fetching more wine. Another slave farther down is holding out a curious thing like a little axe, or fan. The last two feasters are rather damaged. One of them is holding up a garland to the other, but not putting it over his head as they still put a garland over your head, in India, to honour you.

Above the banqueters, in the gable angle, the two great spotted male leopards hang out their tongues and face each other heraldically, lifting a paw, on either side of a little tree. They are the leopards or panthers of the underworld Bacchus, guarding the exits and the entrances of the passion of life.

There is a mystery and a portentousness in the simple scenes which go deeper than commonplace life. It seems all so gay and light. Yet there is a certain weight, or depth of significance that goes beyond aesthetic beauty.

If one once starts looking, there is much to see. But if one glances merely, there is nothing but a pathetic little room with unimposing, half-obliterated, scratchy little paintings in tempera.

There are many tombs. When we have seen one, up we go, a little bewildered, into the afternoon sun, across a tract of rough, tormented hill, and down again to the underground, like rabbits in a warren. The hilltop is really a warren of tombs. And gradually the underworld of the Etruscans becomes more real than the above day of the afternoon. One begins to live with the painted dancers and feasters and mourners, and to look eagerly for them.

A very lovely dance tomb is the *Tomba del Triclinio*, or *del Convito*, both of which mean: Tomb of the Feast. In size and shape this is much the same as the other tombs we have seen. It is a little chamber about fifteen feet by eleven, six feet high at the walls, about eight feet at the centre. It is again a tomb for one person, like nearly all the old painted tombs here. So there is no inner furnishing. Only the farther half of the rock-floor, the pale yellow-white rock, is raised two or three inches, and on one side of this raised part are the four holes where the feet of the sarcophagus stood. For the rest, the tomb has only its painted walls and ceiling.

And how lovely these have been, and still are! The band of dancing figures that go round the room still is bright in colour, fresh, the women in thin spotted dresses of linen muslin and coloured mantles with fine borders, the men merely in a scarf. Wildly the bacchic woman throws back her head and curves out her long, strong fingers, wild and yet contained within herself, while the broad-bodied young man turns round to her, lifting his dancing hand to hers till the thumbs all but touch. They are dancing in the open, past little trees, and birds are running, and a little fox-tailed dog is watching something with the naïve intensity of the young. Wildly and delightedly dances the next woman, every bit of her, in her soft boots and her bordered mantle, with jewels on her arms; till one remembers the old dictum, that every part of the body and of the *anima* shall know religion, and be in touch with the gods. Towards her comes the young man piping on the double flute, and dancing as he comes. He is clothed only in a fine linen scarf with a border, that hangs over his arms, and his strong legs dance of themselves, so full of life. Yet, too, there is a certain solemn intensity in his face, as he turns to the woman beyond him, who stoops in a bow to him as she vibrates her castanets.

She is drawn fair-skinned, as all the women are, and he is of a dark red colour. That is the convention, in the tombs. But it is more than convention. In the early days men smeared themselves with scarlet when they took on their sacred natures. The Red Indians still do it. When they wish to figure in their sacred and portentous selves they smear their bodies all over with red. That must be why they are called Red Indians. In the past, for all serious or solemn occasions, they rubbed red pigment into their skins. And the same today. And today, when they wish to put strength into their vision, and to see true, they smear round their eyes with vermilion, rubbing it into the skin. You may meet them so, in the streets of the American towns.

It is a very old custom. The American Indian will tell you: 'The red paint, it is medicine, make you see!' But he means medicine in a different sense from ours. It is deeper even than magic. Vermilion is the colour of his sacred or potent or god body. Apparently it was so in all the ancient world. Man all scarlet was his bodily godly self. We know the kings of ancient Rome, who were probably Etruscans, appeared in public with their faces painted vermilion with minium. And Ezekiel says (23: 14, 15): 'She saw men pourtrayed upon the wall, the images of the Chaldeans pourtrayed with vermilion ... all of them princes to look to, after the manner of the Babylonians of Chaldea, the land of their nativity.'

It is then partly a convention, and partly a symbol, with the Etruscans, to represent their men red in colour, a strong red. Here in the tombs everything is in its sacred or inner-significant aspect. But also the red colour is not so very unnatural.

When the Italian today goes almost naked on the beach he becomes of a lovely dark ruddy colour, dark as any Indian. And the Etruscans went a good deal naked. The sun painted them with the sacred minium.

The dancers dance on, the birds run, at the foot of a little tree a rabbit crouches in a bunch, bunched with life. And on the tree hangs a narrow, fringed scarf, like a priest's stole; another symbol.

The end wall has a banqueting scene, rather damaged, but still interesting. We see two separate couches, and a man and a woman on each. The woman this time is dark-haired, so she need not be a courtesan. The Etruscans shared the banqueting bench with their wives; which is more than the Greeks or Romans did, at this period. The classic world thought it indecent for an honest woman to recline as the men did, even at the family table. If the woman appeared at all, she must sit up straight, in a chair.

Here, the women recline calmly with the men, and one shows a bare foot at the end of the dark couch. In front of the *lecti*, the couches, is in each case a little low square table bearing delicate dishes of food for the feasters. But they are not eating. One woman is lifting her hand to her head in a strange salute to the robed piper at the end, the other woman seems with the lifted hand to be saying No! to the charming maid, perhaps a servant, who stands at her side, presumably offering the *alabastron*, or ointment-jar, while the man at the end apparently is holding up an egg. Wreaths hang from the ivy-border above, a boy is bringing a wine-jug, the music goes on, and under the beds a cat is on the prowl, while an alert cock watches him. The silly partridge, however, turns his back, stepping innocently along.

This lovely tomb has a pattern of ivy and ivy berries, the ivy of the underworld Bacchus, along the roof-beam and in a border round the top of the walls. The roof-slopes are chequered in red and black, white, blue, brown, and yellow squares. In the gable angle, instead of the heraldic beasts, two naked men are sitting reaching back to the centre of an ivy-covered altar, arm outstretched across the ivy. But one man is almost obliterated. At the foot of the other man, in the tight angle of the roof, is a pigeon, the bird of the soul that coos out of the unseen.

This tomb has been open since 1830, and is still fresh. It is interesting to see, in Fritz Weege's book, *Etruskische Malerei*, a reproduction of an old water-colour drawing of the dancers on the right wall. It is a good drawing, yet, as one looks closer, it is quite often out, both in line and position. These Etruscan paintings, not being in our convention, are very difficult to copy. The picture shows my rabbit all spotted, as if it were some queer cat. And it shows a squirrel in the little tree in front of the piper, and flowers, and many details that have now disappeared.

But it is a good drawing, unlike some that Weege reproduces, which are so Flaxmanized and Greekified; and made according to what our great-grandfathers thought they *ought* to be, as to be really funny, and a warning for ever against thinking how things *ought* to be, when already they are quite perfectly what they are.

We climb up to the world, and pass for a few minutes through the open day. Then down we go again. In the Tomb of the Bacchanti the colours have almost gone. But still we see, on the end wall, a strange wondering dancer out of the mists of time carrying his zither, and beyond him, beyond the little tree, a man of the dim ancient world, a man with a short beard, strong and mysteriously male, is reaching for a wild archaic maiden who throws up her hands and turns back to him her excited, subtle face. It is wonderful, the strength and mystery of old life that comes out of these faded figures. The Etruscans are still there, upon the wall.

Above the figures, in the gable angle, two spotted deer are prancing heraldically towards one another, on either side the altar, and behind them two dark lions, with pale manes and with tongues hanging out, are putting up a paw to seize them on the haunch. So the old story repeats itself.

From the striped border rude garlands are hanging, and on

the roof are little painted stars, or four-petalled flowers. So much has vanished! Yet even in the last breath of colour and form, how much life there is!

In the *Tomba del Morto*, the Tomb of the Dead Man, the banqueting scene is replaced by a scene, apparently, of a dead man on his bed, with a woman leaning gently over to cover his face. It is almost like a banquet scene. But it is so badly damaged! In the gable above, two dark heraldic lions are lifting the paw against two leaping, frightened, backward-looking birds. This is a new variation. On the broken wall are the dancing legs of a man, and there is more life in these Etruscan legs, fragment as they are, than in the whole bodies of men today. Then there is one really impressive dark figure of a naked man who throws up his arms so that his great wine-bowl stands vertical, and with spread hand and closed face gives a strange gesture of finality. He has a chaplet on his head, and a small pointed beard, and lives there shadowy and significant.

Lovely again is the *Tomba delle Leonesse*, the Tomb of the Lionesses. In its gable two spotted lionesses swing their bell-like udders, heraldically facing one another across the altar. Beneath is a great vase, and a flute-player playing to it on one side, a zither-player on the other, making music to its sacred contents. Then on either side of these goes a narrow frieze of dancers, very strong and lively in their prancing. Under the frieze of dancers is a lotus dado, and below that again, all round the room, the dolphins are leaping, leaping all down-wards into the rippling sea, while birds fly between the fishes.

On the right wall reclines a very impressive dark red man wearing a curious cap, or head-dress, that has long tails like long plaits. In his right hand he holds up an egg, and in his left is the shallow wine-bowl of the feast. The scarf or stole of his human office hangs from a tree before him, and the garland of his human delight hangs at his side. He holds up the egg of resurrection, within which the germ sleeps as the soul sleeps in the tomb, before it breaks the shell and emerges again. There is another reclining man, much obliterated, and beside him hangs a garland or chain like the chains of dandelion-stems we used to make as children. And this man has a naked flute-boy, lovely in naked outline, coming towards him.

The *Tomba della Pulcella*, or Tomb of the Maiden, has faded but vigorous figures at the banquet, and very ornate couch-covers in squares and the key-pattern, and very handsome mantles.

The *Tomba dei Vasi Dipinti*, Tomb of the Painted Vases, has great amphorae painted on the side wall, and springing to-wards them is a weird dancer, the ends of his waist-cloth flying. The amphorae, two of them, have scenes painted on them, which can still be made out. On the end wall is a gentle little banquet scene, the bearded man softly touching the woman with him under the chin, a slave-boy standing childishly behind, and an alert dog under the couch. The *kylix*, or wine-bowl, that the man holds is surely the biggest on record; exaggerated, no doubt, to show the very special importance of the feast. Rather gentle and lovely is the way he touches the woman under the chin, with a delicate caress. That again is one of the charms of the Etruscan paintings: they really have the sense of touch; the people and the creatures are all really in touch. It is one of the rarest qualities, in life as well as in art. There is plenty of pawing and laying hold, but no real touch. In pictures especially, the people may be in contact, embracing or laying hands on one another. But there is no soft flow of touch. The touch does not come from the middle of the human being. It is merely a contact of surfaces, and a juxta-position of objects. This is what makes so many of the great masters boring, in spite of all their clever composition. Here, in this faded Etruscan painting, there is a quiet flow of touch that unites the man and the woman on the couch, the timid boy behind, the dog that lifts his nose, even the very garlands that hang from the wall.

Above the banquet, in the triangle, instead of lions or leopards, we have the hippocampus, a favourite animal of the Etruscan imagination. It is a horse that ends in a long, flowing fish-tail. Here these two hippocampi face one another prancing their front legs, while their fish-tails flow away into the narrow angle of the roof. They are a favourite symbol of the seaboard Etruscans.

In the *Tomba del Vecchio*, the Tomb of the Old Man, a beautiful woman with her hair dressed backwards into the long cone of the East, so that her head is like a sloping acorn, offers her elegant, twisted garland to the white-bearded old man, who is now beyond garlands. He lifts his left hand up at her, with the rich gesture of these people, that must mean something each time.

Above them, the prancing spotted deer are being seized in the haunch by two lions. And the waves of obliteration, wastage of time and damage of men, are silently passing over all.

So we go on, seeing tomb after tomb, dimness after dimness, divided between the pleasure of finding so much and the disappointment that so little remains. One tomb after another, and nearly everything faded or eaten away, or corroded with alkali, or broken wilfully. Fragments of people at banquets, limbs that dance without dancers, birds that fly in nowhere, lions whose devouring heads are devoured away! Once it was all bright and dancing: the delight of the underworld; honouring the dead with wine, and flutes playing for a dance, and limbs whirling and pressing. And it was deep and sincere honour rendered to the dead and to the mysteries. It is contrary to our ideas; but the ancients had their own philosophy for it. As the pagan old writer says: 'For no part of us nor of our bodies shall be, which doth not feel religion: and let there be no lack of singing for the soul, no lack of leaping and of dancing for the knees and heart; for all these know the gods.'

Which is very evident in the Etruscan dancers. They know the gods in their very finger-tips. The wonderful fragments of limbs and bodies that dance on in a field of obliteration still know the gods, and made it evident to us.

But we can hardly see any more tombs. The upper air seems pallid and bodiless, as we emerge once more, white with the light of the sea and the coming evening. And spent and slow the old dog rises once more to follow after.

We decide that the *Tomba delle Iscrizioni*, the Tomb of the Inscriptions, shall be our last for today. It is dim but fascinating, as the lamp flares up, and we see in front of us the end wall, painted with a false door studded with pale studs, as if it led to another chamber beyond; and riding from the left, a trail of shadowy tall horsemen; and running in from the right, a train of wild shadowy dancers wild as demons.

The horsemen are naked on the four naked horses, and they make gestures as they come towards the painted door. The horses are alternately red and black, the red having blue manes and hoofs, the black, red ones, or white. They are tall archaic horses on slim legs, with necks arched like a curved knife. And they come pinking daintily and superbly along, with their long tails, towards the dark red death-door.

From the left, the stream of dancers leaps wildly, playing music, carrying garlands or wine-jugs, lifting their arms like revellers, lifting their live knees, and signalling with their long hands. Some have little inscriptions written near them: their names.

And above the false door in the angle of the gable is a fine design: two black, wide-mouthed, pale-maned lions seated back to back, their tails rising like curved stems, between them, as they each one lift a black paw against the cringing head of a cowering spotted deer, that winces to the death-blow. Behind each deer is a smaller dark lion, in the acute angle of the roof, coming up to bite the shrinking deer in the haunch, and so give the second death-wound. For the wounds of death are in the neck and in the flank.

At the other end of the tomb are wrestlers and gamesters; but so shadowy now! We cannot see any more, nor look any further in the shadows for the unconquerable life of the Etruscans, whom the Romans called vicious, but whose life, in these tombs, is certainly fresh and cleanly vivid.

The upper air is wide and pale, and somehow void. We cannot see either world any more, the Etruscan underworld nor the common day. Silently, tired, we walk back in the wind to the town, the old dog padding stoically behind. And the guide promises to take us to the other tombs tomorrow.

There is a haunting quality in the Etruscan representations. Those leopards with their long tongues hanging out: those flowing hippocampi; those cringing spotted deer, struck in flank and neck; they get into the imagination, and will not go out. And we see the wavy edge of the sea, the dolphins curving over, the diver going down clean, the little man climbing up the rock after him so eagerly. Then the men with beards who recline on the banqueting beds: how they hold up the mysterious egg! And the women with the conical head-dress, how strangely they lean forward, with caresses we no longer know! The naked slaves joyfully stoop to the wine-jars. Their nakedness is its own clothing, more easy than drapery. The curves of their limbs show pure pleasure in life, a pleasure that goes deeper still in the limbs of the dancers, in the big, long hands thrown out and dancing to the very ends of the fingers, a dance that surges from within, like a current in the sea. It is as if the current of some strong different life swept through them, different from our shallow current today: as if they drew their vitality from different depths that we are denied.

Yet in a few centuries they lost their vitality. The Romans took the life out of them. It seems as if the power of resistance to life, self-assertion, and overbearing, such as the Romans knew: a power which must needs be moral, or carry morality with it, as a cloak for its inner ugliness: would always succeed in destroying the natural flowering of life. And yet there still are a few wild flowers and creatures.

The natural flowering of life! It is not so easy for human beings as it sounds. Behind all the Etruscan liveliness was a religion of life, which the chief men were seriously responsible for. Behind all the dancing was a vision, and even a science of life, a conception of the universe and man's place in the universe which made men live to the depth of their capacity.

To the Etruscan all was alive; the whole universe lived; and the business of man was himself to live amid it all. He had to draw life into himself, out of the wandering huge vitalities of the world. The cosmos was alive, like a vast creature. The whole thing breathed and stirred. Evaporation went up like breath from the nostrils of a whale, steaming up. The sky received it in its blue bosom, breathed it in and pondered on it and transmuted it, before breathing it out again. Inside the earth were fires like the heat in the hot red liver of a beast. Out of the fissures of the earth came breaths of other breathing, vapours direct from the living physical underearth, exhalations carrying inspiration. The whole thing was alive, and had a great soul, or *anima*: and in spite of one great soul, there were myriad roving, lesser souls: every man, every creature and tree and lake and mountain and stream, was animate, had its own peculiar consciousness. And has it today.

The cosmos was one, and its *anima* was one; but it was made up of creatures. And the greatest creature was earth, with its soul of inner fire. The sun was only a reflection, or off-throw, or brilliant handful, of the great inner fire. But in juxtaposition to earth lay the sea, the waters that moved and pondered and held a deep soul of their own. Earth and waters lay side by side, together, and utterly different.

So it was. The universe, which was a single aliveness with a single soul, instantly changed, the moment you thought of it, and became a dual creature with two souls, fiery and watery, for ever mingling and rushing apart, and held by the great aliveness of the universe in an ultimate equilibrium. But they rushed together and they rushed apart, and immediately they became myriad: volcanoes and seas, then streams and mountains, trees, creatures, men. And everything was dual, or contained its own duality, for ever mingling and rushing apart.

The old idea of the vitality of the universe was evolved long before history begins, and elaborated into a vast religion before we get a glimpse of it. When history does begin, in China or India, Egypt, Babylonia, even in the Pacific and in aboriginal America, we see evidence of one underlying religious idea: the conception of the vitality of the cosmos, the myriad vitalities in wild confusion, which still is held in some sort of array: and man, amid all the glowing welter, adventuring, struggling, striving for one thing, life, vitality, more vitality: to get into himself more and more of the gleaming vitality of the cosmos. That is the treasure. The active religious idea was that man, by vivid attention and subtlety and exerting all his strength, could draw more life into himself, more life, more and more glistening vitality, till he became shining like the morning, blazing like a god. When he was all himself he painted himself vermilion like the throat of dawn, and was god's body, visibly, red and utterly vivid. So he was a prince, a king, a god, an Etruscan Lucumo; Pharaoh, or Belshazzar, or Ashurbanipal, or Tarquin; in a feebler *decrescendo*, Alexander, or Caesar, or Napoleon.

This was the idea at the back of all the great old civilizations. It was even, half-transmuted, at the back of David's mind, and voiced in the Psalms. But with David the living cosmos became merely a personal god. With the Egyptians and Babylonians and Etruscans, strictly there were no personal gods. There were only idols or symbols. It was the living cosmos itself, dazzlingly and gaspingly complex, which was divine, and which could be contemplated only by the strongest soul, and only at moments. And only the peerless soul could draw into itself some last flame from the quick. Then you had a king-god indeed.

There you have the ancient idea of kings, kings who are gods by vividness, because they have gathered into themselves core after core of vital potency from the universe, till they are clothed in scarlet, they are bodily a piece of the deepest fire. Pharaohs and kings of Nineveh, kings of the East, and Etruscan Lucumones, they are the living clue to the pure fire, to the cosmic vitality. They are the vivid key to life, the vermilion clue to the mystery and the delight of death and life. They, in their own body, unlock the vast treasure-house of the cosmos for their people, and bring out life, and show the way into the dark of death, which is the blue burning of the one fire. They, in their own bodies, are the life-bringers and the death-guides, leading ahead in the dark, and coming out in the day with more than sunlight in their bodies. Can one wonder that such dead are wrapped in gold; or were?

The life-bringers, and the death-guides. But they set guards at the gates both of life and death. They keep the secrets, and safeguard the way. Only a few are initiated into the mystery of the bath of life, and the bath of death: the pool within pool within pool, wherein, when a man is dipped, he becomes darker than blood, with death, and brighter than fire, with life; till at last he is scarlet royal as a piece of living life, pure vermilion.

The people are not initiated into the cosmic ideas, nor into the awakened throb of more vivid consciousness. Try as you may, you can never make the mass of men throb with full awakenedness. They *cannot* be more than a little aware. So you must give them symbols, ritual and gesture, which will fill their bodies with life up to their own full measure. Any more is fatal. And so the actual knowledge must be guarded from them, lest knowing the formulae, without undergoing at all the experience that corresponds, they may become insolent and impious, thinking they have the all, when they have only an empty monkey-chatter. The esoteric knowledge will always be esoteric, since knowledge is an experience, not a formula. But it is foolish to hand out the formulae. A little knowledge is indeed a dangerous thing. No age proves it more than ours. Monkey-chatter is at last the most disastrous of all things.

The clue to the Etruscan life was the Lucumo, the religious prince. Beyond him were the priests and warriors. Then came the people and the slaves. People and warriors and slaves did not think about religion. There would soon have been no religion left. They felt the symbols and danced the sacred dances. For they were always kept *in touch*, physically, with the mysteries. The 'touch' went from the Lucumo down to the merest slave. The blood-stream was unbroken. But 'knowing' belonged to the high-born, the pure-bred.

So, in the tombs we find only the simple, uninitiated vision of the people. There is none of the priest-work of Egypt. The symbols are to the artist just wonderforms, pregnant with emotion and good for decoration. It is so all the way through Etruscan art. The artists evidently were of the people, artisans. Presumably they were of the old Italic stock, and understood nothing of the religion in its intricate form, as it had come in from the East: though doubtless the crude principles of the official religion were the same as those of the primitive religion of the aborigines. The same crude principles ran through the religions of all the barbaric world of that time, Druid or Teutonic or Celtic. But the newcomers in Etruria held secret the science and philosophy of their religion, and gave the people the symbols and the ritual, leaving the artists free to use the symbols as they would; which shows that there was no priest-rule.

Later, when scepticism came over all the civilized world, as it did after Socrates, the Etruscan religion began to die, Greeks and Greek rationalism flooded in, and Greek stories more or less took the place of the old Etruscan symbolic thought. Then again the Etruscan artists, uneducated, used the Greek stories as they had used the Etruscan symbols, quite freely, making them over again just to please themselves.

But one radical thing the Etruscan people never forgot, because it was in their blood as well as in the blood of their masters: and that was the mystery of the journey out of life, and into death; the death-journey, and the sojourn in the afterlife. The wonder of their soul continued to play round the mystery of this journey and this sojourn.

In the tombs we see it; throes of wonder and vivid feeling throbbing over death. Man moves naked and glowing through the universe. Then comes death: he dives into the sea, he departs into the underworld.

The sea is that vast primordial creature that has a soul also, whose inwardness is womb of all things, out of which all things emerged, and into which they are devoured back. Balancing the sea is the earth of inner fire, of after-life, and before-life. Beyond the waters and the ultimate fire lay only that

oneness of which the people knew nothing: it was a secret the
Lucumones kept for themselves, as they kept the symbol of it
in their hand.

But the sea the people knew. The dolphin leaps in and out of
it suddenly, as a creature that suddenly exists, out of nowhere.
He was not: and lo! there he is! The dolphin which gives up
the sea's rainbows only when he dies. Out he leaps; then, with
a head-dive, back again he plunges into the sea. He is so much
alive, he is like the phallus carrying the fiery spark of procreation down into the wet darkness of the womb. The diver
does the same, carrying like a phallus his small hot spark into
the deeps of death. And the sea will give up her dead like
dolphins that leap out and have the rainbow within them.

But the duck that swims on the water, and lifts his wings, is
another matter: the blue duck, or goose, so often represented
by the Etruscans. He is the same goose that saved Rome, in the
night.

The duck does not live down within the waters as the fish
does. The fish is the *anima*, the animate life, the very clue to the
vast sea, the watery element of the first submission. For this
reason Jesus was represented in the first Christian centuries as
a fish, in Italy especially, where the people still thought in the
Etruscan symbols. Jesus was the *anima* of the vast, moist ever-
yielding element which was the opposite and the counterpart
of the red flame the Pharaohs and the kings of the East had
sought to invest themselves with.

But the duck has no such subaqueous nature as the fish. It
swims upon the waters, and is hot-blooded, belonging to the
red flame, of the animal body of life. But it dives under water,
and preens itself upon the flood. So it became, to man, the
symbol of that part of himself which delights in the waters,
and dives in, and rises up and shakes its wings. It is the symbol
of a man's own phallus and phallic life. So you see a man holding on his hand the hot, soft, alert duck, offering it to the
maiden. So today the Red Indian makes a secret gift to the
maiden of a hollow, earthenware duck, in which is a little fire
and incense. It is that part of his body and his fiery life that a

-man can offer to a maid. And it is that awareness or alertness in him, that other consciousness, that wakes in the night and rouses the city.

But the maid offers the man a garland, the rim of flowers from the edge of the 'pool', which can be placed over the man's head and laid on his shoulders, in symbol that he is invested with the power of the maiden's mystery and different strength, the female power. For whatever is laid over the shoulders is a sign of power added.

Birds fly portentously on the walls of the tombs. The artist must often have seen these priests, the augurs, with their crooked, bird-headed staffs in their hand, out on a high place watching the flight of larks or pigeons across the quarters of the sky. They were reading the signs and the portents, looking for an indication, how they should direct the course of some serious affair. To us it may seem foolish. To them, hot-blooded birds flew through the living universe as feelings and premonitions fly through the breast of a man, or as thoughts fly through the mind. In their flight the suddenly roused birds, or the steady, far-coming birds, moved wrapped in a deeper consciousness, in the complex destiny of all things. And since all things corresponded in the ancient world, and man's bosom mirrored itself in the bosom of the sky, or *vice versa*, the birds were flying to a portentous goal, in the man's breast who watched, as well as flying their own way in the bosom of the sky. If the augur could see the birds flying *in his heart*, then he would know which way destiny too was flying for him.

The science of augury certainly was no exact science. But it was as exact as our sciences of psychology or political economy. And the augurs were as clever as our politicians, who also must practise divination, if ever they are to do anything worth the name. There is no other way when you are dealing with life. And if you live by the cosmos, you look in the cosmos for your clue. If you live by a personal god, you pray to him. If you are rational, you think things over. But it all amounts to the same thing in the end. Prayer, or thought, or studying the stars, or watching the flight of birds, or studying the entrails of the sacrifice, it is all the same process, ultimately: of divination. All it depends on is the amount of *true*, sincere, religious concentration you can bring to bear on your object. An act of pure attention, if you are capable of it, will bring its own answer. And you choose that object to concentrate upon which will best focus your consciousness. Every real discovery made, every serious and significant decision ever reached, was reached and made by divination. The soul stirs, and makes an act of pure attention, and that is a discovery.

The science of the augur and the haruspex was not so foolish as our modern science of political economy. If the hot liver of the victim cleared the soul of the haruspex, and made him capable of that ultimate inward attention which alone tells us the last thing we need to know, then why quarrel with the haruspex? To him, the universe was alive, and in quivering *rapport*. To him, the blood was conscious: he thought with his heart. To him, the blood was the red and shining stream of consciousness itself. Hence, to him, the liver, that great organ where the blood struggles and 'overcomes death', was an object of profound mystery and significance. It stirred his soul and purified his consciousness; for it was also his victim. So he gazed into the hot liver, that was mapped out in fields and regions like the sky of stars, but these fields and regions were those of the red, shining consciousness that runs through the whole animal creation. And therefore it must contain the answer to his own blood's question.

It is the same with the study of stars, or the sky of stars. Whatever object will bring the consciousness into a state of pure attention, in a time of perplexity, will also give back an answer to the perplexity. But it is truly a question of *divination*. As soon as there is any pretence of infallibility, and pure scientific calculation, the whole thing becomes a fraud and a jugglery. But the same is true not only of augury and astrology, but also of prayer and of pure reason, and even of the discoveries of the great laws and principles of science. Men juggle with prayer today as once they juggled with augury; and in the same way they are juggling with science. Every great discovery or decision comes by an act of divination. Facts are fitted round afterwards. But all attempt at divination, even prayer and reason and research itself, lapses into jugglery when the heart loses its purity. In the impurity of his heart, Socrates often juggled logic unpleasantly. And no doubt, when scepticism came over the ancient world, the haruspex and the augur became jugglers and pretenders. But for centuries they held real sway. It is amazing to see, in Livy, what a big share they must have had in the building up of the great Rome of the Republic.

Turning from birds to animals, we find in the tombs the continual repetition of lion against deer. As soon as the world was created, according to the ancient idea, it took on duality. All things became dual, not only in the duality of sex, but in the polarity of action. This is the 'impious pagan duality'. It did not, however, contain the later pious duality of good and evil.

The leopard and the deer, the lion and the bull, the cat and the dove, or the partridge, these are part of the great duality, or polarity of the animal kingdom. But they do not represent good action and evil action. On the contrary, they represent the polarized activity of the divine cosmos, in its animal creation.

The treasure of treasures is the soul, which, in every creature, in every tree or pool, means that mysterious conscious point of balance or equilibrium between the two halves of the duality, the fiery and the watery. This mysterious point clothes itself in vividness after vividness from the right hand, and vividness after vividness from the left. And in death it does not disappear, but is stored in the egg, or in the jar, or even in the tree which brings forth again.

But the soul itself, the conscious spark of every creature, is not dual; and being the immortal, it is also the altar on which our mortality and our duality is at last sacrificed.

So as the key-picture in the tombs, we have over and over again the heraldic beasts facing one another across the altar, or the tree, or the vase; and the lion is smiting the deer in the hip and the throat. The deer is spotted, for day and night, the lion is dark and light the same.

The deer or lamb or goat or cow is the gentle creature with udder of overflowing milk and fertility; or it is the stag or ram or bull, the great father of the herd, with horns of power set obvious on the brow, and indicating the dangerous aspect of the beasts of fertility. These are the creatures of prolific, boundless procreation, the beasts of peace and increase. So even Jesus is the lamb. And the endless, endless gendering of these creatures will fill all the earth with cattle till herds rub flanks over all the world, and hardly a tree can rise between.

But this must not be so, since they are only half, even of the animal creation. Balance must be kept. And this is the altar we are all sacrificed upon: it is even death; just as it is our soul and purest treasure.

So, on the other hand from the deer, we have lionesses and leopards. These, too, are male and female. These, too, have udders of milk and nourish young; as the wolf nourished the first Romans: prophetically, as the destroyers of many deer, including the Etruscan. So these fierce ones guard the treasure and the gateway, which the prolific ones would squander or close up with too much gendering. They bite the deer in neck and haunch, where the great blood-streams run.

So the symbolism goes all through the Etruscan tombs. It is very much the symbolism of all the ancient world. But here it is not exact and scientific, as in Egypt. It is simple and rudimentary, and the artist plays with it as a child with fairy stories. Nevertheless, it is the symbolic element which rouses the deeper emotion, and gives the peculiarly satisfying quality to the dancing figures and the creatures. A painter like Sargent, for example, is so clever. But in the end he is utterly uninteresting, a bore. He never has an inkling of his own triviality and silliness. One Etruscan leopard, even one little quail, is worth all the miles of him.

4

The Painted Tombs of Tarquinia

2

WE sit at the tin tables of the café above the gate watching the peasants coming in the evening from the fields, with their implements and their asses. As they drift in through the gate the man of the *Dazio*, the town customs, watches them, asks them questions if they carry bundles, prods the pack on the ass, and when a load of brushwood rolls up keeps it halted while he pierces the load with a long steel rod, carefully thrusting to see if he can feel hidden barrels of wine or demijohns of oil, bales of oranges or any other foodstuffs. Because all foodstuffs that come into an Italian town – many other things too, besides comestibles – must pay a duty, in some instances a heavy one.

Probably in Etruscan days the peasants came in very much the same, at evening, to the town. The Etruscans were instinctively citizens. Even the peasants dwelt within walls. And in those days, no doubt, the peasants were serfs very much as they are today in Italy, working the land for no wages, but for a portion of the produce; and working the land intensely, with that careful, almost passionate attention the Italian still gives to the soil; and living in the city, or village, but having straw huts out in the fields, for summer.

But in those days, on a fine evening like this, the men would come in naked, darkly ruddy-coloured from the sun and wind, with strong, insouciant bodies; and the women would drift in, wearing the loose, becoming smock of white or blue linen; and somebody, surely, would be playing on the pipes; and somebody, surely, would be singing, because

the Etruscans had a passion for music, and an inner carelessness the modern Italians have lost. The peasants would enter
the clear, clean, sacred space inside the gates, and salute the
gay-coloured little temple as they passed along the street that
rose uphill towards the arx, between rows of low houses with
gay-coloured fronts painted or hung with bright terra-cottas.
One can almost hear them still, calling, shouting, piping,
singing, driving in the mixed flocks of sheep and goats, that
go so silently, and leading the slow, white, ghostlike oxen
with the yokes still on their necks.

And surely, in those days, young nobles would come
splashing in on horseback, riding with naked limbs on an
almost naked horse, carrying probably a spear, and cantering
ostentatiously through the throng of red-brown, full-limbed,
smooth-skinned peasants. A Lucumo, even, sitting very noble
in his chariot driven by an erect charioteer, might be driving
in at sundown, halting before the temple to perform the brief
ritual of entry into the city. And the crowding populace
would wait; for the Lucumo of the old days, glowing ruddy
in flesh, his beard stiffly trimmed in the Oriental style, the
torque of gold round his neck, and the mantle or wrap bordered
with scarlet falling in full folds, leaving the breast bare, he was
divine, sitting on the chair in his chariot in the stillness of
power. The people drew strength even from looking at him.

The chariot drew a little forward, from the temple: the
Lucumo, sitting erect on his chair in the chariot, and bare-
shouldered and bare-breasted, waits for the people. Then the
peasants would shrink back in fear. But perhaps some citizen
in a white tunic would lift up his arms in salute, and come
forward to state his difficulty, or to plead for justice. And the
Lucumo, seated silent within another world of power, dis-
ciplined to his own responsibility of knowledge for the people,
would listen till the end. Then a few words – and the chariot
of gilt bronze swirls off up the hill to the house of the chief,
the citizens drift on to their houses, the music sounds in the
dark streets, torches flicker, the whole place is eating, feasting,
and as far as possible having a gay time.

It is different now. The drab peasants, muffled in ugly clothing, straggle in across the waste bit of space, and trail home, songless and meaningless. We have lost the art of living; and in the most important science of all, the science of daily life, the science of behaviour, we are complete ignoramuses. We have psychology instead. Today in Italy, in the hot Italian summer, if a navvy working in the street takes off his shirt to work with free, naked torso, a policeman rushes to him and commands him insultingly into his shirt again. One would think a human being was such a foul indecency altogether that life was feasible only when the indecent thing was as far as possible blotted out. The very exposure of female arms and legs in the street is only done as an insult to the whole human body. 'Look at that! It doesn't matter!'

Neither does it! But then, why did the torso of the workman matter?

At the hotel, in the dark emptiness of the place, there are three Japanese staying: little yellow men. They have come to inspect the salt works down on the coast below Tarquinia, so we are told, and they have a Government permit. The salt works, the extracting of salt from the pools shut off from the low sea, are sort of prisons, worked by convict labour. One wonders why Japanese men should want to inspect such places, officially. But we are told that these salt works are 'very important'.

Albertino is having a very good time with the three Japanese, and seems to be very deep in their confidence, bending over their table, his young brown head among the three black ones, absorbed and on the *qui vive*. He rushes off for their food – then rushes to us to see what we want to eat.

'What is there?'

'*Er – c'è –* ' He always begins with wonderful deliberation, as if there was a menu fit for the Tsar. Then he breaks off suddenly, says: 'I'll ask the mamma!' – darts away – returns, and says exactly what we knew he'd say, in a bright voice, as if announcing the New Jerusalem: 'There are eggs – er – and beefsteak – er and there are some little potatoes.' We know the eggs and beefsteak well! However, I decide to have beefsteak once more, with the little potatoes – left over by good fortune from lunch – fried. Off darts Albertino, only to dart back and announce that the potatoes and beefsteak are finished ('by the Chinese,' he whispers), 'but there are frogs.' 'There are what?' '*Le rane*, the frogs!' 'What sort of frogs?' 'I'll show you!' Off he darts again, returns with a plate containing eight or nine pairs of frogs' naked hind-legs. B. looks the other way and I accept frogs – they look quite good. In the joy of getting the frogs safely to port, Albertino skips, and darts off: to return in a moment with a bottle of beer, and whisper to us all the information about the Chinese, as he calls them. They can't speak a word of Italian. When they want a word they take the little book, French and Italian. *Bread*? – eh? They want bread. Er! – Albertino gives little grunts, like commas and semicolons, which I write as *er!* Bread they want, eh? – er! – they take the little book – here he takes an imaginary little book, lays it on the tablecloth, wets his finger and turns over the imaginary leaves – *bread!* – er! – p – you look under 'p' – er! – *ecco! pane! – pane! – si capisce!* – bread! they want bread. Then wine! er! take the little book (he turns over imaginary little leaves with fervour) – er! here you are, *vino! – pane, e vino!* So they do! Every word! They looked out name! Er! you! Er! I tell him, *Albertino*. And so the boy continues, till I ask what about *le rane*? Ah! Er! *Le rane!* Off he darts, and swirls back with a plate of fried frogs' legs, in pairs.

He is an amusing and vivacious boy, yet underneath a bit sad and wistful, with all his responsibility. The following day he darted to show us a book of views of Venice, left behind by the Chinese, as he persists in calling them, and asks if I want it. I don't. Then he shows us two Japanese postage stamps, and the address of one of the Japanese gentlemen, written on a bit of paper. The Japanese gentleman and Albertino are to exchange picture postcards. I insist that the Japanese are not Chinese. 'Er!' says Albertino. 'But the

Japanese are also Chinese!' I insist that they are not, that they live in a different country. He darts off, and returns with a school atlas. 'Er! China is in Asia! Asia! Asia!' – he turns the leaves. He is really an intelligent boy, and ought to be going to school instead of running an hotel at the tender age of fourteen.

The guide to the tombs, having had to keep watch at the museum all night, wants to get a sleep after dawn, so we are not to start till ten. The town is already empty, the people gone out to the fields. A few men stand about with nothing doing. The city gates are wide open. At night they are closed, so that the *Dazio* man can sleep: and you can neither get in nor out of the town. We drink still another coffee – Albertino's morning dose was a very poor show.

Then we see the guide, talking to a pale young fellow in old corduroy velveteen knee-breeches and an old hat and thick boots: most obviously German. We go over, make proper salutes, nod to the German boy, who looks as if he'd had vinegar for breakfast – and set off. This morning we are going out a couple miles, to the farthest end of the necropolis. We have still a dozen tombs to look at. In all, there are either twenty-five or twenty-seven painted tombs one can visit.

This morning there is a stiff breeze from the south-west. But it is blowing fresh and clear, not behaving in the ugly way the *libeccio* can behave. We march briskly along the highway, the old dog trundling behind. He loves spending a morning among the tombs. The sea gives off a certain clearness, that makes the atmosphere doubly brilliant and exhilarating, as if we were on a mountain-top. The omnibus rolls by, from Viterbo. In the fields the peasants are working, and the guide occasionally greets the women, who give him a sally back again. The young German tramps firmly on: but his spirit is not as firm as his tread. One doesn't know what to say to him, he vouchsafes nothing, seems as if he didn't want to be spoken to, and yet is probably offended that we don't talk to him. The guide chatters to him in unfailing cheerfulness, in Italian: but after a while drops back with evident relief to the milder company of B., leaving me to the young German, who has certainly swallowed vinegar some time or other.

But I feel with him as with most of the young people of today: he has been sinned against more than he sins. The vinegar was given him to drink. Breaking reluctantly into German, since Italian seems foolish, and he won't come out in English, I find, within the first half-mile, that he is twenty-three (he looks nineteen), has finished his university course, is going to be an archaeologist, is travelling doing archaeology, has been in Sicily and Tunis, whence he has just returned; didn't think much of either place – *mehr Schrei wie Wert*, he jerks out, speaking as if he were throwing his words away like a cigarette-end he was sick of; doesn't think much of any place; doesn't think much of the Etruscans – *nicht viel wert*; doesn't, apparently, think much of me; knows a professor or two whom I have met; knows the tombs of Tarquinia very well, having been here, and stayed here, twice before; doesn't think much of them; is going to Greece; doesn't expect to think much of it; is staying in the other hotel, not Gentile's, because it is still cheaper: is probably staying a fortnight, going to photograph all the tombs, with a big photographic apparatus – has the Government authority, like the Japs – apparently has very little money indeed, marvellously doing everything on nothing – expects to be a famous professor in a science he doesn't think much of – and I wonder if he always has enough to eat.

He certainly is a fretful and peevish, even if in some ways silent and stoical, young man. *Nicht viel wert!* – not much worth – doesn't amount to anything – seems to be his favourite phrase, as it is the favourite phrase of almost all young people today. Nothings amounts to anything, for the young.

Well, I feel it's not my fault, and try to bear up. But though it is bad enough to have been of the war generation, it must be worse to have grown up just after the war. One can't blame the young, that they don't find that anything amounts to anything. The war cancelled most meanings for—them.

And my young man is not really so bad: he would even rather like to be *made* to believe in something. There is a yearning pathos in him somewhere.

We have passed the modern cemetery, with its white marble headstones, and the arches of a medieval aqueduct mysteriously spanning a dip, and left the highroad, following a path along the long hill-crest, through the green wheat that flutters and ripples in the sea-wind like fine feathers, in the wonderful brilliance of morning. Here and there are tassels of mauve anemones, bits of verbena, many daisies, tufts of camomile. On a rocky mound, which was once a tumulus, the asphodels have the advantage, and send up their spikes on the bright, fresh air, like soldiers clustered on the mount. And we go along this vivid green headland of wheat – which still is rough and uneven, because it was once all tumuli – with our faces to the breeze, the sea-brightness filling the air with exhilaration, and all the country still and silent, and we talk German in the wary way of two dogs sniffing at one another.

Till suddenly we turn off to an almost hidden tomb – the German boy knows the way perfectly. The guide hurries up and lights the acetylene lamp, the dog slowly finds himself a place out of the wind, and flings himself down: and we sink slowly again into the Etruscan world, out of the present world, as we descend underground.

One of the most famous tombs at this far-off end of the necropolis is the Tomb of the Bulls. It contains what the guide calls: *un po' di pornografico!* – but a very little. The German boy shrugs his shoulders as usual: but he informs us that this is one of the oldest tombs of all, and I believe him, for it looks so to me.

It is a little wider than some tombs, the roof has not much pitch, there is a stone bed for sarcophagi along the side walls, and in the end wall are two doorways, cut out of the rock of the end and opening into a second chamber, which seems darker and more dismal. The German boy says this second chamber was cut out later, from the first one. It has no paintings of any importance.

We return to the first chamber, the old one. It is called the Tomb of the Bulls from the two bulls above the doorways of the end wall, one a man-faced bull charging at the '*po*' *di pornografico*', the other lying down serenely and looking with mysterious eyes into the room, his back turned calmly to the second bit of a picture which the guide says is not '*pornografico*' – 'because it is a woman.' The young German smiles with his sour-water expression.

Everything in this tomb suggests the old East: Cyprus, or the Hittites, or the culture of Minos of Crete. Between the doorways of the end wall is a charming painting of a naked horseman with a spear, on a naked horse, moving towards a charming little palm-tree and a well-head or fountain-head, on which repose two sculptured, black-faced beasts, lions with queer black faces. From the mouth of the one near the palm-tree water pours down into a sort of altar-bowl, while on the far side a warrior advances, wearing a bronze helmet and shin-greaves, and apparently menacing the horseman with a sword which he brandishes in his left hand, as he steps up on to the base of the well-head. Both warrior and horseman wear the long, pointed boots of the East: and the palm-tree is not very Italian.

This picture has a curious charm, and is evidently symbolical. I said to the German: 'What do you think it means?' 'Ach, nothing! The man on the horse has come to the drinking-trough to water his horse: no more!' 'And the man with the sword?' 'Oh, he is perhaps his enemy.' 'And the black-faced lions?' 'Ach nothing! Decorations of the fountain.' Below the picture are trees on which hang a garland and a neck-band. The border pattern, instead of the egg and dart, has the sign of Venus, so called, between the darts: a ball surmounted by a little cross. 'And that, is that a symbol?' I asked the German. 'Here no!' he replied abruptly. 'Merely a decoration!' – which is perhaps true. But that the Etruscan artist had no more feeling for it, as a symbol, than a modern house-decorator would have, that we cannot believe.

I gave up for the moment. Above the picture is a sentence lightly written, almost scribbled, in Etruscan. 'Can you read it?' I said to the German boy. He read it off quickly – myself, I should have had to go letter by letter. 'Do you know what it means?' I asked him. He shrugged his shoulders. 'Nobody knows.'

In the shallow angle of the roof the heraldic beasts are curious. The squat centre-piece, the so-called altar, has four rams' heads at the corners. On the right a pale bodied man with a dark face is galloping up with loose rein, on a black horse, followed by a galloping bull. On the left is a bigger figure, a queer galloping lion with his tongue out. But from the lion's shoulders, instead of wings, rises the second neck of a dark-faced, bearded goat: so that the complex animal has a second, backward-leaning neck and head, of a goat, as well as the first maned neck and menacing head of a lion. The tail of the lion ends in a serpent's head. So this is the proper Chimaera. And galloping after the end of the lion's tail comes a winged female sphinx.

'What is the meaning of this lion with the second head and neck?' I asked the German. He shrugged his shoulders, and said: 'Nothing!' It meant nothing to him, because nothing except the ABC of facts means anything to him. He is a scientist, and when he doesn't want a thing to have a meaning it is, *ipso facto*, meaningless.

But the lion with the goat's head springing backwards from its shoulders must mean something, because there it is, very vivid, in the famous bronze Chimaera of Arezzo, which is in the Florence museum, and which Benvenuto Cellini restored, and which is one of the most fascinating bronzes in the world. There, the bearded goat's head springs twisting backwards from the lion's shoulders, while the right horn of the goat is seized in the mouth of the serpent, which is the tail of the lion whipped forward over his back.

Though this is the correct Chimaera, with the wounds

of Bellerophon in hip and neck, still it is not merely a big toy. It has, and was intended to have, an exact esoteric meaning. In fact, Greek myths are only gross representations of certain very clear and very ancient esoteric conceptions, that are much older than the myths: or the Greeks. Myths, and personal gods, are only the decadence of a previous cosmic religion.

The strange potency and beauty of these Etruscan things arise, it seems to me, from the profundity of the symbolic meaning the artist was more or less aware of. The Etruscan religion, surely, was never anthropomorphic: that is, whatever gods it contained were not *beings*, but symbols of elemental powers, just symbols: as was the case earlier in Egypt. The undivided Godhead, if we can call it such, was symbolized by the *mundum*, the plasm-cell with its nucleus: that which is the very beginning; instead of, as with us, by a personal god, a person being the very end of all creation or evolution. So it is all the way through: the Etruscan religion is concerned with all those physical and creative powers and forces which go to the building up and the destroying of the soul: the soul, the personality, being that which gradually is produced out of chaos, like a flower, only to disappear again into chaos, or the underworld. We, on the contrary, say: In the beginning was the Word! – and deny the physical universe true existence. We exist only in the Word, which is beaten out thin to cover, gild, and hide all things.

The human being, to the Etruscan, was a bull or a ram, a lion or a deer, according to his different aspects and potencies. The human being had in his veins the blood of the wings of birds and the venom of serpents. All things emerged from the blood-stream, and the blood-relation, however complex and contradictory it might become, was never interrupted or forgotten. There were different currents in the blood-stream, and some always clashed: bird and serpent, lion and deer, leopard and lamb. Yet the very clash was a form of unison, as we see in the lion which also has a goat's head.

But the young German will have nothing of this. He is a

modern, and the obvious alone has true existence for him. A lion with a goat's head as well as its own head is unthinkable. That which is unthinkable is non-existent, is nothing. So, all the Etruscan symbols are to him non-existent and mere crude incapacity to think. He wastes not a thought on them: they are spawn of mental impotence, hence negligible.

But perhaps also he doesn't want to give himself away, or divulge any secret that is going to make him a famous archaeologist later on. Though I don't think that was it. He was very nice, showing me details, with his flashlight, that I should have overlooked. The white horse, for example, has had its drawing most plainly altered: you can see the old outline of the horse's back legs and breast, and of the foot of the rider, and you can see how considerably the artist changed the drawing, sometimes more than once. He seems to have drawn the whole thing complete, each time, then changed the position, changed the direction, to please his feeling. And as there was no indiarubber to rub out the first attempts, there they are, from at least six hundred years before Christ: the delicate mistakes of an Etruscan who had the instinct of a pure artist in him, as well as the blithe insouciance which makes him leave his alterations for anyone to spy out, if they want to.

The Etruscan artists either drew with the brush or scratched, perhaps, with a nail, the whole outline of their figures on the soft stucco, and then applied their colour *al fresco*. So they had to work quickly. Some of the paintings seemed to me tempera, and in one tomb, I think the Francesco Giustiniani, the painting seemed to be done on the naked, creamy rock. In that case, the blue colour of the man's scarf is marvellously vivid.

The subtlety of Etruscan painting, as of Chinese and Hindu, lies in the wonderfully suggestive *edge* of the figures. It is not outlined. It is not what we call 'drawing'. It is the flowing contour where the body suddenly leaves off, upon the atmosphere. The Etruscan artist seems to have seen living things surging from their own centre to their own surface. And the curving and contour of the silhouette-edge suggests the whole movement of the modelling within. There is actually no modelling. The figures are painted in the flat. Yet they seem of a full, almost turgid muscularity. It is only when we come to the late Tomb of Typhon that we have the figure *modelled*, Pompeian style, with light and shade.

It must have been a wonderful world, that old world where everything appeared alive and shining in the dusk of contact with all things, not merely as an isolated individual thing played upon by daylight; where each thing had a clear outline, visually, but in its very clarity was related emotionally or vitally to strange other things, one thing springing from another, things mentally contradictory fusing together emotionally, so that a lion could be at the same moment also a goat, and not a goat. In those days, a man riding on a red horse was not just Jack Smith on his brown nag; it was a suave-skinned creature, with death or life in its face, surging along on a surge of animal power that burned with travel, with the passionate movement of the blood, and which was swirling along on a mysterious course, to some unknown goal, swirling with a weight of its own. Then also, a bull was not merely a stud animal worth so much, due to go to the butcher in a little while. It was a vast wonder-beast, a well-head of the great, furnace-like passion that makes the worlds roll and the sun surge up, and makes a man surge with procreative force; the bull, the herd-lord, the father of calves and heifers, of cows; the father of milk; he who has the horns of power on his forehead, symbolizing the warlike aspect of the horn of fertility; the bellowing master of force, jealous, horned, charging against opposition. The goat was in the same line, father of milk, but instead of huge force he had cunning, the cunning *consciousness* and self-consciousness of the jealous, hard-headed father of procreation. Whereas the lion was most terrible, yellow and roaring with a blood-drinking energy, again like the sun, but the sun asserting himself in drinking up the life of the earth. For the sun can warm the worlds, like a yellow hen sitting on her eggs.

Or the sun can lick up the life of the world with a hot tongue. The goat says: let me breed for ever, till the world is one reeking goat. But then the lion roars from the other blood-stream, which is also in man, and he lifts his paw to strike, in the passion of the other wisdom.

So all creatures are potential in their own way, a myriad manifold consciousness storming with contradictions and oppositions that are eternal, beyond all mental reconciliation. We can know the living world only symbolically. Yet every consciousness, the rage of the lion, and the venom of the snake, *is*, and therefore is divine. All emerges out of the unbroken circle with its nucleus, the germ, the One, the god, if you like to call it so. And man, with his soul and his personality, emerges in eternal connexion with all the rest. The blood-stream is one, and unbroken, yet storming with oppositions and contradictions.

The ancients saw, consciously, as children now see unconsciously, the everlasting *wonder* in things. In the ancient world the three compelling emotions must have been emotions of wonder, fear, and admiration: admiration in the Latin sense of the word, as well as our sense; and fear in its largest meaning, including repulsion, dread, and hate: then arose the last, individual emotion of pride. Love is only a subsidiary factor in wonder and admiration.

But it was by seeing all things alert in the throb of inter-related passional significance that the ancients kept the wonder and the delight in life, as well as the dread and the repugnance. They were like children: but they had the force, the power and the sensual *knowledge* of true adults. They had a world of valuable knowledge, which is utterly lost to us. Where they were true adults, we are children; and vice versa.

Even the two bits of '*pornografico*' in the Tomb of the Bull are not two little dirty drawings. Far from it. The German boy felt this, as we did. The drawings have the same naïve wonder in them as the rest, the same archaic innocence, accepting life, knowing all about it, and *feeling* the meaning, which is like a stone fallen into consciousness, sending its rings ebbing out and out, to the extremes. The two little pictures have a symbolic meaning, quite distinct from a *moral* meaning – or an immoral. The words moral and immoral have no force. Some acts – what Dennis would call flagrant obscenity – the man-faced bull accepts calmly lying down; against other acts he charges with lowered horns. It is not judgement. It is the sway of passional action and reaction: the action and reaction of the father of milk.

There are beautiful tombs, in this far-off wheat-covered hill. The Tomb of the Augurs is very impressive. On the end wall is painted a doorway to a tomb, and on either side of it is a man making what is probably the mourning gesture, strange and momentous, one hand to the brow. The two men are mourning at the door of the tomb.

'No!' says the German. 'The painted door does not represent the door to the tomb, with mourners on either side. It is merely the painted door which later they intended to cut out, to make a second chamber to the tomb. And the men are not mourning.'

'Then what are they doing?'

Shrug!

In the triangle above the painted door two lions, a white-faced one and a dark-faced, have seized a goat or an antelope: the dark-faced lion turns over and bites the side of the goat's neck, the white-faced bites the haunch. Here we have again the two heraldic beasts: but instead of their roaring at the altar, or the tree, they are biting the goat, the father of milk-giving life, in throat and hip.

On the side walls are very fine frescoes of nude wrestlers, and then of a scene which has started a lot of talk about Etruscan cruelty. A man with his head in a sack, wearing only a skin-girdle, is being bitten in the thigh by a fierce dog which is held, by another man, on a string attached to what is apparently a wooden leash, this wooden handle being fastened to the dog's collar. The man who holds the string wears a peculiar high conical hat, and he stands, big-limbed and excited, striding behind the man with his head in the sack. This victim is by now getting entangled in the string, the long, long cord which holds the dog; but with his left hand he seems to be getting hold of the cord to drag the dog off from his thigh, while in his right hand he holds a huge club, with which to strike the dog when he can get it into striking range.

This picture is supposed to reveal the barbarously cruel sports of the Etruscans. But since the tomb contains an augur, with his curved sceptre, tensely lifting his hand to the dark bird that flies by: and the wrestlers are wrestling over a curious pile of three great bowls; and on the other side of the tomb the man in the conical pointed hat, he who holds the string in the first picture, is now dancing with a peculiar delight, as if rejoicing in victory or liberation: we must surely consider this picture as symbolic, along with all the rest: the fight of the blindfolded man with some raging, attacking element. If it were sport there would be onlookers, as there are at the sports in the Tomb of the Chariots; and here there are none.

However, the scenes portrayed in the tomb are all *so* real, that it seems they must have taken place in actual life. Perhaps there was some form of test or trial which gave a man a great club, tied his head in a sack, and left him to fight a fierce dog which attacked him, but which was held on a string, and which even had a wooden grip-handle attached to its collar, by which the man might seize it and hold it firm, while he knocked it on the head. The man in the sack has very good chances against the dog. And even granted the thing was done for sport, and not as some sort of trial or test, the cruelty is not excessive, for the man has a very good chance of knocking the dog on the head quite early. Compared with Roman gladiatorial shows, this is almost 'fair play'.

But it must be more than sport. The dancing of the man who held the string is too splendid. And the tomb is, some-how, too intense, too meaningful. And the dog – or wolf or lion – that bites the thigh of the man is too old a symbol. We have it very plainly on the top of the Sarcophagus of the

Painted Amazons, in the Florence museum. This sarcophagus comes from Tarquinia – and the end of the lid has a carved naked man, with legs apart, a dog on each side biting him in the thigh. They are the dogs of disease and death, biting at the great arteries of the thigh, where the elementary life surges in a man. The motive is common in ancient symbolism. And the esoteric idea of malevolent influences attacking the great arteries of the thighs was turned in Greece into the myth of Actaeon and his dogs.

Another very fine tomb is the Tomb of the Baron, with its frieze of single figures, dark on a light background going round the walls. There are horses and men, all in dark silhouette, and very fascinating in drawing. These archaic horses are so perfectly satisfying *as* horses: so far more horse-like, to the soul, than those of Rosa Bonheur or Rubens or even Velazquez, though he comes nearer to these: so that one asks oneself, what, after all, is the horsiness of a horse? What is it that man sees, when he looks at a horse? – what is it that will never be put into words? For a man who sees, sees not as a camera does when it takes a snapshot, not even as a cinema-camera, taking its succession of instantaneous snaps; but in a curious rolling flood of vision, in which the image itself seethes and rolls; and only the mind *picks out* certain factors which *shall* represent the image seen. That is why a camera is so unsatisfactory: its eye is flat, it is related only to a negative thing inside the box: whereas inside our living box there is a decided positive.

We go from tomb to tomb, down into the dark, up again into the wind and brilliance; and the day rolls by. But we are moving, tomb by tomb, gradually nearer the city. The new cemetery draws near. We have passed the aqueduct, which crosses the dip, then takes an underground channel towards the town. Near the cemetery we descend into a big tomb, the biggest we have yet seen – a great underground cavern with great wide beds for sarcophagi and biers, and in the centre a massive square pillar or shaft on which is painted a Typhon – the seaman with coiled snake-legs, and wings behind his arms, his hands holding up the roof; two Typhons, another on the opposite face of the pillar, almost identical with the first.

In this place, almost at once, the Etruscan charm seems to vanish. The tomb is big, crude, somehow ugly like a cavern. The Typhon, with his reddish flesh and light-and-shade modelling, is clever, and might be modern, done for effect. He is rather Pompeian – and a little like Blake. But he is done from quite a new consciousness, external; the old inwardness has gone. Dennis, who saw him eighty years ago, thinks him far more marvellous than the archaic dancers. But we do not.

There are some curly-wig dolphins sporting over a curly border which, but for experience, we should not know was the sea. And there is a border of 'roses', really the sacred symbol of the 'one' with its central germ, here for the first time vulgarly used. There is also a fragment of a procession to Hades, which must have been rather fine in the Greco-Roman style. But the true archaic charm is utterly gone. The dancing Etruscan spirit is dead.

This is one of the very latest tombs: said to be of the second century B.C., when the Romans had long been masters of Tarquinia. Veii, the first great Etruscan city to be captured by Rome, was taken about 388 B.C., and completely destroyed. From then on, Etruria gradually weakened and sank, till the peace of 280 B.C., when we may say the military conquest of Etruria was complete.

So that the tombs suddenly change. Those supposed to be of the fifth century, like the Tomb of the Baron, with the frieze of horses and men, or the Tomb of the Leopards, are still perfectly Etruscan, no matter what touch of the Orient they may have, and perfectly charming. Then suddenly we come to the Tomb of Orcus, or Hell, which is given the fourth century as a date, and here the whole thing utterly changes. You get a great gloomy, clumsy, rambling sort of underworld, damp and horrid, with large but much-damaged pictures on the walls.

These paintings, though they are interesting in their way, and have scribbled Etruscan inscriptions, have suddenly lost all Etruscan charm. They still have a bit of Etruscan freedom, but on the whole they are Greco-Roman, half suggesting Pompeian, half suggesting Roman things. They are more free than the paintings of the little old tombs; at the same time, all the motion is gone; the figures are stuck there without any vital flow between them. There is no touch.

Instead of the wonderful old silhouette forms we have modern 'drawing', often quite good. But to me it is an intense disappointment.

When the Roman took the power from the hands of the Etruscan Lucumones – in the fourth century B.C. – and made them merely Roman magistrates, at the best, the mystery of Etruria died almost at once. In the ancient world of king-gods, governing according to a religious conception, the deposition of the chiefs and the leading priests leaves the country at once voiceless and mindless. So it was in Egypt and Babylonia, in Assyria, in the Aztec and Maya lordships of America. The people are governed by the flower of the race. Pluck the flower and the race is helpless.

The Etruscans were not destroyed. But they lost their being. They had lived, ultimately, by the *subjective* control of the great natural powers. Their subjective power fell before the objective power of the Romans. And almost at once the true race-consciousness finished. The Etruscan knowledge became mere superstition. The Etruscan princes became fat and inert Romans. The Etruscan people became expressionless and meaningless. It happened amazingly quickly, in the third and second centuries B.C.

Yet the Etruscan *blood* continued to beat. And Giotto and the early sculptors seem to have been a flowering again of the Etruscan blood, which is always putting forth a flower, and always being trodden down again by some superior 'force'. It is a struggle between the endless patience of life and the endless triumph of force.

There is one other huge late tomb, the Tomb of the

Shields, said to be of the third century. It contains many fragmentary paintings. There is a banqueting scene, with a man on the banqueting bench taking the egg from the woman, and she is touching his shoulder. But they might as well be two chairs from a 'suite'. There is nothing between them. And they have those 'important' sort of faces – all on the outside, nothing inside – that are so boring. Yet they are interesting. They might almost be done today, by an ultra-modern artist bent on being absolutely childlike and naïve and archaic. But after the real archaic paintings, these are empty. The air is empty. The egg is still held up. But it means no more to that man and woman than the chocolate Easter egg does to us. It has gone cold.

In the Tomb of Orcus begins that representation of the grisly underworld, hell and its horrors, which surely was reflected on to the Etruscans from the grisly Romans. The lovely little tombs of just one small chamber, or perhaps two chambers, of the earlier centuries give way to these great sinister caverns underground, and hell is fitly introduced.

The old religion of the profound attempt of man to harmonize himself with nature, and hold his own and come to flower in the great seething of life, changed with the Greeks and Romans into a desire to resist nature, to produce a mental cunning and a mechanical force that would outwit Nature and chain her down completely, completely, till at last there should be nothing free in nature at all, all should be controlled, domesticated, put to man's meaner uses. Curiously enough, with the idea of the triumph over nature arose the idea of a gloomy Hades, a hell and purgatory. To the peoples of the great natural religions the after-life was a continuing of the wonder-journey of life. To the peoples of the Idea the after-life is hell, or purgatory, or nothingness, and paradise is an inadequate fiction. But, naturally enough, historians seized on these essentially non-Etruscan evidences, in the Etruscan late tombs, to build up a picture of a gloomy, hellish, serpent-writhing, vicious Etruscan people who were quite rightly stamped out by the noble Romans. This myth is still not dead. Men *never* want to believe the evidence of their senses. They would far rather go on elaborating some 'classical' author. The whole science of history seems to be the picking of old fables and old lies into fine threads, and weaving them up again. Theopompus collected some scandalous tales, and that is quite enough for historians. It is written down, so that's enough. The evidence of fifty million gay little tombs wouldn't weigh a straw. In the beginning was the Word, indeed! Even the word of a Theopompus!

Perhaps the favourite painting for representing the beauties of the Etruscan tombs is the well-known head of a woman, seen in profile with wheat-ears for a head-wreath, or fillet. This head comes from the Tomb of Orcus, and is chosen because it is far more Greek-Roman than it is Etruscan. As a matter of fact, it is rather stupid and self-conscious – and modern. But it belongs to the classic Convention, and men can only see according to a Convention. We haven't exactly plucked our eyes out, but we've plucked out three-fourths of their vision.

After the Tomb of the Typhon one has had enough. There is nothing really Etruscan left. It is better to abandon the necropolis altogether, and to remember that almost everything we know of the Etruscans from the classic authors is comparable to the paintings in the late tombs. It refers only to the fallen, Romanized Etruscans of the decadence.

It is very pleasant to go down from the hill on which the present Tarquinia stands, down into the valley and up to the opposite hill, on which the Etruscan Tarquinii surely stood. There are many flowers, the blue grape-hyacinth and the white, the mauve tassel anemone, and, in a corner of a field of wheat, the big purple anemone, then a patch of the big pale pink anemone with the red, sore centre – the big-petalled sort. It is curious how the anemone varies. Only in this one place in Tarquinia have I found the whity-pink kind, with the dark, sore-red centre. But probably that is just chance.

The town ends really with the wall. At the foot of the wall is wild hillside, and down the slope is only one little farm, with another little house made of straw. The country is clear of houses. The peasants live in the city.

Probably in Etruscan days it was much the same, but there must have been far more people on the land, and probably there were many little straw huts, little temporary houses, among the green corn: and fine roads, such as the Etruscans taught the Romans to build, went between the hills: and the high black walls, with towers, wound along the hill-crest.

The Etruscans, though they grew rich as traders and metal-workers, seem to have lived chiefly by the land. The intense culture of the land by the Italian peasant of today seems like the remains of the Etruscan system. On the other hand, it was Roman, and not Etruscan, to have large villas in the country, with the great compound or 'factory' for the slaves, who were shut in at night, and in gangs taken out to labour during the day. The huge farms of Sicily and Lombardy and other parts of Italy must be a remains of this Roman system: the big *fattorie*. But one imagines the Etruscans had a different system: that the peasants were serfs rather than slaves: that they had their own small portions of land, which they worked to full pitch, from father to son, giving a portion of the produce to the masters, keeping a portion for themselves. So they were half-free, at least, and had a true life of their own, stimulated by the religious life of their masters.

The Romans changed it all. They did not like the country. In palmy days they built great villas with barracks for slaves, out in the country. But, even so, it was easier to get rich by commerce or conquest. So the Romans gradually abandoned the land, which fell into neglect and prepared the way for the Dark Ages.

The wind blows stiffer and stiffer from the south-west. There are no trees: but even the bushes bend away from it. And when we get to the crown of the long, lonely hill on which stood the Etruscan Tarquinii we are almost blown from our feet, and have to sit down behind a thicket of bushes, for a moment's shelter: to watch the great black-and-white cattle stepping slowly down to the drinking-place, the young bulls curving and playing. All along the hilltop the green wheat ruffles like soft hair. Away inland the green land looks empty, save for a far-off town perched on a hill-top, like a vision. On the next hill, towards the sea, Tarquinia holds up her square towers, in vain.

And we are sitting on what would be the arx of the vanished city. Somewhere here the augurs held up their curved staffs, and watched the birds move across the quarters of the city. We can do so much even today. But of the city I cannot find even one stone. It is so lonely and open.

One can go back up a different road, and in through another gate of the city of today. We drop quickly down, in the fierce wind, down to calm. The road winds up slowly from the little valley, but we are in shelter from the wind. So, we pass the first wall, through the first medieval gateway. The road winds inside the wall, past the *Dazio*, but there are no houses. A bunch of men are excitedly playing *morra*, and the shouts of the numbers come up like explosions, with wild excitement. The men glance at us apprehensively, but laugh as we laugh.

So we pass on through a second frowning gateway, inside the second circle of walls. And still we are not in the town. There is still a third wall, and a third massive gate. And then we are in the old part of the town, where the graceful little palazzos of the Middle Ages are turned into stables and barns, and into houses for poor peasants. In front of the lower storey of one little old palace, now a blacksmith's shop, the smith is shoeing a refractory mule, which kicks and plunges, and brings loud shouts from the inevitable little group of onlookers.

Queer and lonely and slummy the waste corners and narrow streets seem, forlorn, as if belonging to another age. On a beautiful stone balcony a bit of poor washing is drying. The houses seem dark and furtive, people lurking like rats. And then again rises another tall, sharp-edged tower, blank and blind. They have a queer effect on a town, these sharp, rigid, blind, meaningless towers, soaring away with their sharp edges into the sky, for no reason, beyond the house-roofs; and from the far distance, when one sees the little city down far off, suggesting the factory chimneys of a modern town.

They are the towers which in the first place were built for retreat and defence, when this coast was ravaged by sea-rovers, Norman adventurers, or Barbary pirates that were such a scourge to the Mediterranean. Later, however, the medieval nobles built towers just for pure swank, to see who should have the tallest, till a town like Bologna must have bristled like a porcupine in a rage, or like Pittsburg with chimney-stacks – square ones. Then the law forbade towers – and towers, after having scraped the heavens, began to come down. There are some still, however, in Tarquinia, where age overlaps age.

5

Vulci

ANCIENT Etruria consisted of a league, or loose religious Confederacy of twelve cities, each city embracing some miles of country all around, so that we may say there were twelve states, twelve city-states, the famous *dodecapolis* of the ancient world, the Latin *duodecim populi Etruriae*. Of these twelve city-states, Tarquinii was supposed to be the oldest, and the chief. Caere is another city: and not far off, to the north, Vulci.

Vulci is now called Volci – though there is no city, only a hunting ground for treasure in Etruscan tombs. The Etruscan city fell into decay in the decline of the Roman Empire, and either lapsed owing to the malaria which came to fill this region with death, or else was finally wiped out, as Ducati says, by the Saracens. Anyhow there is no life there now.

I asked the German boy about the Etruscan places along the coast: Volci, Vetulonia, Populonia. His answer was always the same: 'Nothing! Nothing! There is nothing there!'

However, we determined to look at Volci. It lies only about a dozen miles north of Tarquinia. We took the train, one station only, to Montalto di Castro, and were rattled up to the little town on the hill, not far inland. The morning was still fairly early – and Saturday. But the town, or village, on the hill was very quiet and dead-alive. We got down from the bus in a sort of nowhere-seeming little piazza: the town had no centre of life. But there was a café, so in we went, asked for coffee, and where could we get a carriage to take us to Volci.

The man in the little café was yellow and slow, with the slow smile of the peasants. He seemed to have no energy at all: and eyed us lethargically. Probably he had malaria – though the fevers were not troubling him at the time. But it had eaten into his life.

He said, did we want to go to the bridge – the *Ponte*? I said yes, the *Ponte dell' Abbadia*: because I knew that Volci was near to this famous old bridge of the monastery. I asked him if we could get a light cart to drive us out. He said it would be difficult. I said, then we could walk: it was only five miles, eight kilometres. 'Eight kilometres!' he said, in the slow, laconic malarial fashion, looking at me with a glint of ridicule in his black eyes. 'It is at least twelve!'

'The book says eight!' I insisted stoutly. They always want to make distances twice as long, if you are to hire a carriage. But he watched me slowly, and shook his head. 'Twelve!' he said. 'Then we must have a carriage,' said I. 'You wouldn't find your way anyhow,' said the man. 'Is there a carriage?' He didn't know. There was one, but it had gone off somewhere this morning, and wouldn't be back till two or three in the afternoon. The usual story.

I insisted, was there no little cart, no *barrocino*, no *carretto*? He slowly shook his head. But I continued to insist, gazing at him fixedly, as if a carriage *must* be produced. So at last he went out, to look. He came back, after a time, shaking his head. Then he had a colloquy with his wife. Then he went out again, and was gone ten minutes.

A dusty little baker, a small man very full of energy, as little Italians often are, came in and asked for a drink. He sat down a minute and drank his drink, eyeing us from his floury face. Then he got up and left the shop again. In a moment the cafe man returned, and said that perhaps there was a *carretto*. I asked where it was. He said the man was coming.

The drive to the Ponte was apparently two hours – then the trip would be six hours. We should have to take a little food with us – there was nothing there.

A small-faced, weedy sort of youth appeared in the doorway: also malaria! We could have the *carretto*. 'For how much?' 'Seventy liras!' 'Too much!' said I. 'Far too much! Fifty, or nothing. Take it or leave it, fifty!' The youth in the doorway looked blank. The café man, always with his faint little sardonic smile, told the youth to go and ask. The youth went. We waited. Then the youth came back, to say all right! So! 'How long?' '*Subito!*' *Subito* means immediately, but it is as well to be definite. 'Ten minutes?' said I. 'Perhaps twenty!' said the youth. 'Better say twenty!' said the café man: who was an honest man, really, and rather pleasant in his silent way.

We went out to buy a little food, and the café man went with us. The shops in the place were just holes. We went to the baker. Outside stood a cart being loaded with bread, by the youth and the small, quicksilver baker. Inside the shop, we bought a long loaf, and a few bits of sliced sausage, and asked for cheese. There was no cheese – but they would get us some. We waited an infinite while. I said to the café man, who waited alongside, full of interest: 'Won't the *carretto* be ready?' He turned round and pointed to the tall, randy mare between the shafts of the bread-cart outside. 'That's the horse that will take you. When the bread is delivered, they will hitch her into the *carretto*, and the youth will drive you.' There was nothing for it but patience, for the baker's mare and the baker's youth were our only hope. The cheese came at last. We wandered out to look for oranges. There was a woman selling them on a low bench beside the road, but B., who was getting impatient, didn't like the look of them. So we went across to a little hole of a shop where another woman had oranges. They were tiny ones, and B. was rejecting them with impatient scorn. But the woman insisted they were sweet, sweet as apples, and full of juice. We bought four and I bought a *finocchio* for a salad. But she was right. The oranges were exquisite, when we came to eat them, and we wished we had ten.

On the whole, I think the people in Montalto are honest and rather attractive, but most of them slow and silent. It must be the malaria every time.

The café man asked if we would stay the night. We said, was there an inn? He said: 'Oh yes, several!' I asked where, and he pointed up the street. 'But,' said I, 'what do you want with several hotels here?' 'For the agents who come to buy agricultural produce,' he said. 'Montalto is the centre of a great agricultural industry, and many agents come, many!' However, I decided that, if we could, we would leave in the evening. There was nothing in Montalto to keep us.

At last the *carretto* was ready; a roomy, two-wheeled gig hung rather low. We got in, behind the dark, mulberry mare, and the baker's youth, who certainly hadn't washed his face for some days, started us on the trip. He was in an agony of shyness, stupefied.

The town is left behind at once. The green land, squares of leaden-dark olives planted in rows slopes down to the railway line, which runs along the coast parallel with the ancient Via Aurelia. Beyond the railway is the flatness of the coastal strip, and the whitish emptiness of the sea's edge. It gives a great sense of nothingness, the sea down there.

The mulberry mare, lean and spare, reaches out and makes a good pace. But very soon we leave the road and are on a wide, wide trail of pinkish clayey earth, made up entirely of ruts. In parts the mud is still deep, water stands in the fathomless mud-holes. But fortunately, for a week it hasn't rained, so the road is passable; most of the ruts are dry, and the wide trail, wide as a desert road which has no confines, is not difficult, only jolty. We run the risk of having our necks jerked out of their sockets by the impatient, long-striding mare.

The boy is getting over his shyness, now he is warmed up to driving, and proves outspoken and straightforward. I said to him: 'What a good thing the road is dry!' 'If it had been fifteen days ago,' he said, 'you couldn't have passed.' But in the late afternoon, when we were returning on the same road and I said: 'In bad wet weather we should have to come through here on horseback,' he replied: 'Even with the *carretto* you can get through.' 'Always?' said I. 'Always!' said he.

And that was how he was. Possibility or impossibility was just a frame of mind with him.

We were on the Maremma, that flat, wide plain of the coast that has been water-logged for centuries, and one of the most abandoned, wildest parts of Italy. Under the Etruscans, apparently, it was an intensely fertile plain. But the Etruscans seem to have been very clever drainage-engineers; they drained the land so that it was a waving bed of wheat, with their methods of intensive peasant culture. Under the Romans, however, the elaborate system of canals and levels of water fell into decay, and gradually the streams threw their mud along the coast and choked themselves, then soaked into the land and made marshes and vast stagnant shallow pools where the mosquitoes bred like fiends, millions hatching on a warm May day; and with the mosquitoes came the malaria, called the marsh fever in the old days. Already in late Roman times this evil had fallen on the Etruscan plains and on the Campagna of Rome. Then, apparently, the land rose in level, the sea-strip was wider but even more hollow than before, the marshes became deadly, and human life departed or was destroyed, or lingered on here and there.

In Etruscan days, no doubt, large tracts of this coast were

covered with pine-forest, as are the slopes of the mountains that rise a few miles inland, and stretches of the coast, still farther north. The pleasant *pineta*, or open, sparse forest of umbrella-pines, once spread on and on, with tall arbutus and heather covering the earth from which the reddish trunks rose singly, as from an endless moor, and tufts of arbutus and broom making thickets. The pine-woods farther north are still delightful, so silent and bosky, with the umbrella roofs.

But the pine will not bear being soaked. So, as the great pools and marshes spread, the trees of Etruscan days fell for ever, and great treeless tracts appeared, covered with an almost impenetrable low jungle of bush and scrub and reeds, spreading for miles, and quite manless. The arbutus, that is always glossy green, and the myrtle, the mastic-tree, heaths, broom, and other spiny, gummy, coarse moorland plants rose up in dense luxuriance, to have their tops bent and whipped off by the ever-whipping winds from the sea, so that there was a low, dark jungle of scrub, less than man-high, stretching in places from the mountains almost to the sea. And here the wild boar roamed in herds; foxes and wolves hunted the rabbits, the hares, the roebuck; the innumerable wild-fowl and the flamingoes walked the sickly, stricken shores of the great pools and the sea.

So the Maremma country lay for centuries, with cleared tracts between, and districts a little elevated, and therefore rich in produce, but for the most part a wilderness, where the herdsmen pastured sheep, if possible, and the buffaloes roamed unherded. In 1828, however, the Grand-duke Leopold of Tuscany signed the decree for the reclaiming of the Maremma, and lately the Italian Government has achieved splendid results – great tracts of farmland added on to the country's resources, and new farms stuck up.

But still there are large tracts of moorland. We bowled along the grassy ruts, towards the distant mountains, and first all was wheat: then it was moorland, with great, grey-headed carrion-crows floating around in the bareness; then a little thicket of ilex-oak; then another patch of wheat; and then a desolate sort of farmhouse, that somehow reminded one of America, a rather dismal farm on the naked prairie, all alone.

The youth told me he had been for two years *guardiano*, or herdsman, at this place. The large cattle were lingering around the naked house, within the wire enclosure. But there was a notice that the place was shut off, because of foot-and-mouth disease. The driver saluted a dismal woman and two children as he drove by.

We made a good pace. The driver, Luigi, told me his father had been also a *guardiano*, a herdsman, in this district, his five sons following him. The youth would look round, into the distance, with that keen, far-off look of men who have always lived wild and apart, and who are in their own country. He knew every sign. And he was so glad to get out again, out of Montalto.

The father, however, had died, a brother had married and lived in the family house, and Luigi had gone to help the baker in Montalto. But he was not happy: caged. He revived and became alert once more out in the Maremma spaces. He had lived more or less alone all his life – he was only eighteen – and loneliness, space, was precious to him, as it is to a moorland bird.

The great hooded crows floated round, and many big meadow-larks rose up from the moor. Save for this, everything to us was silent. Luigi said that now the hunting season was closed: but still, if he had a gun, he could take a shot at those hooded crows. It was obvious he was accustomed to have a gun in his hand when he was out in the long, hot, malarial days, mounted on a pony, watching the herds of cattle roving on the Maremma. Cattle do not take malaria.

I asked him about game. He said there was much in the foothills there. And he pointed away ahead, to where the mountains began to rise, six or eight miles away. Now so much of the Maremma itself is drained and cleared, the game is in the hills. His father used to accompany the hunters in winter: they still arrive in winter-time, the hunters in their hunting outfit, with dogs, and a great deal of fuss and paraphernalia, from Rome or from Florence. And still they catch the wild boar, the fox, the *capriolo*: which I suppose means the roedeer rather than the wild goat. But the boar is the *pièce de résistance*. You may see his bristling carcass in the market-place in Florence, now and again, in winter. But, like every other wild thing on earth, he is becoming scarcer and scarcer. Soon the only animals left will be tame ones: man the tamest and most swarming. Adieu even to Maremma.

'There!' said the boy. 'There is the bridge of the monastery!' We looked into the shallow hollow of green land, and could just see a little, black sort of tower by some bushes, in the empty landscape. There was a long, straight ditch or canal, and digging evidently going on. It was the Government irrigation works.

We left the road and went bowling over rough grass, by tracts of poor-looking oats. Luigi said they would cut these oats for fodder. There was a scrap of a herdsman's house, and new wire fences along the embankment of the big irrigation canal. This was new to Luigi. He turned the mare uphill again, towards the house, and asked the urchin where he was to get through the wire fence. The urchin explained – Luigi had it in a moment. He was intelligent as a wild thing, out here in his own spaces.

'Five years ago,' he said, 'there was none of this' – and he pointed around. 'No canal, no fences, no oats, no wheat. It was all *maremma*, moorland, with no life save the hooded crows, the cattle and the herdsmen. Now the cattle are all going – the herds are only remnants. And the ranch-houses are being abandoned.' He pointed away to a large house some miles off, on the nearest hill-foot. 'There, there are no more cattle, no more herdsmen. The steam-plough comes and ploughs the earth, the machinery sows and reaps the wheat and oats, the people of the Maremma, instead of being more, are fewer. The wheat grows by machinery.'

We were on a sort of trail again, bowling down a slight

incline towards a bushy hollow and a black old ruin with a tower. Soon we saw that in the hollow was a tree-filled ravine, quite deep. And over the ravine a queer bridge, curving up like a rainbow, and narrow and steep and fortified-seeming. It soared over the ravine in one high curve, the stony path nipped in like a gutter between its broken walls, and charging straight at the black lava front of the ruin opposite, which was once a castle of the frontier. The little river in the gully, the Fiora, formed the boundary between the Papal States and Tuscany, so the castle guarded the bridge.

We wanted to get down, but Luigi made us wait, while he ran ahead to negotiate. He came back, climbed in, and drove up between the walls of the bridge. It was just wide enough for the cart: just. The walls of the bridge seemed to touch us. It was like climbing up a sort of gutter. Far below, way down in a thicket of bushes, the river rushed : the Fiora, a mere torrent or rainstream.

We drove over the bridge, and at the far end the lava wall of the monastery seemed to shut us back, the mare's nose almost touched it. The road, however, turned to the left under an arched gateway. Luigi edged the mare round cleverly. There was just room to get her round with the *carretto*, out of the mouth of the bridge and under the archway, scraping the wall of the castle.

So! We were through. We drove a few yards past the ruin, and got down on a grassy place over the ravine. It was a wonderfully romantic spot. The ancient bridge, built in the first place by the Etruscans of Vulci, of blocks of black *tufo*, goes up in the air like a black bubble, so round and strange. The little river is in the bushy cleft, a hundred feet below. The bridge is in the sky, like a black bubble, most strange and lonely, with the poignancy of perfect things long forgotten. It has of course, been restored in Roman and medieval days. But essentially it is Etruscan, a beautiful Etruscan movement.

Pressing on to it, on this side, is the black building of the castle, mostly in ruins, with grass growing from the tops of the walls and from the black tower. Like the bridge, it is built of blocks of reddish black, spongy lava-stone, but its blocks are much squarer.

And all around is a peculiar emptiness. The castle is not entirely ruined. It is a sort of peasant farmstead. Luigi knows the people who live there. And across the stream there are patches of oats, and two or three cattle feeding, and two children. But all on this side, towards the mountains, is heathy, waste moorland, over which the trail goes towards the hills, and towards a great house among trees which we had seen from the distance. That is the *Badia*, or monastery, which gave the name to the bridge. But it has long been turned into a villa. The whole of this property belonged to Lucien Bonaparte, Prince of Canino, brother of Napoleon. He lived here after the death of his brother, as an Italian prince. In 1828 some oxen ploughing the land near the castle suddenly went through the surface of the earth, and sank into a tomb, in which were broken vases. This at once led to excavations. It was the time when the 'Grecian urn' was most popular. Lucien Bonaparte had no interest in vases. He hired an overseer to superintend the excavating, giving orders that every painted fragment must be saved, but that coarse ware must be smashed, to prevent the cheapening of the market. So that the work went savagely on, vases and basketfuls of broken pieces were harvested, the coarse, rough black Etruscan ware was smashed to pieces, as it was discovered, the overseer guarding the workmen with his gun over his knees. Dennis saw this still happening in 1846, when Lucien was dead. But the work was still going on, under the Princess's charge. And vainly Dennis asked the overseer to spare him some of the rough black ware. Not one! Smash they went to earth, while the overseer sat with his gun over his knees ready to shoot. But the bits of painted pottery were most skilfully fitted together, by the Princess's expert workmen, and she would sell some patera or amphora for a thousand crowns, which had been a handful of potsherds. The tombs were opened, rifled, and then filled in with earth again. All the landed proprietors with property in the neighbourhood carried on excavations, and endless treasure was exhumed. Within two months of the time when he started excavating, Lucien Bonaparte had got more than two thousand Etruscan objects out of tombs occupying a few acres of ground. That the Etruscans should have left fortunes to the Bonapartes seems an irony; but so it was. Vulci had mines indeed: but mostly of painted vases, those 'brides of quietness' which had been only too much ravished. The tombs have little to show now.

We ate our food, the mare cropping the grass. And I wondered, seeing youths on bicycles, four or five, come swooping down the trail across the stream, out of emptiness, dismount and climb the high curve of the bridge, then disappear into the castle. From the mountains a man came riding on an ass: a pleasant young man in corduroy velveteens. He was riding without a saddle. He had a word with Luigi, in the low, secretive tones of the country, and went on towards the bridge. Then across, two men on mules came trotting down to the bridge: and a peasant drove in two bullocks, whose horns pricked the sky from the tall poise of the bridge.

The place seemed very populous for so lonely a spot. And still, all the air was heavy with isolation, suspicion, guardedness. It was like being in the Middle Ages. I asked Luigi to go to the house for some wine. He said he didn't know if he could get it: but he went off, with the semi-barbaric reluctance and fear of approaching a strange place.

After a while he came back, to say the *dispensa* was shut, and he couldn't get any. 'Then,' said I, 'let us go to the tombs! Do you know where they are?' He pointed vaguely into the distance of the moorland, and said they were there, but that we should want candles. The tombs were dark, and no one was there. 'Then let us get candles from the peasants,' I said. He answered again, the *dispensa* was shut, and we couldn't get candles. He seemed uneasy and depressed, as the people always are when there is a little difficulty. They are so afraid and mistrustful of one another.

We walked back to the black ruin, through a dark gateway that had been portcullised, into a half-ruined black courtyard, curiously gloomy. And here seven or eight men were squatting or standing about, their shiny bicycles leaning against the ruined walls. They were queer-looking men, youngish fellows, smallish, unshaven, dirty; not peasants, but workmen of some sort, who looked as if they had been swept together among the rubbish. Luigi was evidently nervous of them: not that they were villains, merely he didn't know them. And he had one friend among them: a queer young fellow of about twenty, in a close-fitting blue jersey, a black, black beard on his rather delicate but *gamin* face, and an odd sort of smile. This young fellow came roving round us, with a queer, uneasy, half-smiling curiosity. The men all seemed like that, uneasy and as it were outcast, but with an unknown quality too. They were, in reality, the queer, poorest sort of natives of this part of the Maremma.

The courtyard of the castle was black and sinister, yet very interesting in its ruined condition. There were a few forlorn rat-like signs of peasant farming. And an outside staircase, once rather grand, went up to what was now apparently the inhabited quarter, two or three rooms facing the bridge.

The feeling of suspicion and almost of opposition, negative rather than active, was still so strong we went out again and on to the bridge. Luigi, in a dilemma, talked mutteringly to his black-bearded young friend with the bright eyes: all the men seemed to have queer, bright black eyes, with a glint on them such as a mouse's eyes have.

At last I asked him, flatly: 'Who are all those men?' He muttered that they were the workmen and navvies. I was puzzled to know *what* workmen and navvies, in this loneliness. Then he explained they were working on the irrigation works, and had come in to the *dispensa* for their wages and to buy things – it was Saturday afternoon – but that the overseer, who kept the *dispensa*, and who sold wine and necessaries to the workmen, hadn't come yet to open the place, so we couldn't get anything.

At least, Luigi didn't explain all this. But when he said these were the workmen from the irrigation diggings, I understood it all.

By this time, we and our desire for candles had become a feature in the landscape. I said to Luigi, why didn't he ask the *peasants*. He said they hadn't any. Fortunately at that moment an unwashed woman appeared at an upper window in the black wall. I asked her if she couldn't sell us a candle. She retired to think about it – then came back to say, surlily, it would be sixty centimes. I threw her a lira, and she dropped a candle. So!

Then the black-bearded young fellow glintingly said we should want more than one candle. So I asked the woman for another, and threw her fifty centimes – as she was contemplating giving me the change for the lira. She dropped another candle.

B. and I moved towards the *carretto*, with Luigi. But I could see he was still unhappy. 'Do you know where the tombs are?' I asked him. Again he waved vaguely: 'Over there!' But he was unhappy. 'Would it be better to take one of those men for a guide?' I said to him. And I got the inevitable answer: 'It is as you think.' 'If *you* don't know the tombs well,' I said to him, 'then find a man to come with us.' He still hesitated, with that dumb uncertainty of these people. 'Find a man anyhow,' I said, and off he went, feebly.

He came back in relief with the peasant, a short but strong *maremmano* of about forty, unshaven but not unclean. His name was Marco, and he had put on his best jacket to accompany us. He was quiet and determined-seeming – a brownish blond, not one of the queer black natives with the queer round soft contours. His boy of about thirteen came with him, and they two climbed on to the back of the *carretto*.

Marco gave directions, and we bowled down the trail, then away over a slight track, on to the heathy strong moorland. After us came a little black-eyed fellow on a bicycle. We passed on the left a small encampment of temporary huts made of planks, with women coming out to look. By the trail were huge sacks of charcoal, and the black charcoal-burners, just down from the mountains, for the week-end, stood aside to look at us. The asses and mules stood drooping.

This was the winter camp of the charcoal-burners. In a week or so, Marco told me, they would abandon this camp and go up into the mountains, out of reach of the fevers which begin in May. Certainly they looked a vigorous bunch, if a little wild. I asked Marco if there was much fever – meaning malaria. He said: 'Not much,' I asked him if he had had any attacks. He said: 'No, never.' It is true he looked broad and healthy, with a queer, subdued, explosive sort of energy. Yet there was a certain motionless, rather worn look in his face, a certain endurance and sallowness, which seemed like malaria to me. I asked Luigi, our driver, if he had had any fever. At first he too said no. Then he admitted he had had a touch now and then. Which was evident, for his face was small and yellowish, evidently the thing had eaten into him. Yet he too, like Marco, had a strong, *manly* energy, more than the ordinary Italians. It is evidently the thing, in these parts, to deny that the malaria has ever touched you.

To the left, out of the heath, rose great flattish mounds, great tumuli, bigger than those of Cerveteri. I asked Marco were those the tombs? He said those were the tumuli, Coccumella and Coccumelletta – but that we would go first to the river tombs.

We were descending a rocky slope towards the brink of the ravine, which was full of trees, as ever. Far away, apparently, behind us to the right, stood the lonely black tower of the castle, across the moorland whence we had come. Across the ravine was a long, low hill, grassy and moorland: and farther down the stream were the irrigation works. The country was all empty and abandoned-seeming, yet with that peculiar, almost ominous, poignancy of places where life has once been intense. 'Where do they say the city of Vulci was?' I asked Marco. He pointed across stream, to the long, low elevation along the opposite side of the ravine. I guessed it had been there – since the tombs were on this side. But it looked very low and undefended, for an Etruscan site: so open to the world! I supposed it had depended upon its walls, seawards, and the ravine inland. I asked Marco if anything was there; some sign of where the walls had gone round. He said: 'Nothing!' It has evidently not been a very large city, like Caere and Tarquinia. But it was one of the cities of the League, and very rich indeed, judging from the thousands of painted vases which have been found in the tombs here.

The rocky descent was too uneven. We got out of the cart, and went on foot. Luigi left the mare, and Marco led us on, down to a barb-wire fence. We should never, never have found the place ourselves. Marco expertly held the wire apart, and we scrambled through on to the bushy, rocky side of the ravine. The trees rose from the riverside, some leaves bright green. And we descended a rough path, past the entrance-passage to a tomb most carefully locked with an iron gate, and defended with barbed wire, like a hermit's cave with the rank vegetation growing up to choke it again.

Winding among rank vegetation and fallen rocks of the face of the ravine, we came to the openings of the tombs, which were cut into the face of the rock, and must have been a fine row once, like a row of rock-houses with a pleasant road outside, along the ravine. But now they are gloomy holes down which one must clamber through the excavated earth. Once inside, with the three candles – for the black-faced youth on the bicycle had brought a stump too – we were in gloomy wolves' dens of places, with large chambers opening off one another as at Cerveteri, damp beds of rock for the coffins, and huge grisly stone coffins, seven feet long, lying in disorder, among fallen rocks and rubble, in some of them the bones and man-dust still lying dismally. There was nothing to see but these black, damp chambers, sometimes cleared, sometimes with coarse great sarcophagi and broken rubbish and excavation-rubble left behind in the damp-grisly darkness.

Sometimes we had to wriggle into the tombs on our bellies,

over the mounds of rubble, going down into holes like rats, while the bats flew blindly in our faces. Once inside, we clambered in the faint darkness over huge pieces of rock and broken stone, from dark chamber to chamber, four or five or even more chambers to a tomb, all cut out of the rock and made to look like houses, with the sloping roof-tilts and the central roof-beam. From these roofs hung clusters of pale brown furry bats, in bunches, like bunches of huge furry hops. One could hardly believe they were alive, till I saw the squat little fellow of the bicycle holding his candle up to one of the bunches, singeing the bats' hair, burning the torpid creatures, so the skinny wings began to flutter, and half-stupefied, half-dead bats fell from the clusters of the roof, then groped on the wing and began to fly low, staggering towards the outlet. The dark little fellow took pleasure in burning them. But I stopped him at it, and he was afraid, and left them alone.

He was a queer fellow – quite short, with the fat, soft, round curves, and black hair and sallow face and black bats' eyes of a certain type of this district. He was perhaps twenty years old, and like a queer burrowing dumb animal. He would creep into holes in the queerest way, with his queer, soft, round hind-quarters jutting behind: just like some uncanny animal. And I noticed the backs of his ears were all scaly and raw with sores; whether from dirt or some queer disease, who can say. He seemed healthy and alive enough, otherwise. And he seemed quite unconscious of his sore ears, with an animal unconsciousness.

Marco, who was a much higher type, knew his way about, and led us groping and wriggling and clambering from tomb to tomb, among the darkness and brokenness and bats and damp, then out among the fennel and bushes of the ravine top, then in again into some hole. He showed us a tomb whence only last year they had taken a big stone statue – he showed me where it had stood, there, in the innermost chamber, with its back to the wall. And he told me of all the vases, mostly broken pieces, that he too had lifted from the dirt, on the stone beds.

But now there is nothing, and I was tired of climbing into these gruesome holes, one after another, full of damp and great fallen rocks. Nothing living or beautiful is left behind – nothing. I was glad when we came to the end of the excavated tombs, and saw beyond only the ravine bank grown over with bushes and fennel and great weeds. Probably many a vase and many a stone coffin still lie hidden there – but let them lie.

We went back along the path the way we had come, to climb back to the upper level. As we came to the gangway leading to the locked tomb Marco told me that in here were paintings and some things left behind. Probably it was the famous François tomb with the paintings that are copied in the Vatican museum. It was opened by the excavator François in 1857, and is one of the very, very few painted tombs found at Vulci.

We tried in vain to get in. Short of smashing the lock, it was impossible. Of course, in these expeditions, one should arm oneself with official permits. But it means having officials hanging round.

So we climbed up to the open world, and Luigi made us get into the *carretto*. The mare pulled us jolting across towards the great tumuli, which we wanted to see. They are huge grassy-bushy mounds, like round, low hills. The band of stonework round the base, if it be there, is buried.

Marco led us inside the dense passage of brambles and bushes which leads to the opening into the tumulus. Already this passage is almost blocked up, overgrown. One has to crawl under the scratching brambles, like a rabbit.

And at last one is in the plain doorway of the tumulus itself. Here, even in 1829, two weird stone sphinxes guarded the entrance. Now there is nothing. And inside the passage or at the angles were lions and griffins on guard. What now shall we find as we follow the candlelight in the narrow, winding passage? It is like being in a mine, narrow passages winding on and on, from nowhere to nowhere. We had not any great length of candle left: four stumps. Marco left one stump burning at the junction of the passages as a signpost, and on and on we went, from nowhere to nowhere, stooping a little, our hats brushing the clusters of bats that hung from the ceiling as we went on, one after the other, pinned all the time in the narrow stone corridors that never led anywhere or did anything. Sometimes there was a niche in the wall – that was all.

There must, surely, be a central burial chamber, to which the passages finally lead. But we didn't find it. And Marco said there was no such thing – the tumulus was all passages and nothing but passages. But Dennis says that when the tumulus was opened in 1829 there were two small chambers in the heart of the mound, and rising from these, two shafts of masonry which passed up to the apex of the mound, and probably these supported great monuments, probably the phallic cippi. On the floor of the chamber were fragments of bronze and frail gold. But now there is nothing; the centre of the tumulus is no doubt collapsed.

It was like being burrowing inside some ancient pyramid. This was quite unlike any other Etruscan tomb we had seen: and if this tumulus was a tomb, then it must have been a very important person whose coffin formed the nut inside all this shell – a person important as a Pharaoh, surely. The Etruscans were queer people, and this tumulus, with no peripheral tombs, only endless winding passages, must be either a reminiscence of prehistoric days or of Egyptian pyramids.

When we had had enough of running along passages in nowhere we got out, scrambled through the bramble tangle, and were thankful to see clear heaven again. We all piled into the *carretto*, and the mare nobly hauled us up to the trail. The little dark fellow sailed ahead silently, on his bicycle, to open the gate for us. We looked round once more at the vast mound of the Coccumella, which strange dead hands piled in soft earth over two tiny death-chambers, so long ago: and even now it is weirdly conspicuous across the flat Maremma. A strange, strange nut indeed, with a kernel of perpetual mystery! And once it rose suave as a great breast, tipped with the budded monuments of the cippi! It is too problematic. We turn our back on it all as the *carretto* jolts over the tomb-rifled earth. There is something gloomy, if rather wonderful, about Vulci.

The charcoal-burners were preparing to wash their faces for Sunday, in the little camp. The woman stood smiling as we drove by on the moor. 'Oh, how fat thou hast got!' Luigi shouted to one plump and smiling woman. '*You* haven't though!' she shouted back at him. '*Tu pure no!*'

At the bridge we said good-bye to Marco and his boy, then we pulled over the arch once more. But on the other side Luigi wanted to drink. So he and I scrambled down to the spring, the old, thin-trickling spring, and drank cool water. The river rushed below: the bridge arched its black, soaring rainbow above, and we heard the shouts of mule-drivers driving the mules over the arch.

Once this old bridge carried an aqueduct, and it is curious to see the great stalactitic mass that hangs like a beard down the side facing the mountains. But the aqueduct is gone, the muddy stalactitic mass itself is crumbling. Everything passes!

So we climbed up and into the *carretto*, and away went the mare at a spanking pace. We passed the young man in velveteens, on the donkey – a peasant from the hills, Luigi said he was. And we met horsemen riding towards us, towards the hills, away from Montalto. It was Saturday afternoon, with a bright sea-wind blowing strong over the Maremma, and men travelling away from work, on horseback, on mules, or on asses. And some drove laden donkeys out to the hills.

'It would be a good life,' I said to Luigi, 'to live here, and have a house on the hills, and a horse to ride, and space: except for the malaria!'

Then, having previously confessed to me that the malaria was still pretty bad, though children often escaped it, but grown people rarely; the fever inevitably came to shake them sometimes; that Montalto was more stricken than the open country; and that in the time of rains the roads were impassable – one was cut off – now Luigi changed his tune: said there was almost no fever any more; the roads were always passable; in Montalto people came at bathing season to bathe in the sea, having little cane huts on the coast: the roads were always easily passable, easily! and that you never got fever at all if you were properly fed, and had a bit of meat now and then, and a decent glass of wine. He wanted me so much to come and have some abandoned house in the foothills; and he would look after my horses, and we would go hunting together – even out of season, for there was no one to catch you.

B. dozed lightly while we drove joltingly on. It was a dream too. I would like it well enough – if I were convinced about that malaria. And I would certainly have Luigi to look after the horses. He hasn't a grand appearance, but he is solitary and courageous and surely honest, solitary, and far more manly than the townsmen or the grubbing peasants.

So, we have seen all we could see of Vulci. If we want to see what the Etruscans buried there we must go to the Vatican, or to the Florence museum, or to the British Museum in London, and see vases and statues, bronzes, sarcophagi and jewels. In the British Museum lie the contents, for the most part, of the famous Tomb of Isis, where lay buried a lady whom Dennis thought was surely Egyptian, judging from her statue, that is stiff and straight, and from the statuette of 'Isis', the six ostrich eggs and other imported things that went to the grave with her: for in death she must be what she was in life, as exactly as possible. This was the Etruscan creed. How the Egyptian lady came to Vulci, and how she came to be buried there along with a lady of ancient Etruria, down in that bit of the Vulci necropolis now called Polledrara, who knows? But all that is left of her is now in the British Museum. Vulci has nothing. Anyhow she was surely not Egyptian at all. Anything of the archaic east Mediterranean seemed to Dennis Egyptian.

So it is. The site of Vulci was lost from Roman times till 1828. Once found, however, the tombs were rapidly gutted by the owners, everything precious was taken away, then the tombs were either closed again or abandoned. All the thousands of vases that the Etruscans gathered so lovingly and laid by their dead, where are they? Many are still in existence. But they are everywhere except at Vulci.

6

Volterra

VOLTERRA is the most northerly of the great Etruscan cities of the west. It lies back some thirty miles from the sea, on a towering great bluff of rock that gets all the winds and sees all the world, looking out down the valley of the Cecina to the sea, south over vale and high land to the tips of Elba, north to the imminent mountains of Carrara, inward over the wide hills of the Pre-Apennines, to the heart of Tuscany.

You leave the Rome–Pisa train at Cecina, and slowly wind up the valley of the stream of that name, a green, romantic, forgotten sort of valley, in spite of all the come-and-go of ancient Etruscans and Romans, medieval Volterrans and Pisans, and modern traffic. But the traffic is not heavy. Volterra is a sort of inland island, still curiously isolated, and grim.

The small, forlorn little train comes to a stop at the Saline de Volterra, the famous old salt works now belonging to the State, where brine is pumped out of deep wells. What passengers remain in the train are transferred to one old little coach across the platform, and at length this coach starts to creep like a beetle up the slope, up a cog-and-ratchet line, shoved by a small engine behind. Up the steep but round slope among the vineyards and olives you pass almost at walking-pace, and there is not a flower to be seen, only the beans make a whiff of perfume now and then, on the chill air, as you rise and rise, above the valley below, coming level with the high hills to south, and the bluff of rock with its two or three towers, ahead.

After a certain amount of backing and changing, the fragment of a train eases up at a bit of a cold wayside station, and is finished. The world lies below. You get out, transfer yourself to a small ancient motor-omnibus and are rattled up to the final level of the city, into a cold and gloomy little square, where the hotel is.

The hotel is simple and somewhat rough, but quite friendly, pleasant in its haphazard way. And what is more, it has central heating, and the heat is on, this cold, almost icy, April afternoon. Volterra lies only 1800 feet above the sea, but it is right in the wind, and cold as any Alp.

The day was Sunday, and there was a sense of excitement and fussing, and a bustling in and out of temporarily important persons, and altogether a smell of politics in the air. The waiter brought us tea, of a sort, and I asked him what was doing. He replied that a great banquet was to be given this evening to the new *podestà* who had come from Florence to govern the city, under the new regime. And evidently he felt that this was such a hugely important 'party' occasion we poor outsiders were of no account.

It was a cold, grey afternoon, with winds round the hard dark corners of the hard, narrow medieval town, and crowds of black-dressed, rather squat little men and pseudo-elegant young women pushing and loitering in the streets, and altogether that sense of furtive grinning and jeering and threatening which always accompanies a public occasion – a political one especially – in Italy, in the more out-of-the-way centres. It is as if the people, alabaster-workers and a few peasants, were not sure which side they wanted to be on, and therefore were all the more ready to exterminate anyone who was on the other side. This fundamental uneasiness, indecision, is most curious in the Italian soul. It is as if the people could never be wholeheartedly anything: because they can't trust anything. And this inability to trust is at the root of the political extravagance and frenzy. They don't trust themselves, so how can they trust their 'leaders' or their 'party'?

Volterra, standing sombre and chilly alone on her rock, has always, from Etruscan days on, been grimly jealous of her own independence. Especially she has struggled against the Florentine yoke. So what her actual feelings are, about this new-old sort of village tyrant, the *podestà*, whom she is banqueting this evening, it would be hard, probably, even for the Volterrans themselves to say. Anyhow the cheeky girls salute one with the 'Roman' salute, out of sheer effrontery: a salute which has nothing to do with me, so I don't return it. Politics of all sorts are anathema. But in an Etruscan city which held out so long against Rome I consider the Roman salute unbecoming, and the Roman *imperium* unmentionable.

It is amusing to see on the walls, too, chalked fiercely up: *Morte a Lenin!* though that poor gentleman has been long enough dead, surely even for a Volterran to have heard of it. And more amusing still is the legend permanently painted: *Mussolini ha sempre ragione!* Some are born infallible, some achieve infallibility, and some have it thrust upon them.

But it is not for me to put even my little finger in any political pie. I am sure every post-war country has hard enough work to get itself governed, without outsiders interfering or commenting. Let those rule who can rule.

We wander on, a little dismally, looking at the stony stoniness of the medieval town. Perhaps on a warm sunny day it might be pleasant, when shadow was attractive and a breeze welcome. But on a cold, grey, windy afternoon of April, Sunday, always especially dismal, with all the people in the streets, bored and uneasy, and the stone buildings peculiarly sombre and hard and resistant, it is no fun. I don't care about the bleak but truly medieval piazza: I don't care if the Palazzo Pubblico has all sorts of amusing coats of arms on it: I don't care about the cold cathedral, though it is rather nice really, with a glow of dusky candles and a smell of Sunday incense: I am disappointed in the wooden sculpture of the taking down of Jesus, and the bas-reliefs don't interest me. In short, I am hard to please.

The modern town is not very large. We went down a long, stony street, and out of the Porta dell'Arco, the famous old Etruscan gate. It is a deep old gateway, almost a tunnel, with the outer arch facing the desolate country on the skew, built at an angle to the old road, to catch the approaching enemy on his right side, where the shield did not cover him. Up handsome and round goes the arch, at a good height, and with that peculiar weighty richness of ancient things; and three dark heads, now worn featureless, reach out curiously and inquiringly, one from the keystone of the arch, one from each of the arch bases, to gaze from the city and into the steep hollow of the world beyond.

Strange, dark old Etruscan heads of the city gate, even now they are featureless they still have a peculiar, out-reaching life of their own. Ducati says they represented the heads of slain enemies hung at the city gate. But they don't hang. They stretch with curious eagerness forward. Nonsense about dead heads. They were city deities of some sort.

And the archaeologists say that only the doorposts of the outer arch, and the inner walls, are Etruscan work. The Romans restored the arch, and set the heads back in their old positions. (Unlike the Romans to set anything back in its old position!) While the wall above the arch is merely medieval.

But we'll call it Etruscan still. The roots of the gate, and the dark heads, these they cannot take away from the Etruscans. And the heads are still on the watch.

The land falls away steeply, across the road in front of the arch. The road itself turns east, under the walls of the modern city, above the world: and the sides of the road, as usual outside the gates, are dump-heaps, dump-heaps of plaster and rubble, dump-heaps of the white powder from the alabaster works, the waste edge of the town.

The path turns away from under the city wall, and dips down along the brow of the hill. To the right we can see the tower of the church of Santa Chiara, standing on a little platform of the irregularly-dropping hill. And we are going there. So we dip downwards above a Dantesque, desolate world, down to Santa Chiara, and beyond. Here the path follows the top of what remains of the old Etruscan wall. On the right are little olive-gardens and bits of wheat. Away beyond is the dismal sort of crest of modern Volterra. We walk along, past the few flowers and the thick ivy, and the bushes of broom and marjoram, on what was once the Etruscan wall, far out from the present city wall. On the left the land drops steeply, in uneven and unhappy descents.

The great hilltop or headland on which Etruscan 'Volterra', *Velathri, Vlathri*, once stood spreads out jaggedly, with deep-cleft valleys in between, more or less in view, spreading two or three miles away. It is something like a hand, the bluff steep of the palm sweeping in a great curve on the east and south, to seawards, the peninsulas of fingers running jaggedly inland. And the great wall of the Etruscan city swept round the south and eastern bluff, on the crest of steeps and cliffs, turned north and crossed the first finger, or peninsula, then started up hill and down dale over the fingers and into the declivities, a wild and fierce sort of way, hemming in the great crest. The modern town occupies merely the highest bit of the Etruscan city site.

The walls themselves are not much to look at, when you climb down. They are only fragments, now, huge fragments of embankment, rather than wall, built of uncemented square masonry, in the grim, sad sort of stone. One only feels, for some reason, depressed. And it is pleasant to look at the lover and his lass going along the top of the ramparts, which are now olive-orchards, away from the town. At least they are alive and cheerful and quick.

On from Santa Chiara the road takes us through the grim and depressing little suburb-hamlet of San Giusto, a black street that emerges upon the waste open place where the church of San Giusto rises like a huge and astonishing barn. It is so tall, the interior should be impressive. But no! It is merely nothing. The architects have achieved nothing, with all that tallness. The children play around with loud yells and ferocity. It is Sunday evening, near sundown, and cold.

Beyond this monument of Christian dreariness we come to the Etruscan walls again, and what was evidently once an Etruscan gate: a dip in the wall-bank, with the groove of an old road running to it.

Here we sit on the ancient heaps of masonry and look into weird yawning gulfs, like vast quarries. The swallows, turning their blue backs, skim away from the ancient lips and over the really dizzy depths, in the yellow light of evening, catching the upward gusts of wind, and flickering aside like lost fragments of life, truly frightening above those ghastly hollows. The lower depths are dark grey, ashy in colour, and in part wet, and the whole things looks new, as if it were some enormous quarry all slipping down.

This place is called *Le Balze* – the cliffs. Apparently the waters which fall on the heights of Volterra collect in part underneath the deep hill and wear away at some places the lower strata, so that the earth falls in immense collapses. Across the gulf, away from the town, stands a big, old, picturesque, isolated building, the *Badia* or Monastery of the Camaldolesi, sad-looking, destined at last to be devoured by *Le Balze*, its old walls already splitting and yielding.

From time to time, going up to the town homewards, we come to the edge of the walls and look out into the vast glow of gold, which is sunset, marvellous, the steep ravines sinking in darkness, the farther valley silently, greenly gold, with hills breathing luminously up, passing out into the pure, sheer gold gleams of the far-off sea, in which a shadow, perhaps an island, moves like a mote of life. And like great guardians the Carrara mountains jut forward, naked in the pure light like flesh, with their crests portentous: so that they seem to be advancing on us: while all the vast concavity of the west roars with gold liquescency, as if the last hour had come, and the gods were smelting us all back into yellow transmuted oneness.

But nothing is being transmuted. We turn our faces, a little frightened, from the vast blaze of gold, and in the dark, hard streets the town band is just chirping up, brassily out of tune as usual, and the populace, with some maidens in white, are streaming in crowds towards the piazza. And, like the band, the populace also is out of tune, buzzing with the inevitable suppressed jeering. But they are going to form a procession.

When we come to the square in front of the hotel, and look out from the edge into the hollow world of the west, the light is sunk red, redness gleams up from the far-off sea below, pure and fierce, and the hollow places in between are dark. Over all the world is a low red glint. But only the town, with its narrow streets and electric light, is impervious.

The banquet, apparently, was not till nine o'clock, and all was hubbub. B. and I dined alone soon after seven, like two orphans whom the waiters managed to remember in between whiles. They were so thrilled getting all the glasses and goblets and decanters, hundreds of them, it seemed, out of the big chiffonnier-cupboard that occupied the back of the dining-room, and whirling them away, stacks of glittering glass, to the banquet-room: while out-of-work young men would poke their heads in through the doorway, black hats on, overcoats hung over one shoulder, and gaze with bright inquiry through the room, as though they expected to see Lazarus risen, and not seeing him, would depart again to the nowhere whence they came. A banquet is a banquet, even if it is given to the devil himself; and the *podestà* may be an angel of light.

Outside was cold and dark. In the distance the town band tooted spasmodically, as if it were short-winded this chilly Sunday evening. And we, not bidden to the feast, went to bed. To be awakened occasionally by sudden and roaring noises – perhaps applause – and the loud and unmistakable howling of a child, well after midnight.

Morning was cold and grey again, with a chilly and forbidding country yawning and gaping and lapsing away beneath us. The sea was invisible. We walked the narrow cold streets, whose high, cold, dark stone walls seemed almost to press together, and we looked in at the alabaster workshops, where workmen, in Monday-morning gloom and half-awakedness, were turning the soft alabaster, or cutting it out, or polishing it.

Everybody knows Volterra marble – so called – nowadays, because of the translucent bowls of it which hang under the electric lights, as shades, in half the hotels of the world. It is nearly as transparent as alum, and nearly as soft. They peel it down as if it were soap, and tint it pink or amber or blue, and turn it into all those things one does not want: tinted alabaster lampshades, light-bowls, statues, tinted or untinted, vases, bowls with doves on the rim, or vine-leaves, and similar curios. The trade seems to be going strong. Perhaps it is the electric-light demand: perhaps there is a revival of interest in 'statuary'. Anyhow there is no love lost between a Volterran alabaster worker and the lump of pale Volterran earth he turns into marketable form. Alas for the goddess of sculptured form, she has gone from here also.

But it is the old alabaster jars we want to see, not the new. As we hurry down the stony street the rain, icy cold, begins to fall. We flee through the glass doors of the museum, which has just opened, and which seems as if the alabaster inside had to be kept at a low temperature, for the place is dead-cold as a refrigerator.

Cold, silent, empty, unhappy the museum seems. But at last an old and dazed man arrives, in uniform, and asks quite scared what we want. 'Why, to see the museum!' '*Ah! Ah! Ah sì – sì!*' It just dawns upon him that the museum is there to be looked at. '*Ah sì, sì, Signori!*'

We pay our tickets, and start in. It is really a very attractive and pleasant museum, but we had struck such a bitter cold April morning, with icy rain falling in the courtyard, that I felt as near to being in the tomb as I have ever done. Yet very soon, in the rooms with all those hundreds of little sarcophagi, ash-coffins, or urns, as they are called, the strength of the old life began to warm one up.

Urn is not a good word, because it suggests, to me at least, a vase, an amphora, a round and shapely jar: perhaps through association with Keats' *Ode to a Grecian Urn* – which vessel no doubt wasn't an urn at all, but a wine-jar – and with the 'tea-urn' of children's parties. These Volterran urns, though correctly enough used for storing the ashes of the dead, are not round, they are not jars, they are small alabaster sarcophagi. And they are a peculiarity of Volterra. Probably because the Volterrans had the alabaster to hand.

Anyhow here you have them in hundreds, and they are curiously alive and attractive. They are not considered very highly as 'art'. One of the latest Italian writers on Etruscan things, Ducati, says: 'If they have small interest from the artistic point of view, they are extremely valuable for the scenes they represent, either mythological or relative to the beliefs in the after-life.'

George Dennis, however, though he too does not find much 'art' in Etruscan things, says of the Volterran ash-chests: 'The touches of Nature on these Etruscan urns, so simply but eloquently expressed, must appeal to the sympathies of all – they are chords to which every heart must respond; and I envy not the man who can walk through this museum unmoved, without feeling a tear rise in his eye'

> *And recognizing ever and anon*
> *The breeze of Nature stirring in his soul.*

The breeze of Nature no longer shakes dewdrops from our eyes, at least so readily, but Dennis is more alive than Ducati to that which is alive. What men mean nowadays by 'art' it would be hard to say. Even Dennis said that the Etruscans never approached the pure, the sublime, the perfect beauty which Flaxman reached. Today, this makes us laugh: the Greekified illustrator of Pope's *Homer*! But the same instinct lies at the back of our idea of 'art' still. Art is still to us something which has been well cooked – like a plate of spaghetti. An ear of wheat is not yet 'art'. Wait, wait till it has been turned into pure, into perfect macaroni.

For me, I get more real pleasure out of these Volterran ash-chests than out of – I had almost said, the Parthenon frieze. One wearies of the aesthetic quality – a quality which takes the edge off everything, and makes it seem 'boiled down'. A great deal of pure Greek beauty has this boiled-down effect. It is too much cooked in the artistic consciousness.

In Dennis's day a broken Greek or Greekish amphora would fetch thousands of crowns in the market, if it was the right 'period', etc. These Volterran urns fetched hardly anything. Which is a mercy, or they would be scattered to the ends of the earth.

As it is, they are fascinating, like an open book of life, and one has no sense of weariness with them, though there are so many. They warm one up, like being in the midst of life.

The downstairs rooms of ash-chests contain those urns representing 'Etruscan' subjects: those of sea-monsters, the sea-man with fish-tail, and with wings, the sea-woman the same: or the man with serpent-legs, and wings, or the woman the same. It was Etruscan to give these creatures wings, not Greek.

If we remember that in the old world the centre of all power was at the depths of the earth, and at the depths of the sea, while the sun was only a moving subsidiary body: and that the serpent represented the vivid powers of the inner earth, not only such powers as volcanic and earthquake, but the quick powers that run up the roots of plants and establish the great body of the tree, the tree of life, and run up the feet and legs of man, to establish the heart: while the fish was the symbol of the depths of the waters, whence even light is born: we shall see the ancient power these symbols had over the imagination of the Volterrans. They were a people faced with the sea, and living in a volcanic country.

Then the powers of the earth and the powers of the sea take life as they give life. They have their terrific as well as their prolific aspect.

Someone says the wings of the water-deities represent evaporation towards the sun, and the curving tails of the dolphin represent torrents. This is part of the great and controlling ancient idea of the come-and-go of the life-powers, the surging up, in a flutter of leaves and a radiation of wings, and the surging back, in torrents and waves and the eternal downpour of death.

Other common symbolic animals in Volterra are the beaked griffins, the creatures of the powers that tear asunder and, at the same time, are guardians of the treasure. They are lion and eagle combined, of the sky and of the earth with caverns. They do not allow the treasure of life, the gold, which we should perhaps translate as consciousness, to be stolen by thieves of life. They are guardians of the treasure: and then, they are the tearers asunder of those who must depart from life.

It is these creatures, creatures of the elements, which carry men away into death, over the border between the elements. So is the dolphin, sometimes; and so the hippicampus, the sea-horse; and so the centaur.

The horse is always the symbol of the strong animal life of man: and sometimes he rises, a sea-horse, from the ocean: and sometimes he is a land creature, and half-man. And so he occurs on the tombs, as the passion in man returning into the sea, the soul retreating into the death-world at the depths of the waters: or sometimes he is a centaur, sometimes a female centaur, sometimes clothed in a lion-skin, to show his dread aspect, bearing the soul back, away, off into the other-world.

It would be very interesting to know if there were a definite connexion between the scene on the ash-chest and the dead whose ashes it contained. When the fishtailed sea-god entangles a man to bear him off, does it mean drowning at sea? And when a man is caught in the writhing serpent-legs of the Medusa, or of the winged snake-power, does it mean a fall to earth; a death from the earth, in some manner; as a fall, or the dropping of a rock, or the bite of a snake? And the soul carried off by a winged centaur: is it a man dead of some passion that carried him away?

But more interesting even than the symbolic scenes are those scenes from actual life, such as boar-hunts, circus-games, processions, departures in covered wagons, ships sailing away, city gates being stormed, sacrifice being performed, girls with open scrolls, as if reading at school; many banquets with man and woman on the banqueting couch, and slaves playing music, and children around: then so many really tender fare-well scenes, the dead saying good-bye to his wife, as he goes on the journey, or as the chariot bears him off, or the horse waits; then the soul alone, with the death-dealing spirits standing by with their hammers that gave the blow. It is as Dennis says, the breeze of Nature stirs one's soul. I asked the

gentle old man if he knew anything about the urns. But no!
no! He knew nothing at all. He had only just come. He coun-
ted for nothing. So he protested. He was one of those gentle,
shy Italians too diffident even to look at the chests he was
guarding. But when I told him what I thought some of the
scenes meant he was fascinated like a child, full of wonder,
almost breathless. And I thought again, how much more
Etruscan than Roman the Italian of today is: sensitive, diffident, craving really for symbols and mysteries, able to be
delighted with true delight over small things, violent in
spasms, and altogether without sternness or natural will-to-
power. The will-to-power is a secondary thing in an Italian,
reflected on to him from the Germanic races that have almost
engulfed him.

The boar-hunt is still a favourite Italian sport, the grandest
sport of Italy. And the Etruscans must have loved it, for they
represent it again and again, on the tombs. It is difficult to
know what exactly the boar symbolized to them. He occupies
often the centre of the scene, where the one who dies should
be: and where the bull of sacrifice is. And often he is attacked,
not by men, but by young winged boys, or by spirits. The
dogs climb in the trees around him, the double axe is swinging to come down on him, he lifts up his tusks in a fierce wild
pathos. The archaeologists say that it is Meleager and the boar
of Calydon, or Hercules and the fierce brute of Erymanthus.
But this is not enough. It is a symbolic scene: and it seems as if
the boar were himself the victim this time, the wild, fierce
fatherly life hunted down by dogs and adversaries. For it is
obviously the boar who must die: he is not, like the lions and
griffins, the attacker. He is the father of life running free in the
forest, and he must die. They say too he represents winter:
when the feasts for the dead were held. But on the very oldest
archaic vases the lion and the boar are facing each other, again
and again, in symbolic opposition.

Fascinating are the scenes of departures, journeyings in
covered wagons drawn by two or more horses, accompanied
by driver on foot and friend on horseback, and dogs, and met

by other horsemen coming down the road. Under the arched tarpaulin tilt of the wagon reclines a man, or a woman, or a whole family: and all moves forward along the highway with wonderful slow surge. And the wagon, as far as I saw, is always drawn by horses, not by oxen.

This is surely the journey of the soul. It is said to represent even the funeral procession, the ash-chest being borne away to the cemetery, to be laid in the tomb. But the *memory* in the scene seems much deeper than that. It gives so strongly the feeling of a people who have trekked in wagons, like the Boers, or the Mormons, from one land to another.

They say these covered-wagon journeys are peculiar to Volterra, found represented in no other Etruscan places. Altogether the feeling of the Volterran scenes is peculiar. There is a great sense of *journeying*: as of a people which remembers its migrations, by sea as well as land. And there is a curious restlessness, unlike the dancing surety of southern Etruria: a touch of the Gothic.

In the upstairs rooms there are many more ash-chests, but mostly representing Greek subjects: so called. Helen and the Dioscuri, Pelops, Minotaur, Jason, Medea fleeing from Corinth, Oedipus, and the Sphinx, Ulysses and the Sirens, Eteocles and Polynices, Centaurs and Lapithae, the Sacrifice of Iphigenia – all are there, just recognizable. There are so many Greek subjects that one archaeologist suggested that these urns must have been made by a Greek colony planted there in Volterra after the Roman conquest.

One might almost as well say that *Timon of Athens* was written by a Greek colonist planted in England after the overthrow of the Catholic Church. These 'Greek' ash-chests are about as Grecian as *Timon of Athens* is. The Greeks would have done them so much 'better'.

No, the 'Greek' scenes are innumerable, but it is only just recognizable what they mean. Whoever carved these chests knew very little of the fables they were handling: and fables they were, to the Etruscan artificers of that day, as they would be to the Italians of this. The story was just used as a peg upon which the native Volterran hung his fancy, as the Elizabethans used Greek stories for their poems. Perhaps also the alabaster cutters were working from old models, or the memory of them. Anyhow, the scenes show nothing of Hellas.

Most curious these 'classic' subjects: so unclassic! To me they hint at the Gothic which lay unborn in the future, far more than at the Hellenistic past of the Volterran Etruscan. For, of course, all these alabaster urns are considered late in period, after the fourth century B.C. The Christian sarcophagi of the fifth century A.D. seem much more nearly kin to these ash-chests of Volterra than do contemporary Roman chests: as if Christianity really rose, in Italy, out of Etruscan soil, rather than out of Greco-Roman. And the first glimmering of that early, glad sort of Christian art, the free touch of Gothic within the classic, seems evident in the Etruscan scenes. The Greek and Roman 'boiled' sort of form gives way to a raggedness of edge and a certain wildness of light and shade which promises the later Gothic, but which is still held down by the heavy mysticism from the East.

Very early Volterran urns were probably plain stone or terra-cotta. But no doubt Volterra was a city long before the Etruscans penetrated into it, and probably it never changed character profoundly. To the end, the Volterrans burned their dead: there are practically no long sarcophagi of Lucumones. And here most of all one feels that the *people* of Volterra, or Velathri, were not Oriental, not the same as those who made most show at Tarquinii. This was surely another tribe, wilder, cruder, and far less influenced by the old Aegean influences. In Caere and Tarquinii the aborigines were deeply overlaid by incoming influences from the East. Here not! Here the wild and untamable Ligurian was neighbour, and perhaps kin, and the town of wind and stone kept, and still keeps, its northern quality.

So there the ash-chests are, an open book for anyone to read who will, according to his own fancy. They are not more than two feet long, or thereabouts, so the figure on the lid is queer and stunted. The classic Greek or Asiatic could not have borne that. It is a sign of barbarism in itself. Here the northern spirit was too strong for the Hellenic or Oriental or ancient Mediterranean instinct. The Lucumo and his lady had to submit to being stunted, in their death-effigy. The head is nearly life-size. The body is squashed small.

But there it is, a portrait-effigy. Very often, the lid and the chest don't seem to belong together at all. It is suggested that the lid was made during the lifetime of the subject, with an attempt at real portraiture: while the chest was bought ready-made, and apart. It may be so. Perhaps in Etruscan days there were the alabaster workshops as there are today, only with rows of ash-chests portraying all the vivid scenes we still can see: and perhaps you chose the one you wished your ashes to lie in. But more probably, the workshops were there, the carved ash-chests were there, but you did not select your own chest, since you did not know what death you would die. Probably you only had your portrait carved on the lid, and left the rest to the survivors.

So maybe, and most probably, the mourning relatives hurriedly *ordered* the lid with the portrait-bust, after the death of the near one, and then chose the most appropriate ash-chest. Be it as it may, the two parts are often oddly assorted: and so they were found with the ashes inside them.

But we must believe that the figure on the lid, grotesquely shortened, is an attempt at a portrait. There is none of the distinction of the southern Etruscan figures. The heads are given the 'imperious' tilt of the Lucumones, but here it becomes almost grotesque. The dead nobleman may be wearing the necklace of office and holding the sacred patera or libation-dish in his hand; but he will not, in the southern way, be represented ritualistically as naked to below the navel; his shirt will come to his neck: and he may just as well be holding the tippling wine-cup in his hand as the sacred patera; he may even have a wine-jug in his other hand, in full carousal. Altogether the peculiar 'sacredness', the inveterate symbolism of the southern Etruscans, is here gone. The religious power is broken.

It is very evident in the ladies: and so many of the figures are ladies. They are decked up in all their splendour, but the mystical formality is lacking. They hold in their hands wine-cups or fans or mirrors, pomegranates or perfume-boxes, or the queer little books which perhaps were the wax tablets for writing upon. They may even have the old sexual and death symbol of the pine-cone. But the *power* of the symbol has almost vanished. The Gothic actuality and idealism begins to supplant the profound *physical* religion of the southern Etruscans, the true ancient world.

In the museum there are jars and bits of bronze, and the pateras with the hollow knob in the middle. You may put your two middle fingers in the patera, and hold it ready to make the last libation of life, the first libation of death, in the correct Etruscan fashion. But you will not, as so many of the men on these ash-chests do, hold the symbolic dish upside down, with the two fingers thrust into the 'mundus'. The torch upside down means the flame has gone below, to the underworld. But the patera upside down is somehow shocking. One feels the Volterrans, or men of Velathri, were slack in the ancient mysteries.

At last the rain stopped crashing down icily in the silent inner courtyard; at last there was a ray of sun. And we had seen all we could look at for one day. So we went out, to try to get warmed by a kinder heaven.

There are one or two tombs still open, especially two outside the Porta a Selci. But I believe, not having seen them, they are of small importance. Nearly all the tombs that have been opened in Volterra, their contents removed, have been filled in again, so as not to lose two yards of the precious cultivable land of the peasants. There were many tumuli: but most of them are levelled. And under some were curious round tombs built of unsquared stones, unlike anything in southern Etruria. But then, Volterra is altogether unlike southern Etruria.

One tomb has been removed bodily to the garden of the archaeological museum in Florence: at least its contents have. There it is built up again as it was when discovered in Volterra in 1861, and all the ash-chests are said to be replaced as they stood originally. It is called the Inghirami Tomb, from the famous Volterran archaeologist Inghirami.

A few steps lead down into the one circular chamber of the tomb, which is supported in the centre by a square pillar, apparently supposed to be left in the rock. On the low stone bed that encircles the tomb stand the ash-chests, a double row of them, in a great ring encircling the shadow.

The tomb belongs all to one family, and there must be sixty ash-chests, of alabaster, carved with the well-known scenes. So that if this tomb is really arranged as it was originally, and the ash-chests progress from the oldest to the latest counter-clockwise, as is said, one ought to be able to see certainly a century or two of development in the Volterran urns.

But one is filled with doubt and misgiving. Why, oh why, wasn't the tomb left intact as it was found, where it was found? The garden of the Florence museum is vastly instructive, if you want object-lessons about the Etruscans. But who wants object-lessons about vanished races? What one wants is a contact. The Etruscans are not a theory or a thesis. If they are anything, they are an *experience*.

And the experience is always spoilt. Museums, museums, museums, object-lessons rigged out to illustrate the unsound theories of archaeologists, crazy attempts to coordinate and get into a fixed order that which has no fixed order and will not be coordinated! It is sickening! Why must all experience be systematized? Why must even the vanished Etruscans be reduced to a system? They never will be. You break all the eggs, and produce an omelette which is neither Etruscan nor Roman not Italic nor Hittite, nor anything else, but just a systematized mess. Why can't incompatible things be left incompatible? If you make an omelette out of a hen's egg, a plover's, and an ostrich's, you won't have a grand amalgam or unification of hen and plover and ostrich into something we may call 'oviparity'. You'll have that formless object, an omelette.

So it is here. If you try to make a grand amalgam of Cerveteri and Tarquinia, Vulci, Vetulonia, Volterra, Chiusi, Veii, then you won't get the essential *Etruscan* as a result, but a cooked-up mess which has no life-meaning at all. A museum is not a first-hand contact: it is an illustrated lecture. And what one wants is the actual vital touch. I don't want to be 'instructed'; nor do many other people.

They could take the more homeless objects for the museums, and still leave those that *have* a place in their own place: the Inghirami Tomb here at Volterra.

But it is useless. We walk up the hill and out of the Florence gate, into the shelter under the walls of the huge medieval castle which is now a State prison. There is a promenade below the ponderous walls, and a scrap of sun, and shelter from the biting wind. A few citizens are promenading even now. And beyond, the bare green country rises up in waves and sharp points, but it is like looking at the choppy sea from the brow of a tall ship; here in Volterra we ride above all.

And behind us, in the bleak fortress, are the prisoners. There is a man, an old man now, who has written an opera inside those walls. He had a passion for the piano: and for thirty years his wife nagged him when he played. So one day he silently and suddenly killed her. So, the nagging of thirty years silenced, he got thirty years of prison, and *still* is not allowed to play the piano. It is curious.

There were also two men who escaped. Silently and secretly they carved marvellous likenesses of themselves out of the huge loaves of hard bread the prisoners get. Hair and all, they made their own effigies lifelike. Then they laid them in the bed, so that when the warder's light flashed on them he should say to himself: 'There they lie sleeping, the dogs!'

And so they worked, and they got away. It cost the governor, who loved his household of malefactors, his job. He was kicked out. It is curious. He should have been rewarded, for having such clever children, sculptors in bread.

MORE ABOUT PENGUINS
AND PELICANS

Penguinews, which appears every month, contains details of all the new books issued by Penguins as they are published. From time to time it is supplemented by *Penguins in Print,* which is a complete list of all available books published by Penguins. (There are well over four thousand of these.)

A specimen copy of *Penguinews* will be sent to you free on request. For a year's issues (including the complete lists) please send 30p if you live in the United Kingdom, or 60p if you live elsewhere. Just write to Dept EP, Penguin Books Ltd, Harmondsworth, Middlesex, enclosing a cheque or postal order, and your name will be added to the mailing list.

Note: *Penguinews* and *Penguins in Print* are not available in the U.S.A. or Canada

Evelyn Waugh

WHEN THE GOING WAS GOOD

'From 1928 until 1937,' Evelyn Waugh has written, 'I had no fixed home and no possessions which would not conveniently go on a porter's barrow. I travelled continuously, in England and abroad.' Of those years, when more countries were accessible than are so today, he wrote four travel books, and from these four he has selected all that he wishes to preserve under the ironic title, *When the Going was Good*.

O. R. *Gurney*

THE HITTITES

The Hittites as a legendary Palestinian tribe are familiar to us from our schooldays. In this book the story is told of the rediscovery of the historical Hittites during the last eighty years, as the result of excavation and the decipherment of cuneiform and hieroglyphic documents. The Hittites of history were a great nation of Asia Minor, whose kings treated on equal terms with those of Egypt, Babylon, and Assyria, during a period of about two hundred years in the second millennium B.C. There was an Indo-European strain in them which is revealed in their language and perhaps in the physical types of some of the Hittite prisoners represented on Egyptian monuments. Their earliest social organization also shows some points of resemblance to that of the heroic age of Greece. Their religion on the other hand seems to have been largely that of the indigenous population, who must be supposed to have inhabited the country before the Indo-European reached it. They developed a rupestrian art, which has its roots in the soil of Mesopotamia, but exhibits a strong and independent style of its own.

This is an attempt to present a balanced picture of what is known of the Hittites and in the chapter on literature to give some impression of the more important types of documents found among their archives.

A PELICAN BOOK

I. E. S. Edwards

THE PYRAMIDS OF EGYPT

When *The Pyramids of Egypt* was first published – as a Pelican – in 1947, it was immediately recognized as a work of real importance in the field of Egyptology. Since then many new facts have been unearthed and recorded.

In this new edition the author, who is Keeper of Egyptian Antiquities at the British Museum, has completely revised his text and incorporated the latest knowledge. He presents us with the most up-to-the-minute answer to that eternal question: 'How and why did the ancient Kings of Egypt build their gigantic geometrical monuments?' For today it is possible to trace their early history with some exactitude and to follow the gradual evolution from the simple pre-dynastic tomb to the Step Pyramid of Zoser.

A very comprehensive bibliography of the greatly increased literature on the Pyramids is included, and many new line-drawings and half-tone illustrations have been added.

G. C. Vaillant

THE AZTECS OF MEXICO

SECOND EDITION

In the eleventh century A.D. the Aztecs arrived in Mexico from the north. In less than a hundred years they developed an extraordinary civilization. Here is the strange story of that rise, and of the even swifter fall under the impact of Cortés and his followers. Dr Vaillant discusses the basic beliefs of its society in relation to government, education, and law. At the same time he captures the spirit of the age, and in one fascinating chapter takes us on a conducted tour of the great city of Tenochtitlan in the heyday of its power.

Further excavation and study, and improved techniques of dating archaeological material have thrown new light on the story. This thorough revision by his wife Suzannah Vaillant has lost none of the flavour of the original, which remains the most important account of one of the great civilizations of the world.

A PELICAN BOOK

Graham Greene

THE LAWLESS ROADS

In the late thirties Graham Greene was commissioned to visit Mexico and find out how the ordinary people had reacted to the brutal anti-clerical purges of President Calles. His journey took him through the tropical states of Chiapas and Tabasco, where all the churches had been destroyed or closed and the priests driven out or shot; and it provided him with setting and theme for one of his greatest novels, *The Power and the Glory*.

'He gives, with something like genius, the impression of a deeper and further combat between Darkness and Light, Sin and Forgiveness, which lies behind the decay of Mexico' – *Tablet*

D. H. LAWRENCE

D. H Lawrence is now acknowledged as one of the greatest writers of the twentieth century. Nearly all his works are available in Penguins:

NOVELS

Aaron's Rod*   Kangaroo*
Lady Chatterley's Lover*
The Lost Girl*   The Plumed Serpent
The Rainbow*   The Trespasser
The White Peacock
Women in Love*
The Boy in the Bush (with M. L. Skinner)*
Sons and Lovers

SHORT STORIES

The Prussian Officer*   England, My England*
St Mawr & The Virgin and the Gipsy
Love Among the Haystacks*
The Woman Who Rode Away*
Three Novellas: The Fox, The Ladybird, The Captain's Doll*
The Princess and other stories*
The Mortal Coil and other stories*
The Virgin and the Gipsy

TRAVEL BOOKS AND OTHER WORKS

Mornings in Mexico & Etruscan Places
Sea and Sardinia*
Twilight in Italy*   Selected Essays*
Selected Letters*   Selected Poems*
A Selection from Phoenix*
Fantasia of the Unconscious & Psychoanalysis and the Unconscious*
Studies in Classic American Literature*

*NOT FOR SALE IN THE U.S.A.
REMAINDER NOT FOR SALE IN THE U.S.A. OR CANADA